Motoring My Way

1 *W.O Bentley MBE*

MOTORING MY WAY

Stanley Sedgwick

B T Batsford Ltd, London

First published 1976

ISBN 0 7134 3262 4

Filmset by
Servis Filmsetting Ltd, Manchester
Printed by The Anchor Press Ltd
Tiptree, Essex
for the publishers BT Batsford
4 Fitzhardinge Street, London WC1H 0AH

Dedication

I humbly dedicate this book to the late Walter Owen Bentley – the man whose products and achievements captured my imagination from boyhood.

I was not among those fortunate enough to have witnessed the Bentleys racing in their heyday, but the Bentley tradition was well established when I left school. For me there was only one motor car – the Bentley. W.O. was an enigmatic, unknown figure whose name ranked in one's teenage hall of fame with Louis Armstrong, Jack Hobbs and the like. Little did I dream when I gazed in awe upon the great green Bentleys that one day I would come to know their legendary creator – indeed to number myself among his friends and to be privileged to drive thousands of miles in a variety of cars with him as a contented passenger.

When I met W.O. for the first time after the war and told him that I was helping to revive the Bentley Drivers Club, it was clear to me that the idea of encouraging ownership and preservation of the old Bentleys was an enterprise which he regarded with little enthusiasm and considerable misgiving.

W.O., disillusioned by the adversities which he had endured in the thirties, was in no hurry to reopen a chapter of his life which he had tried to forget, but in due course he accepted the Club's invitation to become Patron and as the Club grew and grew, so blossomed its association with W.O. His attendance at sporting and social gatherings up and down the country, always accompanied by his wife, Margaret, was a source of pleasure to all concerned.

The cottage at Shamley Green was the Mecca of Bentley enthusiasts who beat a path to his door from all corners of the globe. He was too kindly a man to turn away even the most importunate visitor.

Humility and a sense of humour were, perhaps, his most endearing attributes. He could never understand the hero-worship apparent at gatherings of Bentley owners and was embarrassed when those meeting him for the first time thanked him for the pleasure he had brought into their lives. He was a man who never sought the limelight and would never make a speech in public. To have insisted on his doing so would have spoiled his enjoyment of the occasion, but it is characteristic of him smilingly to have found refuge in his later years in the philosophy that people would have been disappointed if he had changed his Trappist image. Nevertheless, overcoming his natural shyness, he yielded to pressure to appear on television and radio programmes on several occasions and proved himself a match for the most experienced interviewers.

W.O. was held in high esteem far beyond the immediate circle of Bentley owners. The French Minister of Youth and Sport conferred upon him the Mérite Sportif Français on the occasion of the Silver Jubilee Celebration of the marque at Le Mans in 1969. There are many who consider that the honour bestowed upon W.O. by a grateful Government at home was less than his due; that he merited the accolade no less than many of his contemporaries.

Few people are known widely by their initials alone. Those of W.O. will long be remembered, and his memory is enshrined in the cars which bear his name and show every sign of sharing the longevity of the man who conceived them.

W.O. said that the pleasure he derived in the post-war years from Club activities; from making new friends among its members; and from seeing the loving care bestowed upon 'his' cars, had more than compensated for all his earlier disappointments. I count myself fortunate in having played some part in creating the opportunities for this great man to enjoy a belated sense of fulfilment.

Acknowledgment

The majority of the photographs in this book are from the author's own collection – for those which are not the author gratefully acknowledges their use as follows; Richmond Pike for illustration 9, Michael Cooper for illustration 59, Louis Klementaski for illustration 76 and *Motor* for the drawings on page 149.

Preface

Only those who have undertaken a similar task can know the sheer hard work and application involved in writing a book of this kind in one's spare time.

I do not think I could have embarked upon the job at all if it had not been for two things – firstly, my penchant for hoarding piles and piles of papers, notes, magazines, letters and suchlike just in case I should need them for reference and, secondly, the vast accumulation of self-processed photographs lying about in my study. I have thus been able to draw freely upon my writings in a variety of motoring periodicals over the years and to dig out sufficient source material to enable me to cover subjects and episodes not before recounted.

My reward has been the pleasure derived from reliving my motoring life in retrospect. I do not flatter myself that readers will share every moment with me – indeed one colleague who kindly read the manuscript said that some people would be exhausted merely by reading of some of my more marathon exploits – but I hope that everyone will find something to their liking.

It will be found that I enjoy driving alone, but most of my experiences have been shared with other like-minded enthusiasts. I gratefully acknowledge my indebtedness to all these friends for their co-operation and partnership. My thanks go to my niece, Anthea, who typed the book from very messy manuscripts; to John Croxson who undertook the unenviable task of suggesting deletions to meet the publisher's length limitations and succeeded without impairing our long-standing friendship; and to Hugh Young who also read the manuscript and painstakingly checked the proofs.

I have given this book to the custodians of The W. O. Bentley Memorial Fund and, therefore, unashamedly express the hope that in so doing I have done the right thing – in other words, that the book will sell well.

Stanley Sedgwick

Contents

Appreciation

This autobiography would be incomplete without an expression of appreciation of the immense contribution which my understanding wife, Con, has made to my enjoyment of motoring.

Herself a keen driver, preferring open cars, she took her driving test on my $4\frac{1}{2}$-litre Bentley and failed because an ill-informed examiner could not understand how or why she changed gears without using the clutch – a procedure which I had taught her because she found it an uncomfortable stretch to depress the pedal fully. There was a bright side, however, for Con's father bought her a second-hand TC MG as a more suitable car in which to take her test. She did indeed throw away her L plates as soon as a new test could be arranged, and her liking for the marque was to continue through the TD, TF, MGA and MGB series, now superseded by an Alfa Romeo 1750 Spyder.

Con has shared in many of my motoring adventures and has tolerated my idiosyncracies when I took off on long-distance solo ventures. By reason of my involvement with motoring clubs and organizations, she has borne with fortitude unconscionable intrusions upon our domestic life at all times of day and night. Con, too, has shared the many treasured friendships formed throughout the world and feels rewarded, as I do, for the thought and effort devoted to motoring activities of one sort or another.

2 *Con with her 1750 Alfa Romeo*

Mainly about Bentleys

The 3-litre Bentley

I can remember that during my schooldays there existed for me only one make of car; it was, of course, the Bentley. When I left school at sixteen I vowed that I would never own a car until I could afford a Bentley and twelve years passed before I became the owner of a Bentley – and could not afford it! During the war, I bought a 3-litre 'Red Label' unseen through the post from an RAF officer, one John Stone stationed near Dundee, for £150. Some will deem such an incautious procedure a clear manifestation of my youth and inexperience, but I have no regrets and am still on speaking terms with the previous owner. Owing to petrol restrictions and the exigencies of the Service it was not possible for the Bentley to be driven to Surrey from Scotland. It was, therefore, entrusted to the railway, which conveyed it on a flat truck for a sum approximating one-sixth of the cost of the car. My eyes first fell upon my new acquisition as it stood in the cattle yard at King's Cross. A quick survey showed that it had not been damaged in transit. Then followed an inspection of the unfamiliar controls and a final study of the vendor's instructions on how to start the car. A veil must be drawn over the drive home to Cobham – it would have taken something much more substantial to muffle the noise which issued from the protesting gearbox. On arriving home the 3-litre was put on blocks until more propitious times permitted it to be put on the road once more. This car gave me two years of uncomplaining service. Very little had to be spent on maintenance once the ravages of war-time hibernation had been dealt with. The gearbox was soon mastered, and indeed I have yet to meet a Bentley owner

3 *The author's first car, a 1925 3-litre Bentley, as it arrived home in June 1942. Note the wartime masks on the headlamps*

who does not admit to causing horrible noises once in a while!

I enjoyed many thousands of miles of motoring in this 3-litre. Many were the convoys of Bentleys I led to Prescott at speeds of up to 80 mph in those post-war days when opportunities to indulge one's interest in motor sport were few indeed.

A 3-litre owner's greatest problem is the ever-present ambition to own a 4½-litre and, as so many others have done before and since, I eventually succumbed to temptation. The 3-litre is now owned by a young enthusiast living only ten miles away and is unquestionably in better condition than when I parted with it twenty-five years ago.

The 4½-litre Bentley

The 4½-litre which I was able to acquire fortuitously in November 1947 was quite well known amongst Bentley enthusiasts before the war when owned by Roddy Seys, and became available only as a result of his untimely death on active service. (It was featured in the *Autocar* 'Talking of Sports Cars' series on 14 March 1941.) When I first saw this car, it was looking rather bedraggled through being laid up for several years but a short run confirmed the impression of good, sound motor car underneath the surface shabbiness. This was as it should be, for the Bentley had been cared for by L.C. McKenzie, known to all vintage Bentley enthusiasts as the 'high priest'.

It was one of the very few TT Replicas. The compression ratio had been raised by milling 6 mm off the cylinder block; twin sloping SU carburettors, which are reputed to give 6 bhp more than the vertical type, were fitted, and special ribbed brake drums, manufactured in high-carbon steel by Krupps at Essen, had been substituted for the standard type.

This car was driven home with great pride and new-found pleasure in the additional horses under the bonnet. Alas, ten days after taking delivery, misfortune overtook the 4½. Returning home in the early hours from a BARC dance in London, I was driving along the Kingston Bypass when I noticed a haystack on fire in a field alongside the road. Glancing back at this disturbing sight I saw sparks in the road behind me which I thought to be strays from the burning stack. Another look revealed a trail of sparks behind the car, and I realized at once that my Bentley was on fire. My cry to Con, who had been asleep, that the car was on fire was met with a sleepy enquiry as to whether she should get out – needless to say full consciousness returned rapidly and was followed by a speedy exit. This car had a stoneguard on the petrol tank in the form of wooden slats strapped on over felt. Flames were coming from this stoneguard underneath the tank, and I can only conclude that war-time storage had resulted in the tank becoming perforated, impregnating the felt with petrol. One of the leather retaining straps had broken and, possibly, a spark from the buckle trailing on the road had started the fire. Frantic efforts to tear off the stone-guard with bare hands and to smother the flames with a rug were of no avail. The fire-extinguisher that I had observed on the car when I bought it proved to be empty. It seemed hours before a car came into sight and the flames were really getting a hold by the time the driver of this car brought his extinguisher to bear. The fire was now too fierce to be doused by ordinary methods and the good Samaritan went off to call the fire brigade from Esher. They arrived in a creditably short time though it seemed an age, and were soon at work on the flames, which by then were twenty feet high from the bulkhead to the back of the car. We gratefully accepted a lift home from the driver who had come to our assistance and reached home in a very depressed state, having left the erstwhile beautiful Bentley a smoking, soaking wreck at the roadside.

Next day, the wreck was towed to McKenzie's workshop by the 'high priest' himself, while Avery, his foreman, choked by wind-blown

4 *The 1925 3-litre Bentley still going strong thirty-two years later (October 1974). Now owned by Roy Baker of Guildford*
5 *The 4½-litre Bentley one week after acquisition*

6 *The $4\frac{1}{2}$-litre Bentley after the burn-up on the Bypass*

ash and cinders, steered the burnt-out remains.

The next six months were occupied by The Great Rebuild, not the least difficult part of which was the search for replacement parts. Fellow Bentley enthusiasts were most helpful; such things as a prop-shaft, bulkhead, Autovac, instruments and steering column were soon acquired, and advantage was taken of an opportunity to instal a 'D'-type gearbox in place of the original 'A'-type. The chassis and engine were not damaged, but the body was a complete write-off. Mac fitted a Borg & Beck clutch and lightened the flywheel considerably.

It was clear that the biggest headache was going to be finding a new body. The one which had been destroyed was a Vanden Plas open four-seater, but it was different from the body usually fitted to Bentleys in that the rear panel swept inwards at the bottom to make room for the 25-gallon petrol tank. It was, in fact, a replica of the one fitted to the car driven by Humphrey Cook in the TT. Then a million-to-one stroke of luck came my way – Bill Shortt presented me with the body which came off the actual Humphrey Cook car! I collected my prize from a grassy grave and delivered it to the coachbuilders, who stripped off the rotted fabric, replaced rotten timber, mounted it on the chassis and re-covered the body with leather inside and out. That doyen of Vintage Bentley owners, the late Forrest Lycett, gave me a windscreen from an earlier version of his 8-litre, which required little alteration to form an admirable fold-flat screen for the rapidly forming 'new' $4\frac{1}{2}$-litre Bentley. Hood and tonneau cover were added – mercifully the hood irons were not beyond repair after the fire. A coat of green paint, new tyres, new electric wiring, windscreen wiper driven by a motor under the scuttle and the car was ready for the road once again.

It was indeed a case of an ill wind, for the $4\frac{1}{2}$ was now in far better shape than when I had bought it and the insurance company had contributed more than half the cost of the rebuild.

I collected the car in Putney at the end of May and next day left for a 2,000-mile Continental tour with four up and luggage.

Novice abroad

This was to be my first venture by car on to the Continent of Europe and I was pleased to have the guidance and, for part of the trip, the company of Johnnie Green in his open Vanden Plas 3-litre Bentley. We joined Johnnie at Dover on 20 May 1948 to catch the midnight ferry to Dunkerque. Here we met Gerry Crozier – destined to become one of my closest friends but, alas, no longer with us – driving his 38/250 Mercedes-Benz drophead coupé. This car had the biggest petrol tank I have ever seen – 50 gallons, I think – and, despite the thirsty engine, he expected to reach Italy without having to replenish the tank.

The first day's driving brought us to Paris. The following afternoon we all went to the Paris Grand Prix at Montlhéry, but my enjoyment was marred by having damaged the 4½ earlier in the day in a collision with a taxi near the Opéra – the result of my unfamiliarity with the operation of the priority from the right rule when bowling down a wide boulevard. The race, though almost a procession, was very enjoyable, and it was grand to be on a real race track once again. P.A.T. Garland was placed fifth in his Delage and because he was a lone hand from England we found him afterwards and went driving through Paris streets straight off the track, sans silencer, sans licence, sans number plates, sans almost everything except a terrific performance. The gendarmes couldn't have cared less and waved us on with a welter of Citroëns and Renaults. It was through Garland that I was fortunate enough to meet Henri Trillaud and his partner, the racing-driver Albert Divo, who immediately undertook to straighten the frame of the 4½ and render it mobile once again. It turned out that three new spring main leaves had to be made. In view of the indefinite delay in prospect, Con and our two friends went on to Interlaken by night train. The 3-litre and the Mercedes also went on their way to Interlaken, having very sportingly delayed their departure until it was certain that the 4½ was under treatment.

The springs were fitted by Divo and I collected the car three days later, setting off for Switzerland in pouring rain. After a brief stop at Barbizon for an excellent dinner at Les Pléiades, I pressed on to Interlaken on a non-stop run of 350 miles. It rained all night, and two incidents have stuck in my mind. The first was when I turned left with the road in Auxerre only to find myself right in the middle of a conglomeration of railway tracks. I was so surprised that I stopped, until it soon struck me that it was not such a very good idea to remain there. The second moment was when, climbing over the mountains to Pontarlier in thick mist, the first streaks of dawn just appearing, the road surface became so bad that I thought I had left the road and entered a farm. After reversing downhill for half a mile I noticed no side turning and that the telegraph wires followed the supposed road, so I went ahead again. This atrocious road went on for some miles, and then suddenly broadened out into a good metalled surface as if it had never been anything else.

After a couple of hours sleep our reunited party left to keep an appointment in Bern with a great enthusiast Ditlev Scheel, then a junior diplomat and now Danish Ambassador to a number of South American countries. On the way we met Johnnie in the 3-litre; he had trickled down from Paris via Dijon and Ouchy. We drove round the Bremgarten circuit already being prepared for the Swiss Grand Prix, and then partook of a sumptuous repast at the home of the Scheels. We still talk about the vast quantities of strawberries and cream which came as a revelation to us rationed Britons.

The Merc. had now arrived at Krebs Hotel in Interlaken and the convoy went out pass-storming the next day. The Susten Pass was climbed to within a mile of the summit at which point it was blocked by snow. As the Grimsel and Furka were also impassable, the journey next day to Lugano necessitated a detour via Lucerne and a climb over the St Gotthard Pass. Lugano was reached before dinner, and the next morning we spent looking round and buying lire and French francs with our surplus Swiss currency – a highly recommended piece of arbitrage at the time.

After lunch we parted company with the 3-litre and the Merc. and left for Italy. Como and the Italian customs behind us, we entered the autostrada for Milan and covered 30 kilometres in just under 15 minutes, an average speed of 75 mph. This road was not then twin track, the surface had not been touched since the war, and it was pretty busy with heavy commercial traffic. We arrived in Milan somewhat buffetted from the fast run with screen flat, and were circling the square outside the Cathedral looking for a car park when an HRG wearing GB plates shot across the square, the owner (Charles Meisl) shouting some crack about it being '. . . the only time you get enough petrol, Sedgwick.'

After tea we set out for Genoa without knowing where we would spend the night. Hunger forced us to stop for a meal at a roadside service station where our lack of knowledge of Italian was only partly overcome by mime, for we thought we had ordered chicken, but were served up with a poached egg in soup! Genoa was reached at 11 pm and a wrong turn landed us in the dock area.

Now whether it was the darkness or the ignorance of the language I do not know, but everything looked sinister and menacing. It appeared to us as if a revolution might start at any minute as we prowled around looking for a hotel at which to spend the night. We did not find anything in that district and left on the road to Ventimiglia. After some miles we stopped in a small watering-place to debate our plans; we were almost reconciled to spending the night in the car by then. It appeared, however, that we were outside a hotel and some Italians – presumably acting on the mad-dog-the-Englishman-theory and not in the least surprised to find four people in an open car long after midnight – guessed we wanted to sleep and knocked to awaken the porter without further ado.

Then followed an altercation which appeared to be concerned with finding a garage to house the machine. The porter, who had dragged a pair of trousers over his pyjamas, mounted the step of the 4½ and directed us half a mile down the road to a garage which was definitely shut. The original locals again appeared and the knocking business started again – this time it was poor Ricardo who was being called from his bed. The car garaged, the procession returned to the albergo on foot with all the luggage, and a very comfortable night – or what remained of it – was spent.

It was not until after breakfast that we found out the name of the village; it was Arenzano. A short delay to complete certain petroleum transactions and to convert into French francs enough lire notes to paper a bathroom and we set off along the coast road for Nice.

We stayed on the Côte d'Azur a day longer than planned which made it necessary to attempt the run to Paris – over six hundred miles – in one day. We left Nice at 7 am, planning to arrive in Paris at midnight. After an hour, however, a headlamp post was seen to be leaning drunkenly inwards and investigation showed that the universal on the perrot shaft operating the front brake had given up the ghost – a latent defect as a result of the prang in Paris, now just showing itself. An hour's delay proved that nothing could be done about it, so we continued to limp on our way using only the hand-brake. Lyon was reached at 6 pm, where tea was taken, petrol vouchers converted into coupons, another 100 litres of petrol taken aboard and all set for the second 300 miles. A further delay occurred when a back tyre punctured and necessitated a wheel change. A belated dinner of Lucullan description was taken at 9.30 pm at the Hôtel de la Poste at Saulieu. We left there for Paris at 10.30. Incidentally, only one headlamp was working and as no relief driver was in the crew three short naps had to be taken before we eventually reached Paris just as the street lights went out at 4 am. On checking in at the hotel we were informed that the Merc. was within, but that the 3-litre had not yet reported.

After lunch the following day we left, with the Merc., for Le Touquet. Here we found the 3-litre outside the hotel, but the owner was out and we did not see him again until the following day on the dockside at Calais. A pleasant crossing, tea with friends in Folkestone, a fast run up the London road (how smooth after those on the Continent), a quick cup of coffee at the home of Bill and Marion Cook – ever since a recognized staging-post when going to, or returning from, the Continent – and the final lap to Cobham concluded a most enjoyable holiday. By this time I had become very adept at progressing quite rapidly with only the handbrake working, a skill which was to stand me in good stead in later years.

We had covered nearly 2,300 miles and, believe it or not, the *net* cost of petrol was 7s. 6d. (37½p) per head! My first motoring holiday on the Continent truly had been an exciting experience. The two passengers – the late Edgar Baker and his wife – who covered the whole distance (including the Nice to Paris in a day effort) in the back of the 4½ with the luggage, bought a 3-litre Bentley soon after their return to England. Whether this was because they were so impressed with vintage Bentley motoring or whether, as some unbeliever suggested, they were determined never to ride in the back of one again, I never knew for sure.

It is not easy for those accustomed to the autoroute era to visualize road and traffic conditions in France and Italy in those early post-war years. There were few bypasses, and one had to drive through village after village – often behind a crawling camion – on road surfaces still bearing the ravages of armoured vehicles and almost total war-time neglect. Average speeds achieved on long drives considered to be very creditable in those days would now be regarded as a snail's pace.

Across France in a day

May 1950 saw the 4½ once more heading across France towards the Mediterranean, this time in the company of two more 4½-litres belonging to Geoffrey Kramer and Harry Kemp-Place; the former being the Pacey-Hassan in its then two-seater road-going guise and surely having the least ground clearance of any vintage Bentley.

It had been decided to go away towards the end of May with the object of including visits to the Grands Prix of Monaco, Monza and Bern which were to be held on three consecutive weekends.

We planned to go to the same places and hotels at more or less the same time, but each car was to be a law unto itself. The Kramer and Kemp-Place équipes, each having only one driver, arranged to take two days to cross France and accordingly took the Dover to Dunkerque night ferry on Thursday, 18 May. They were delayed on arrival while the customs officials had breakfast but reached Dijon before nightfall, and pressed on to Monte-Carlo next day, reaching their destination at 11.30 pm. Geoffrey and Anne bore physical and psychological signs of the unremitting battle between the low hard-sprung 4½ and the pavé. The car had shed a headlamp and broken a spare-wheel mounting bracket.

I took the opportunity of fulfilling a wish of long-standing to cross France in one day. Co-driver Bob Gregory and our wives were talked into this marathon run and we left England on the night ferry 24 hours behind our colleagues. We were fortunate in clearing customs at Dunkerque without delay and at 5.05 am turned the Bentley's radiator southwards determined to see the Mediterranean before we slept again. The first 200 miles were covered in pouring rain in five hours, including stops totalling 25 minutes. Only another 560 miles to go! Our route lay through Péronne, Soissons, Sézanne, and Troyes to Dijon, where we partook of our first French meal at the Hôtel du Nord. We were informed that two other Bentleys had spent the night there and left early that morning. The 'others' had, indeed, selected the same hotel by coincidence for an overnight stop. We were still less than half-way and left almost $1\frac{1}{2}$ hours later for Mâcon, Lyon and points South. The 25-gallon tank, which was filled with rationed petrol at Dover to save precious currency, became empty at Mâcon (400 miles) and received its first dose of 'super-carburant'. We resumed our journey through Lyon, Valence and Avignon, stopped for dinner just after leaving Avignon and continued in darkness grateful for the unaccustomed warmth now making itself felt in the air. Through Aix-en-Provence to Fréjus, we then took the road over the hills to Cannes and the coast road to Nice and beyond.

The Bentley came to rest, after a trouble-free run, at 2 am outside the Beau Rivage Hotel – alas, since replaced by an apartment block with the same name – overlooking Monte-Carlo harbour and we retired to bed having ascertained that the other two Bentleys and their crews were safely within. We were delighted to learn that Johnnie Green, 3-litre and parents were there also. We had covered the 760 miles in 21 hours including stops; nothing outstanding, but an ambition, however senseless, achieved.

Next morning we awoke to eat a late breakfast on our bedroom balcony, while watching final preparations for the world-famous Monaco Grand Prix. We strolled round the town before lunch, running across other Club members and British drivers, then we took up positions on our respective balconies ready for the Race of a Thousand Corners.

The pack of cars arriving at the first corner after the start took our breath away and we were agog to see them re-appear along the harbour's edge. They came, and then the disaster struck. Farina spun round and the following eight cars telescoped into each other. Seen from our vantage point it seemed like a dodgem track. Each driver bounced up into the air when his car collided with the one in front and was then bounced again as another car hit him in the back. It looked as if the race was washed out, but some of the drivers managed to stop before the wreckage and remained there blipping until a gap was made to allow them through. The field was halved and much of the interest went out of the race but we enjoyed seeing Fangio drive through to win on an Alfa Romeo, and it was a pleasure to see Bob Gerard acquit himself so creditably with a car so much slower than the leaders.

Much of the rest of that week was spent in idleness. One day spent crossing the hills to Grasse for lunch and Castellane for tea, a trip prompted by a desire to see if the road really was as bad as it had appeared under sheet-ice during the Monte-Carlo Rally, and also by the reference to the Grand Canyon du Verdon in Rodney Walkerley's book. We left Castellane after tea to do the circular tour recommended by R.L.de B.W.; although it seemed a long time before we reached the gorge, the grandeur revealed at our first glimpse took our breath away. The road climbed higher and higher along the side of the canyon – sometimes on a ledge, sometimes in a tunnel – and every minute the view became more and more awe-inspiring. The route lived up to its reputation and the scenery equalled any I had seen in Switzerland.

To the regret of the sea-bathers and sun-worshippers, departure day came all too soon, and three heavily-laden Bentleys departed eastwards. Our route lay along the coast road to Genoa – where my $4\frac{1}{2}$ fractured a lamp bracket and shed the headlamp – and then via the Autostrada to Milan. We were headed for the fabulous Villa d'Este at Cernobbio on Lake Como. We were able to stop at this palatial hotel only by reason of a personal introduction by Club member Max Colombi, Banqueting Manager of 'The Dorchester', to M. Willy Dombré, the owner, who gave us luxurious rooms at incredibly low charges. Nevertheless, our stay here made a considerable dent in our currency allowances; we could not afford to dine in the hotel but were otherwise monarchs for a day.

Early next morning, the five males clambered into my Bentley and we were soon back on the Autostrada for Milan. We visited the Alfa Romeo works and were made most welcome. Dr Alessio, the Managing Director, allowed us to examine closely one of the racing cars (the one driven by Reg Parnell a fortnight earlier at Silverstone) and the prototype of the new production 2-litre 100 mph saloon. While we were climbing in and out of the cockpit and poking about in the engine-room of the Type 158, workers in the factory crowded round the door outside to catch a glimpse of the racing car. Dr Alessio placed at our disposal a chauffeur-driven Alfa Romeo and arranged for the Export Manager, Tony Compari, to accompany us to Monza to see the practice for the next day's Grand Prix of the Autodrome.

Early next morning we left Cernobbio for breakfast with Count Lurani at his villa at Cernusco. I was in front and put up a black by leading the convoy through villages where Dunlop (or even Pirelli) tread had never been seen before. Before regaining the correct road we had squeezed by bullock carts and left entire populations speculating upon our passing. Eventually, the three 4½s swept into the drive at Cernusco where we all tucked into breakfast with several of Johnny's friends assembled for the racing. The menfolk found it hard to tear themselves away from the famous garage where the white-washed walls were covered with the autographs of dozens of racing drivers and personalities. We were privileged to add our own signatures in black chalk and noted other familiar names – Pomeroy, Lycett, Nockolds, etc – among the famous Caracciola, Nuvolari, Varzi and a hundred more.

7 *Havoc at the Tabac – the first lap pile-up when Farina spun in the Monaco Grand Prix of 1950*

The convoy then left for Monza – three 4½-litre Bentleys sandwiched between a couple of 1500 cc Fiat saloons and Johnny's new 1100 cc model. The gatekeeper at the track was overwhelmed by the heavy metal and the Bentleys were soon parked alongside the course in the Paddock.

I was invited to lunch by the President of the Automobile Club of Milan and met several prominent figures in the Italian motor-racing world; all were unanimous in their sincere desire to have the BRM offer some worthwhile opposition. When I sat down to lunch our proposed itinerary was to take us to St Moritz that evening, back into Italy over the Bernina

Pass the next day and thence to Innsbruck via an, as yet, undetermined route. When I arose to resume watching the racing, the plot had undergone a complete re-routing, chiefly at the instance of Signor Lombardini, Racing Manager of Pirelli's. On the back of a menu was drawn a route considered to be far more worthwhile than our original itinerary – and so it turned out.

After the racing we returned to Johnny's place, and left, not for the Maloja Pass, but for Gardone on Lake Garda. One of Johnny's friends conducted us some miles on our way to point out the gorge which formed the background in the classical painting 'La Gioconda'. Thereafter, we traversed some 15 miles of second-class road towards Bergamo. Hermetically sealed Aprilias and Pinin Farinas may have been all right off the main roads in Italy but not open cars such as ours – unless one liked to be enveloped in choking white dust and enjoyed surfaces on which the pavé of northern France had nothing. We arrived, very dirty and tired, at the Grand Hotel Fasano on the shores of Lake Garda in good time for a meal before turning in.

8 *The 4½-litre Bentley at Johnny Lurani's home at Cernusco*

Following the recommendations of our Italian friends we then drove northwards on the road built by Mussolini along the steeply rising banks of Lake Garda and at the northern extremity turned south following the other shore of this beautiful lake. The leisurely progress round the lake soon gave way to a rapid run along the Autostrada to Venice. We obtained rooms and set out to explore the famous city. Some time was spent next morning in further exploration, but we were not sorry to leave Venice on this occasion. Beautiful as the city undoubtedly is, we found our nasal reactions outweighed visual appreciation. At one time it seemed likely that one, if not two, of the ladies, suffering from food-poisoning, might not be fit to travel, and it was a thankful group of fellow-travellers who lunched at a roadside restaurant overlooking the Lake of S. Croce on the road to Cortina d'Ampezzo. After passing through Cortina we turned westwards to drive over the famous Dolomiti Road to Bolzano and Austria.

At the top of the first of three passes, the Falzárego, we stopped to play with the first snow we had encountered. We then proceeded to climb the Pordoi Pass. I was driving at the time, in front of the other two Bentleys, thoroughly enjoying the prospect of a long climb of countless hairpins. Inexcusably, I looked upwards to trace the zigzag path of the road over the mountainside.

As my eyes returned to the road I saw that I was running on to the grass verge on the near side. I corrected, but not in time to prevent the front hub hitting the end of a rock wall holding up the mountain. Then things began to happen with astounding rapidity. The steering-wheel was wrenched out of my hands, the suitcase secured to the near-side step disintegrated as it, too, hit the wall; then the back wheel hit as well. This last impact flung the back of the car across the road, and it came to rest at right-angles driving its nose into the wall. I stopped the engine and got out thinking 'This can't happen to me'. But it had. The passengers were shaken but fortunately unhurt. Not so the poor 4½. She was lying there looking to my inexpert eyes a complete write-off. The other two Bentleys arrived and none of us could really believe our eyes. The front axle was pushed back about five inches, having sheared the dowel-pin; the back spring had been broken clean off at the front end, and the rear axle had moved back and split the petrol tank; both off-side wheels were bent beyond use and the tyres and tubes were torn into shreds; the dumb iron was considerably bent; and the wings were creased, and there was other subsidiary damage.

I could not have wished to have the help of more able or willing chaps than Bob, Harry and Geoffrey who proceeded to tackle the problem without delay.

The two spare wheels were put on; the car dragged sideways by means of a tow-rope; the front axle was unbolted from the spring and refixed nearer to its correct location; the back spring was sledge-hammered roughly into place so that the free, repeat free, end of the main leaf was bearing on its bracket; and the back brake was disconnected to prevent braking torque from dislodging the spring from its temporary resting place. A trial proved that the car could be driven under its own power in spite of its crippled condition – the back and front axles were eight inches out of track. It was decided to limp on, so somehow we transferred part of our luggage and both Con and Marjorie Gregory into the other Bentleys – a rearrangement which caused much discomfort to all concerned. The convoy then went up and up to the summit of the pass, where we stopped to see how the car was faring. A leak manifested itself in the radiator; it was running out of the honeycomb like a tap. All stocks of radiator panaceas were put in to no avail.

We reached a village as darkness was falling and Bob and I persuaded the rest of the party to press on to Bolzano for a meal and thence to Innsbruck where we had reservations at the Maria Theresia Hotel. As their tail-lights disappeared up the street I think we felt something like Edge and Jarrott must have felt when trouble overtook them during the famous intercity races of long ago. Neither of us spoke a word of Italian and we were in a village which rivalled any Balkan ditto in the crudity of its amenities. The radiator continued to empty itself, and we dared not tackle the Costalunga Pass without means of replenishing the cooling water. After protracted negotiations with the local motor repairer through a semi-intoxicated native who spoke an obscure French patois, I found a jerrican in a shed and purchased it for a bag of gold. Thus armed we set off into the night. A book could be filled with the diverse methods by which we procured water that night. Suffice it to say that the radiator had to be filled every 10 kilometres and was boiling almost continuously. We were thankful that we were in a country full of streams, springs and pumps. Eventually we pulled into a petrol station in Bolzano just as the others were preparing to leave after a meal. We left before the other Bentleys, took a wrong turn in the town, and the other cars passed on before we regained the main road. We heard afterwards that they drove fast to catch us, but after some time concluded that we just could not have gone that fast and must have run out of road into a ravine. Actually we slogged on with countless stops for water, climbed the Brenner Pass, crossed the frontier into Austria in the small hours and reached Innsbruck just as it was getting light at 4 am.

Noon found us at a radiator repairer's workshop where we were told that the hole would be repaired by 6 pm. The springs had remained in place and, as the car seemed no worse for its journey after the accident, we decided to go on to Interlaken, where we were to stay for a few days, and to have the springs fixed and the chassis straightened in Switzerland. We left Innsbruck at 6.30 pm, some six hours behind the other two Bentleys, and headed for the Arlberg Pass. For some reason the battery had run down and we had to resort to second gear to get sufficient current to light the headlamps. It seems incredible now, but we negotiated the Arlberg Pass with the aid of a torch shone upon the trees lining the road. At midnight, we parked above the Walensee and picnicked – this was the first stop, apart from the frontier, since leaving Innsbruck. After another couple of hours we decided that it was useless to go on with virtually no lights when it would be daylight in half an hour or so. Once again we stopped and all went to sleep in situ. Con awoke to find four mystified Swiss faces peering out of a cottage window at the strange sight of an open car full of sleeping bodies. We reached Krebs Hotel at Interlaken at 9 am in time for breakfast and only 12 hours behind schedule.

The 4½ had survived nearly 400 miles since the prang – I venture to think that only a vintage Bentley would perform thus. The Kemp-Places were at the hotel, but the Kramer outfit had not turned up. To everyone's relief Geoffrey and Anne arrived during the morning; unhurt, but the 4½ had suffered damage. The sprag – as we called the protruding end of the hand-brake lever – had inevitably grounded and resulted in a split brake drum. The front brakes were therefore disconnected. While cautiously descending the Arlberg Pass the rear brakes were insufficient to bring the slowly moving car, confronted with a road blocked by two parked lorries just round a hairpin corner, to a standstill. Geoffrey had aimed the expensive parts through the inadequate gap between the two vehicles, and wings and windscreen were torn adrift. They had decided, not surprisingly, to call it a day and spent the night in the next village completing the journey into Interlaken the next morning.

I snatched a few hours sleep and at lunchtime drove the 4½ into the Bahnhof Garage where Herr Zimmermann and his staff set to work to straighten out the Bentley. They worked with a will and skill refreshing to behold. A new spring leaf was made; the chassis, track-rod and front-axle – the latter found to be slightly bent when dismantled – were straightened, the damaged wings roughly beaten out and painted; and the car was ready for the road at 6 pm two days later.

On Sunday Geoffrey left for Paris, conscious of his poor brakes, and the rest of us went into Bern to witness the Swiss Grand Prix. In addition to the Alfa Romeos of Farina, Fangio and Fagioli fighting it out, we saw the Heath/Abecassis team of H.W.M.s acquit themselves well in the Formula II event and the British motorcycles do well in both solo and sidecar races.

How different were those Grands Prix to the 'slot racing' between Armco barriers to which we have now become accustomed. If a driver left the road and hit a bank at Monte-Carlo it tended to be Barclays, and big solid trees bordered much of the Bremgarten Circuit at Bern. How long will it be before driverless cars are radio controlled from the pits?

The next day we left early for Paris 390 miles away. Motoring steadily all day, we reached the capital in time for dinner. The Kramers had arrived the previous evening, and had experienced only one bad moment on the way when an approaching camion driver had apparently fallen asleep while overtaking another camion – Geoffrey meanwhile had come to a standstill and was looking for reverse. When only twenty yards or so away the driver was roused by his mate and the camion scraped by without touching the Bentley.

The next morning was spent shopping; it was always a good plan to visit Paris at the end of a trip so that the available balance of currency could be calculated with an accuracy all too real. After lunch, we gazed into the windows of the motor accessory shops in the Avenue de la Grande Armée and left Paris at 6 pm for Dunkerque and the night ferry. We dined royally at the Maison Godbert in Amiens – another Walkerley recommendation – and did not leave that town until 10 pm. Then the headlamp which had been temporarily remounted became loose upon its pillar and swung round to the right. It was secured with insulating tape, but this broke several times and we drove with the light shining at right angles to the road for the last 20 miles. As we threaded our way through the docks at Dunkerque midnight chimed, and the Bentley was safely garaged on board.

So ended a memorable holiday and a hundred and one unrecorded incidents now crowd into my mind: innumerable, seemingly interminable, settlings-up ('I have paid the hotel bills, that's 22,195 lire including 15% service; deduct the extra eggs Bob had for breakfast, Jack's doctor's bill, and Geoff's drinks; that leaves 18,215 lire divided by five, but I paid for that last lot of petrol in Swiss francs and Harry owes me 1,000 French francs for his window at the Monaco Grand Prix and I don't want Austrian schillings if they are not convertible into Swiss francs, so if Bob gives me £2 when we get home and Geoff pays 50% of all our lunches at Innsbruck we shall be all square if Harry buys the programmes at Bern, etc, etc.'); . . . Con swigging Chianti out of a litre flask on the beach at Ventimiglia; heady waves of oleander perfume sweeping across the road; the Mille Miglia Ferrari on show in Milan; being shadowed and taken for fire-raisers when out for a stroll late at night in Interlaken; the Union Flag hoisted when Fergus Anderson won the motorcycle race at Bern; Geoffrey running his 4½ on the ferry alongside the trains because his 'sprags' wouldn't let him up the car ramp . . . and so many other things which served to whet the appetite for the next time.

Two trips on the Continent and two accidents was not a record to be proud of. I must have learnt my lesson, for in thousands of miles driving in many different cars since those days I have had only two traffic brushes – one with (or rather by) a Swiss army truck when my car was stationary; the other with an improvised agricultural snowplough meandering across an ice-bound road, again in Switzerland.

More Continental motoring

The year 1951 was a very busy one for me. I had taken on the editorship of a new glossy motoring magazine, *Autocourse*, which was to be published quarterly in four languages. This was the first time that an effort had been made to report in depth on a regular basis the Grand Prix races counting towards the World Championship and certain other important races. This involved personal attendance at nearly all of them (fortunately most Grands Prix took place within the confines of Europe at that time), and afterwards the production, analysis and interpretation of charts showing the relative positions at the end of each lap, and the lap times for every lap, of every competitor. These were compiled from the official time sheets obtained from the race organizers and I must draw a veil over the number of inaccuracies therein that I found necessary to correct in order to make sense of them.

Most of the travelling was done by air, but I did take the Bentley to Spa, Reims and Le Mans on consecutive weekends, leaving it in a hangar at Le Touquet during the intervening weeks and flying to and fro to collect it. These trips, too, had their highlights – as do all Continental excursions by road – and I call to mind the lap of the Reims circuit, on the eve of the race, when the 4½ took exactly twice Fangio's time even though she was doing just under 'the ton' down the straight; a 10 minute run on the Jabbeke-Aeltre road at an average speed of 87½ mph by kilometre stones and stopwatch; the thrill of the 24 hour race 'from the outside';

and searching for a hotel on arrival in Reims and finishing up over a dance-hall in most unusual circumstances (all the bedrooms had red doors!).

At the end of August we set off again in the $4\frac{1}{2}$ for a Continental holiday, this time accompanied by Horace Wilmshurst in 'Bluebell', the $4\frac{1}{2}$-litre Bentley built by Mac, the 'high priest', for his own use in hill-climbs, and owned after the War by Gordon Alexander and then Bill Cook.

We crossed the Channel by the now familiar Dover-Dunkerque midnight ferry, pleased to find a new ship, the 'Saint Germain', in service, and were off the boat very early the next morning. It was raining (I had yet to leave Dunkerque on a fine day). Our destination that evening was Interlaken, some 510 miles away, and our route lay via Arras, Reims, Châlons-sur-Marne, Chaumont, Besançon, Pontarlier and Bern. Geoffrey and Anne Kramer were travelling in my car as far as Bern, thence by train to Geneva to stay with friends until we picked them up on our return from the South of France a fortnight later. Geoffrey wondered, 'A 1150-mile hitch – is this a record?'

We pressed on in the rain with hoods up until we stopped at Laon at 8.45 am, having covered 147 miles. Oh, yes – there was one stop before this and it had the makings of being a permanent one. I had just crossed one of those nasty wooden-surfaced, hump-backed temporary bridges which abounded at that time in northern France and noticed too late that I should have turned immediately right. I stopped and backed up a bit, ready to take the correct course, when I perceived the other Bentley crossing the bridge. Horace braked, ready to follow me to the right, but all four wheels locked and the car slid on the slippery wood straight towards me, without any perceptible deceleration. Mercifully, there was three yards of pavé between the end of the wooden bridge and my car, and the front tyres of the approaching 'Bluebell' found some adhesion and came to rest less than an inch from my rear lamps. Having revived the fainting bystanders . . .!

After breakfast and refuelling 'Bluebell' – whose four SUs demanded a gallon every 12 miles and whose tank limited the distance between fill-ups to about 150 miles – we continued our journey, still in the rain, straight through Reims, resisting the temptation to race round the Grand Prix circuit just outside the city. We stopped in Châlons to lower hoods, the rain having ceased at last, and left for Chaumont. Here both cars were refuelled, coats were shed and windscreens lowered; at last we were beginning to realize that our holiday had really started. It was our intention to travel via Besançon, but we missed the left turn south of Langres, and consequently decided to go on through Dijon and lunch at the Hôtel du Nord, which we did.

We continued on and just before entering Pontarlier, a majority vote called for a cup of tea and out came the stove and kettle. The interval was enlivened by 'Bluebell's' ammeter needle disappearing on the discharge side while a wisp of smoke from under the dash promised an incipient fire if ignored. The fault was traced to the cut-out, temporarily rectified, and the journey continued through the customs and into Switzerland. As we came within striking distance of Bern it occurred to me that if we hurried it would be possible for the Kramers to catch the 7.22 pm train to Geneva; and so it turned out. The last few kilometres into the centre of Bern will long be remembered by those concerned, and probably also by those residents of Bern who saw two Bentleys dash to a stop outside the station, all the passengers and luggage disgorge on to the road, and two people hurriedly disappear into the station. Passengers and luggage caught the train with less than a minute to spare – not bad after nearly 500 miles. Then on to Interlaken in time for dinner at Krebs Hotel, where Bentley owners are always welcome. If perchance you should visit this hostelry, ask to see the visitor's book for the early '50s.

The next day included a short run up to the top of the Susten Pass, and a visit to the Aar Gorge and the Reichenbach Falls. The following day we all piled into my car and went shopping in Bern before a rapid run down to Lausanne for lunch at the Château d'Ouchy, overlooking Lake Léman. The return to Interlaken, after a visit to the Château de Chillon at Montreux, was made via the Col du Pillon.

We were to leave Interlaken the next day, Friday, August 31, intending to cover half a dozen of the highest passes in Europe on the way to Innsbruck. An early start was made, overcast skies and a promise of rain replacing the customary hot sunshine. The first pass negotiated was the Grimsel, and as we reached the first dam the rains came. It poured and poured for the rest of the day. We were very wet before we abandoned the hope that 'it was only a shower' and put up the hoods. The Furka Pass was climbed in a thunderstorm, and we decided to curtail our proposed 'pass-storming' route and settle for the Oberalp and Arlberg Passes. (This was the third occasion on which my desire to climb the Stelvio had been foiled and it is one of the few Alpine passes which I have yet to cross.)

After crossing the Austrian frontier, we stopped for a meal at a pleasant-looking gasthof – this was, I think, the only bad meal we had during that holiday – and then came round a bend to see a fellow countryman making fruitless efforts to extinguish flames under the bonnet of his elderly Austin. Horace put the fire out with one squirt from his 'Pyrene', and we moved on to reach Innsbruck at 10.15 pm. Imagine our surprise and anger when we were told by the manager that, as we had not arrived by 9 pm, he had let our rooms! He was unrepentant and maintained that this was an accepted practice. I pointed out that I had made similar reservations the previous year and arrived at 4 am to find the rooms still available, and what the hell! All he could or would do was offer us one large double room with three beds. Eventually, tired and dispirited, I told him to push in another bed and we all four shared the one room that night. I still like this hotel, but really . . .

The next morning we made a pre-arranged call at the B.P. depot to collect some benzole awaiting our arrival, and at lunch-time left for Salzburg via the southern tip of Germany near Berchtesgaden. This in spite of the fact that one of my magnetos had ceased to function. I put this down to failure of the insulation and steeled myself to cover the remaining 2,000 miles on one mag. – if it lasted – and, if necessary, have another flown out.

Hotel accommodation in Salzburg was at a premium, but we found satisfactory rooms at the fifth attempt and then repaired to the Goldener Hirsch for dinner. Afterwards, we went up to the castle to a folk-dancing and yodelling concert where a real live Austrian zither player played the very popular 'Harry Lime Theme' to the obvious satisfaction of all present.

The next day, after a visit to the mirth-provoking Schloss at Hellbron, we turned southwards over the famous Grossglockner Pass to Cortina d'Ampezzo. My 4½ did this trip, including the 8,438-ft climb, on one mag., and Horace streaked up the beautifully-engineered Grossglockner road as if at Prescott.

We left Cortina next morning to traverse the well-known Dolomiti Road (on which I had disgraced myself the previous year by driving the Bentley into the mountain side) over the Falzárego Pass, the Pordoi Pass and the Costalunga Pass to Bolzano, and then down to Fasano on the shore of Lake Garda. This was to prove an eventful day. The clouds were low and much of the beautiful scenery was obscured. While descending the first pass, Horace discovered, as a result of a door that refused to shut, that his chassis had cracked on the left side just behind the rear engine bearer. His wife transferred herself to the back seat of my car, and Horace decided that he would drive on slowly into civilization. The roads were under repair in parts and there were many miles of very bad surface indeed. We all felt every bump and jolt, and before long the crack developed into a clean break. The radiator trunnion clamp was removed to obviate the possibility of the flexing chassis splitting the matrix, and the magneto advance and retard control was disconnected. We eventually arrived at Lake Garda with no further worsening of this state of affairs.

A telephone call to Count Maggi, the man behind the Mille Miglia, sent us scurrying next morning to Brescia and the garage of the Lancia agent, Cantoni. Willing hands set to work on our arrival at 10.20 am and the job was finished at 3 pm, the frame member having been welded and boxed. Meantime, 20 minutes work on my ailing magneto by a Marelli mechanic cured the fault. Immediately, we headed for the Autostrada to Milan and arrived at Johnny Lurani's home at Cernusco in time for tea. Less than an hour later we were on our way to nearby Monza, where to our delight we found Farina indulging in some brake tests in a G.P. Alfa. He lapped consistently in 1 min. 57 secs. – well inside the lap record and a whole minute less than Horace in 'Bluebell' later in the day. We then did a lap in a new experimental 1900 Alfa Romeo with lights on and Guidotti driving. We were impressed more than somewhat. Then back to Johnny's house, where he had kindly invited us to spend the night.

Next morning was spent in Milan, and after lunch we turned south for Genoa and the Mediterranean. After a very pleasant drive along the coast road through Alassio, we reached Monte-Carlo in time for dinner; a visit to the Casino, of course, to add a modicum of our currency allowance to the coffers of that establishment; a visit to the Sporting Garage for benzole and a much-needed 'lavage de route'; then, along the coast to Juan-les-Pins where we anticipated four days of lazy bathing and generally taking things easy. We were all very disappointed in both the town and the hotel. The hotel had very small bedrooms, and only one bathroom in commission for those unfortunate enough not to possess the not inconsiderable means to pay for a room with bath. We coped with the town by leaving it every morning for a secluded beach near Antibes.

Telephone calls to and from a fellow Bentley enthusiast, Arnold Stenhouse, at Ste. Maxime, and artist Roy Nockolds at St. Jean Cap Ferrat, resulted in a run down to Ste. Maxime, where a most enjoyable swimming party took place.

Tales of bad weather at home made us reluctant to leave the almost too hot weather of the South of France, but the end of our stay approached. We left Juan-les-Pins at 7 am on Monday, September 10, and went via the Route Napoléon to Geneva, breakfasting in Castellane and lunching in Grenoble. At Geneva we were met by the Kramers, who had made reservations for us at the then new and highly satisfactory Hôtel du Rhône.

Early next morning we left for Paris and, thanks to the Michelin Guide, partook of an excellent lunch at Vieux Morvan at Rouvray, just north of Saulieu – the Omelette Meringué really was something! Resuming our course at a steady pace, we approached Paris rather more slowly than usual – the effects of the lunch, I think – and on reaching our destination parked the Bentley outside the Hôtel Continentale (now the Inter-Continental) in Rue Castiglione.

We had but 24 hours to spend in Paris and proceeded to make the most of it. After the lengthy ablutions which naturally follow a day's run in an open car on the Continent, we all six piled into the four-seater Bentley and went to eat at La Grenouille, or 'Roger the Frog's' as it was known to its habitues. The Michelin Guide describes this eating place as 'Fantasie et bonne humeur – au coude à coude', and is quite right. The menu was scribbled in chalk on a blackboard and you were handed a pair of opera glasses to read it; the place was a series

9 *The 4½-litre Bentley in Vintage Sports-Car Club driving tests at Slough, December 1953*

of small rooms surrounding the kitchen; ancient theatre posters and odd souvenirs decorated the walls and waiters were, to say the least of it, less formal than usual. Our waiter talked one of the girls in our party into having a sweet called 'Maison de Chef' – suffice to say that it was a confection of ice cream and fruit in a form which reduced all within sight to helpless laughter, but which in London (at that time) would have left the most broad-minded Watch Committee at a loss for words.

About six o'clock the following evening we reluctantly left Paris to catch the night ferry at Dunkerque – or so we thought. During dinner at the Moderne in Arras an old friend on his way to Monza told us of floods in south-east England and broken dock gates at Dunkerque. This chance encounter and a subsequent telephone call to the RAC Port Officer at Dunkerque from the police station at Béthune, saved us a fruitless journey to Dunkerque for a non-existent ferry-boat and sent us beetling off to Calais from which the 'Dinard' was making a special trip in the small hours. During the latter part of this trip I passed a car of the 'tin-box' variety with British plates and, thinking that it was probably heading for Dunkerque, slowed down alongside and called out to the driver that the lock was 'out' and that we were being diverted via Calais. Far from a word of thanks for this friendly act, the driver of the termite reacted as if I personally had run into the lock gates.

So back to England, many pounds poorer, but richer in experience, and having thoroughly enjoyed yet another spell of Vintage motoring on the mainland of Europe. We had covered 3,106 miles in the course of which some 240 gallons of petrol had been used.

The next year (1952) I clocked up over 2,500 miles on the 4½ in France and Switzerland, including a visit to Le Mans for the 24 Hour Race – the latter trip enlivened by the presence in the back seat of cartoonist Russell Brockbank.

I had the $4\frac{1}{2}$-litre for a few more years, enjoyed every mile in it and took part in many rallies, sprints and driving test competitions with it, but at the end of 1952 I acquired 'for business purposes' another car – a Rolls-Royce Phantom III of which more later – and tended to use this for Continental journeys. In addition, my health began to deteriorate, as a result of which I spent six months during the winter of 1955/6 in a sanatorium with T.B., which effectively curtailed my motoring activities for a spell.

I sold my $4\frac{1}{2}$ to David Braxton in August 1956, but not until I had my sights firmly on the next step up the Vintage Bentley ladder – a $6\frac{1}{2}$-litre; specifically, the unique Speed Six belonging to John Norris.

Speed Six

Thus, I graduated from the ruddy thump of a four-cylinder to the smoother torque of a six – but what a six!

My first ride, not drive, in a Speed Six – indeed in any Bentley – was during World War II when a G/Capt. E.M. Jones very kindly took me some miles up and down the A5 in his Barker-bodied boat-tailed $6\frac{1}{2}$-litre with torpedo running-boards and matching mudguards. At the time, this trip was a highlight in the midst of gloom and I hardly dared contemplate whether such opportunities would still arise when Peace broke out.

'AC 260' – my Speed Six – was often referred to by its registration number and will always be remembered for its battleship grey four-seater body (the rear two seats being in a tonneau-covered hole); for its five carburettors; and for its large third headlamp mounted centrally in front of the radiator.

John Norris had owned AC 260 since 1945 when he acquired it from John Morris. The latter, who held a senior position with SU Carburetters, devised and installed a five-carburettor lay-out which worked extremely well. Five carburettors for a six-cylinder engine sounds crazy until it is realized that there are three small carburettors which function all the time, and two large ones, which only come into operation when the throttle pedal is pressed beyond a certain point. The effect is not unlike the blower coming into operation on the 38/250 Mercedes-Benz. John Norris drove the Speed Six with zest on the road and in competition during his leave periods in the U.K. His eyes sparkled as he told of 100 mph plus over Salisbury at dead of night, and he once put it alongside Mavrogordato's Birkin Blower (now in the Sears' collection) and offered to toss him 'double or quits' – the winner to take both cars! His 1957 home leave coincided with the period of petrol rationing imposed upon us as a result of 'the Suez business', so he turned to his other love, sailing, and sold the car to me.

Would-be 'record-breakers'

It was in November 1957, when glancing through a copy of the V.S.C.C. Bulletin, that I was reminded of Tom Plowman's magnificent 106.9 miles in an hour at Montlhéry in August 1953, in his 30/98 Vauxhall. To me and many other Bentley enthusiasts this was a performance which could not forever remain unchallenged, and having recently acquired the Speed Six – not a fair comparison with a 30/98, I know – my thoughts turned to the possibility of my car, and perhaps Forrest Lycett's famous 8-litre, putting rather more than a hundred miles into the hour at Monza. At this stage it was only a pipe-dream, and not until I broke a connecting rod in my $6\frac{1}{2}$-litre during the Lagonda November Handicap Rally, thus making an engine overhaul necessary earlier than previously anticipated did I seriously consider the project.

My Bentley was towed to Hofmann & Burton's works at Henley-on-Thames and whilst being driven home afterwards by George Burton I gave him an inkling of my plot, and as a postscript asked him if he would like to bring his

10 *6½-Litre (Speed Six) waiting its turn at VSCC driving test meeting at Charterhouse*

4½ as well. He said 'Yes' just like that, and within 24 hours I was in a flurry of letter-writing and telephone calls making preliminary investigations as to the practicability of the operation. When should we go? Would the track be available and, if so, how much would it cost to hire for a day? Would the right kind and size of tyres be available? A host of other problems had to be settled before any real steps could be taken.

I called a meeting at my house of all concerned. Geoffrey Kramer agreed to join the party as Assistant Chef d'Equipe and Gerry Crozier, one-time owner of the Barnato-Hassan, agreed to drive my Speed Six – family and business considerations deterring me from doing the job myself. Don McKenzie found himself in the party committed to take part with his 3-litre Bentley, once owned by Forrest Lycett. Forrest Lycett, after careful consideration, decided not to participate in the venture. An invitation to Stanley Sears to join in with his beautifully rebuilt supercharged 4½-litre Birkin Team car was reluctantly declined by the owner, who, understandably, hesitated to expose such a precious possession to the risk of breakage or damage.

And so the party comprised three Bentleys – my Speed Six to be driven by Gerry Crozier, George Burton's 4½-litre and Don McKenzie's 3-litre.

An exchange of letters with Johnny Lurani and Mr. Bacciagalupi, Track Manager at Monza, revealed that the 'Circuito di Velocita' could be hired for Wednesday, 9 April, at a figure which looked astronomical in lire, but less frightening when converted to sterling. The date was cunningly chosen so that a 10-day trip bracketing the Easter week-end would mean the loss of only four working days. Meantime, Norman Freeman of Dunlops had started enquiries about the availability of suitable tyres. It turned out that special racing covers would have to be made for the project – *if* the moulds were still in existence. Many years had passed since there had been a demand for tyres for 18-inch and 19-inch wheels to carry cars weighing nearly two tons at over 100 mph. After several panic periods, during which Harold Smets and Dick Jeffery acquired not a few grey hairs as first one and then another size was eliminated when old plant proved to be unusable, Dunlops turned up trumps and produced sufficient 6.00 × 19, 7.00 and 6.50 × 19 covers to make the venture possible. These covers were buffed at the Works, reducing the tread-depth by 3 mm to lessen the likelihood of thrown treads.

All three participants were meeting the cost of preparing their own cars, sharing the hire of the track and paying all their own expenses throughout the venture. The idea was to chalk up one more prestige performance for the Vintage Bentleys – in other words, we were doing it for the hell of it. Nevertheless, we wished to reduce the cost to ourselves if at all possible. Esso, very sportingly I think, agreed to supply the oil and petrol needed for the journey out and home and for the high-speed runs at Monza. Silver City Airways made a special reduction in the cross-channel air ferry charges, and Lodge provided suitable plugs. I think that all this co-operation was forthcoming because the Vintage Bentley was (and still is) held in high esteem everywhere.

The problem of finding a suitable vehicle for the transport of wheels, tyres and spares was solved when Roney Messervy of Rolls-Royce Motor Car Division secured for us the loan of a brand-new Commer 30 cwt van.

Each month there was a 'Monza Meeting' at my home, when all the problems – administrative, technical and logistic – were fully discussed. The party was joined by Derek and Mary Waller, who were to do the lap-scoring and timing; Bob Gregory and Fred Hofmann, who were to drive the van carrying the spares; and John Tate and Ivor Kramer, who were to make a film of the whole thing. Bill Cook came along to assist generally, and his 300 SL Mercedes-Benz gull-wing coupe acted as a surprising 'tail-end Charlie' for many miles in trek across Europe.

The Speed Six engine was rebuilt with modified exhaust valves and lighter pistons. The chassis was 'gone over', all steering parts crack tested, and a 2.8 rear axle fitted, giving 34 mph per 1,000 rpm with 6.50 × 19 tyres.

The 4½-litre of George Burton had distinguished itself at the hands of its owner at race meetings, sprints and hill-climbs up and down the country, and was undoubtedly one of the three fastest 4½s in existence. The power behind the disarming 3-litre radiator had shaken more than one driver of a modern sports car. Each winter had brought its quota of 'mods.' and it is not surprising that the suspension and road-holding were selected for particular attention during the winter of 1957–8. I was surprised, however, to learn that George proposed to convert the rear of the 4½ to De Dion suspension of his own design using mainly Bentley parts. This conversion was carried out using Bentley springs and differential unit (now containing a 2.8 ratio lent by Forrest Lycett for the occasion). The De Dion tube was of mammoth proportions and the whole thing proved to be a most workmanlike job. There are those who will disapprove of this modification to a Vintage Bentley and regret yet another departure from the original design. This viewpoint is certainly a valid one, but it is extremely difficult to know where to draw the line, to decide when a Bentley is not a Bentley. Is the internal modification of the engine more open to criticism than the fitting of hydraulic brakes? Is the use of wheels smaller than those originally fitted (21-inch!) more anachronous than an oil cooling radiator? Whatever one's view, the fact remains that a De Dion type rear end is almost as old as motoring itself and, in this case, it worked extremely well.

Don McKenzie, with the smallest Bentley in the party, was faced with the most difficult

11 *The author at the wheel of the Speed Six in touring trim*

12 *Don McKenzie's 3-litre circulating at Monza*

problem of all: how to make a 3-litre in more or less touring trim cover 100 miles in the hour. It was asking a lot from a car which had left the factory 31 years previously. What combination of axle ratio and tyre size would enable the car to maintain its peak revs for one hour? There were many problems arising from sustained high-speed motoring which could not be resolved until we reached Monza, as we were to find out to our cost.

To my lot had fallen the task of making all the arrangements connected with the movement of the party to and from Monza. This involved a considerable amount of work. Few would relish the problem of finding hotel accommodation for single nights for 18 people along a 700 mile route across Europe during the Easter holidays. Other things, too, occupied my mind. Obtaining a currency allowance from the Bank of England; French and Italian petrol coupons; a permit to drive a van through France; lots of copies in English and French of the formidable list of spare parts to be taken, showing the value of each item (ever tried to translate 'rear-axle pinion-sleeve securing bolt' into French?); personal accident insurance; and a great deal of other paper work inevitable before a convoy of six cars and a van could set forth on such a Continental foray.

At last the day of departure arrived and Good Friday saw the three Vintage Bentleys, my Mark VI Bentley (which was to be a maid of all work) and the DB2/4 Aston Martin of our film unit, assembled at Lydd for the cross-channel flight to Le Touquet. The Commer was crossing by the Dover-Boulogne boat accompanied by the 300 SL, and bore a vast quantity of spares. It is said that the unfortunate customers of Hofmann & Burton and McKenzie Motors could hardly get a plug changed during 'Monza week' as the stores were very bare indeed while the gaffers were away. Some wag, seeing the pile of 17 wheels in the van, made an uncalled-for remark about customers' cars being jacked up for a fortnight.

The whole party joined up at Reims for the first night, and left next morning for Lucerne. This day's run was enjoyed by everyone, not the least amusing feature being the faces of the astonished Frenchmen, who saw first one Vintage Bentley, then another and finally a third pass through their village in thunderous procession.

Passing motorists, cyclists and pedestrians stared in wonder at the phalanx and Bill Cook, taking up the rear had to take many an avoiding action to preserve the lives of absent-minded road-users still wondering if the Paris-Madrid was on again. Many times did Russell Brockbank's famous cartoon, 'Citron Pressé', come to life, hard-pressed DS 19's giving up the unequal struggle as, one after the other, the three Bentleys thundered by. The only incident of note was the collapse of one of the rear wheels on the Speed Six – a 'slave' wheel not rebuilt for the occasion – which proved to have 27 broken spokes when inspected as a slight wobble became a formidable one.

At Lucerne next morning the cars were lined up outside the Schweizerhof Hotel prior to departure, and quite a crowd gathered to gaze at the cavalcade. Just as we were about to leave for Milan, George Burton came up to me and said: 'I've just pressed my starter button and all I got was an ominous clonk. I think I'm in trouble.' So, instead of making an impressive departure, we slunk one by one to the back of the hotel to investigate the trouble. Someone had commented during the previous day on the steam issuing from the $4\frac{1}{2}$'s exhaust, but only when the removal of a plug from No. 1 cylinder produced a veritable fountain of water was the possibility of a leak into the cylinder fully realized. George motored apprehensively on three cylinders to a nearby garage, where a large quantity of a well-known crack filling preparation was poured into the radiator.

By lunch-time it had been decided that the 3-litre and Speed Six, accompanied by the DB 2/4 and the 300 SL, should press on, whilst I should stay behind in the Mk. VI to cope with the problems arising from the $4\frac{1}{2}$. Fortunately, the Commer had not made an early start that morning and was standing by the disabled Bentley. It soon became evident that the cylinder block was well and truly cracked internally and that nothing short of a proper welding job would yield results – and perhaps not even that. It was decided that the van should tow the $4\frac{1}{2}$ to Monza so that the car would be on the spot and in a place where work could be carried out in comfort, within reach of adequate engineering facilities. So we started off towards Göschenen to board the train through the tunnel to Airolo.

As we neared the mountains the road surface became badly pot-holed and the gradient steeper. The Commer made light enough work of towing the $4\frac{1}{2}$, but its speed was considerably reduced on these gradients, and George in the Bentley could not see the holes in time to avoid them. Time was passing and the prospect of a long tow in the dark in this terrain was not without its hazards. We decided, therefore, to entrain the $4\frac{1}{2}$ and its occupants at Erstfeld, some 14 miles before Göschenen, the van going on ahead to board a train at Göschenen and to wait for the $4\frac{1}{2}$ further on at Airolo, where it would arrive at 6.10 pm.

Having seen the $4\frac{1}{2}$ safely on to its wagon – arranged by the Swiss Railway with no advance notice – I left to catch the van. The Mk. VI and the Commer took the same train through the tunnel and, whilst awaiting the arrival of the $4\frac{1}{2}$ at Airolo, I enquired if the train to which the wagon was attached was going any further. It was, so I decided to make arrangements for the disabled car to continue its journey by train to Chiasso and again sent on the van to await its arrival. When George and Margaret stepped out of the train at Airolo, I told them what I had done and to get back into the train. Just then a booking clerk came running up to say that he had made a mistake and that the train went only as far as Bellinzona. Then, as he rushed away with all the tickets to get different ones, George dropped the bomb-shell that he had left his wallet containing carnet and nearly everything else on the station at Erstfeld.

The train was held up while the station-master telephoned to arrange for the portfolio to be sent on the next train to the frontier station of Chiasso. The booking clerk came running back with the tickets and a refund, and George and Margaret got back into the train. I then set off in the Mk VI in an attempt to overtake the Commer before it reached Bellinzona, for otherwise the towing vehicle would be well on its way to the Italian frontier to wait for the arrival of the $4\frac{1}{2}$. Of course, I didn't overtake the van before Bellinzona – although I did beat the train by twenty minutes – and it was now well and truly dark. What was to be done now? I went to the station-master and explained the position in my halting French. The train was due in a few minutes. Could he attach the wagon with the 4½ to another train leaving for Chiasso that evening? It was now 7.45 pm. Yes, he would send it on a train leaving at 8.50 pm, due at Chiasso at 10 pm. Good, I thought, and asked him to telephone to his colleague at Chiasso to tell him what was happening and to say that if two Englishmen turned up asking about the 4½ to tell them it would be in at 10 o'clock. This done, I once again went to greet the Burtons as they stepped from the train – this time to whisk them into the buffet for a meal during the shunting operation.

Hunger satisfied, I left for Chiasso and drove as fast as conditions permitted. I was amazed on arrival at the station there to find no trace of the van nor of the portfolio, which should by then have arrived from Erstfeld! Once again I had arrived before the train and found that the station authorities did not know that the car was on the train now due in seven minutes' time. It seemed that the telephone call from Bellinzona had coincided with a change of shift, and Bob Gregory (as I discovered later) was told that the 4½ couldn't arrive until the next morning. Thus misinformed, he crossed the frontier and high-tailed it for Milan, intending to return the next morning for his tow. Immediate arrangements were made for the 4½'s wagon to be shunted to a siding where the car was off-loaded by pushing. At this moment, the missing portfolio was found by a luggage clerk, but we were still not in the clear for we had no towing vehicle. Fortunately, the tow-rope was still attached to the 4½, so I fixed the other end of it to the rear bumper of the Mark VI and drove to the frontier about 100 yards away, where I fervently hoped to find the Commer. It was not to be. I was told that it had waited for some time and then departed southwards.

I decided that the Mk VI could tow the 4½ the 30-odd miles into Milan, and after many minutes on the telephone filled with 'Prontos' I was able to tell Geoffrey Kramer at the hotel in Milan that I was bringing the 4½ and expected to arrive at 12.15 am. Thus I left the Customs driving the Mark VI, which carried five passengers, a boot full of luggage, four suitcases on a roof-rack, and a 4½-litre Bentley containing two persons and their luggage on a rope behind. The car went remarkably well and barely seemed to notice the added load. At the entrance to the Autostrada I asked George if he would be all right if I went a bit faster. He said 'Yes.' The night was clear. The Autostrada was deserted. The speed crept up. I could see the line of roadside reflectors and an empty road for miles ahead. The 50 mph I had had in mind was soon reached and, as speed is always relative, a mile-a-minute seemed a mere crawl after a short while. Much of the Autostrada was covered at 70 mph and there was a sustained 80 on the clock on more than one occasion. The Burtons stepped out of the car at the end of this stage without any visible signs of wear, George remarking laconically about the Mk VI: 'These cars really are a magic carpet, aren't they?'

We arrived at the hotel on time and were welcomed by the whole party, for everyone had stayed up to greet us. And so we were all in Milan on schedule. And here a brief tribute to my long-suffering passengers would not be out of place – Con and daughter Carol, Marjorie Gregory and Anne Kramer – who had borne the day's activities with fortitude and good temper. (I soon learned that, provided they were regularly 'fed and watered', they would put up with almost anything.)

The 4½ was towed to Monza next morning by the Commer, and the block lifted to reveal a T-shaped crack which ran for almost one inch across the top of No. 1 cylinder and about the same distance downwards between Nos. 1 and 2 cylinders. It was Easter Monday and nothing in the way of welding could be done until the block could be taken to a welding wizard the following morning.

Meanwhile work proceeded on preparing all three cars for the high-speed runs. We intended to do the runs in touring trim, but decided to remove lamps, mudguards and full-width windscreens for reasons of safety. Apart from this, the cars ran in the same trim in which they had been driven from England.

Dunlop's fitter, Sid West, supervised the fitting of the wheels with the racing covers, and arrangements were made to obtain a supply of Esso Extra from the pumps at the track. The Speed Six and the 3-litre were almost ready for the fray before the 4½-litre's block came back from the welding shop. All hands set to work at tea time, on the day before THE DAY, to re-assemble the 4½ engine. This was completed in a few hours and the car was left standing overnight whilst we all kept our fingers crossed hoping that yet another tin of magic would complete the sealing operation. It was not to be, however, and next morning George made repeated efforts in the Paddock to get the engine to fire on all four cylinders whilst the other two cars were completing their qualifying laps.

Every driver using the 4.25 kilometre banked circuit at Monza was required to do 10 laps at gradually increasing speeds up to 70 per cent of the target speed set for the actual record attempt or high-speed trial. These familiarization laps were undoubtedly of great value, even to experienced racing drivers who had not before driven on a banked circuit. Both Don McKenzie and Gerry Crozier confessed that an increase of only 10 mph on the lap speed gave one quite a different impression of the circuit. The Speed Six and the 3-litre, having completed their qualifying laps, put in a couple of fast ones for Dunlops, whose French Racing Manager, Henri Lallement, had flown down from Paris to pass judgment on tyre temperatures. The cool weather no doubt contributed to the happy verdict that no speed limitation was to be imposed. Nevertheless, the 50 lbs pressure insisted upon gave the drivers a very bumpy ride indeed, and on the worst parts they bounced six inches off their seats.

Poor George came out of the Paddock on three cylinders to do his qualifying laps, hoping that No. 1 cylinder would 'chime in' when he really got going. He did his first two qualifying laps on three cylinders in second gear to keep the revs up but he was out of luck, and also caused some consternation by having greatly exceeded his qualifying speeds. The timely intervention of Johnny Lurani averted the imposition of a 5,000 lire fine. George then went out to do one fast lap for Dunlops and all four cylinders were in for part of this lap; his lap speed was 110 mph. His luck was right out, however, and further work on the car being of no avail he was forced to abandon the attempt.

The Speed Six had now started its Hour Run. After four laps at just over 118 mph Gerry Crozier came in because he had lost all his power quite suddenly and suspected the need for hotter plugs. Whilst the plugs were changed – no speedy operation on the inlet side – Don McKenzie took out the 3-litre on its One Hour Run. It was now 3 pm and less than three hours of track time remained available. He lapped consistently for 40 minutes at nearly 98 mph, then our hearts sank as he came low off the banking and headed for the pits. As he came to a stop the engine sounded uneven, but his real complaint was that he had no clutch and no brakes. A cursory inspection revealed that the pedal cross-shaft had come adrift at one end, and a glance under the valve cover revealed that a valve had broken. The Speed Six was now ready for another go and Gerry set off once more whilst Don, not one whit daunted, proceeded to take the block off the 3-litre to replace the broken valve, hoping that no further damage had been done.

The 6½-litre sounded and looked magnificent. The first four laps were covered at over 118 mph, the next two a good deal slower, and we feared the same trouble had recurred. However, the engine picked up and seemed to be going well until Gerry brought the car in after 12 laps with a most uneven beat. Further examination revealed that an inlet valve had broken, thus putting paid to the Speed Six's effort. It was great while it lasted and we couldn't forget the wonderful sight and sound as it came past the pits at over 120 mph. Its fastest lap was 119.4 mph and it had covered 50 kms at 110.3 mph.

Don's valve job was progressing apace with the assistance of Fred Hofmann, who had left his fruitless labours on the $4\frac{1}{2}$. At 5.30 pm Don was back on the starting line, having changed the valve, fixed the loose pedal-shaft and refuelled in $1\frac{3}{4}$ hours. We wondered if this augured new piece-work rates at Thornton Heath.

It was now a case of all our hopes resting on Don McKenzie's shoulders. He soon got his lap time down to a steady 1′ 39.6″ (96.5 mph). When complimented on his consistent lappery at the end of his first attempt, he replied that there was nothing to congratulate him about; it just wouldn't go any faster, it was flat out all the time.

The tension built up among those of us standing at the pits as Don circulated, and time never went so slowly. Lap after lap went by. Then, with only 10 minutes to go, he came past a minute late and more slowly; the engine sounded a bit rough. Two slowish laps later he stopped and said, 'It's happened again. I've broken another valve. I don't think it will drop in so I think I'll go on and finish the Hour on three cylinders.' And so he did. He covered 89.19 miles in the hour and had covered 100 kilometres at a speed of 96.54 mph before his engine blew up. His fastest lap was 98.63 mph. For sheer grit and determination, Don's work at Monza on that day took a lot of beating.

We all returned to Milan feeling disappointed about the day's happenings – indeed more than one of the womenfolk had shed a tear – but there was not the overwhelming sense of despair which might have been expected with the prospect before us of all three Vintage Bentleys lying out of action in garages at Monza.

It was agreed that the Aston Martin and the Mercedes-Benz should leave for Lausanne during the morning according to plan. The blocks were to be lifted off the Speed Six and the 3-litre and new valves fitted and if no further irreparable damage was discovered they would start for Lausanne later in the day. Bob was to make a solid tow-bar to couple the $4\frac{1}{2}$-litre to the back of the Commer. The van had to be loaded and the wings and lamps put back on the Bentleys. I left Monza in the Mark VI at 2.30 pm and after a miserable three hours spent before, in, and after, the Simplon Tunnel, checked in at the Château d'Ouchy in Lausanne about 11 pm. It was bitterly cold and snowing part of the way. We felt really sorry for those in the open Bentleys, especially for George and Margaret Burton, faced with a tow all the way home without any engine heat and, of course, no hood or sidescreens.

The van and its tow left Monza at 5 pm and reached Lausanne at 2.30 am. On arrival at Lausanne I had received a message from Geoffrey Kramer at Domodossola that the Speed Six and 3-litre were on the last train through the tunnel and they hoped to be in by 3 am, this after having worked on their engines for five or six hours. They arrived at 4 am and were frozen; it had been snowing most of the 100 miles from Brig and to cap it all, they had missed a badly placed diversion sign in Brig. It was some time before they realized that the fallen trees, rocks and snow drifts were not meant and that they were in fact climbing the closed Simplon Pass back into Italy. The necessary reversal of direction was a hazardous business undertaken on a narrow precipitous road, made none the more pleasant by Fred Hofmann's assertions that a Bentley exhaust could easily start an avalanche. Over a very early morning cup of tea in the hotel kitchen, we decided that we would make for Paris the next day as planned, but would defer our departure until lunch-time.

Again the Aston and the Mercedes went ahead with a request to confirm the room reservations at the Hotel Continental, the rest of the convoy leaving about mid-day. Everybody was in good heart, especially the Burtons, for whom our admiration grew as they progressed on their long 'graunch' home behind the Commer. We found snow on the roads in the Jura Mountains and there was a bitterly cold east wind blowing all day. Suffice to say we all reached Paris, the van arriving at 2 am.

The next day was spent resting, and in the evening we dined at the Lido. When more comely chassis were not demanding our attention, we were having a technical post-mortem. It was the considered opinion that there must be some peculiar valve-spring period at sustained peak revs which led to the valves breaking, for all three valves (two in the 3-litre and one in the Speed Six) were made from KE 965, though by two different manufacturers. We recalled the similar trouble experienced by W.O. with the streamlined 3-litre at Montlhéry in 1926. It was gratifying to those responsible for preparing the cars that these breakages were of new components of standard design and could not possibly have been foreseen.

It was then that I heard somebody say, 'If we go again, we must do so and so.' Later on the tone of the conversation changed to *when* instead of *if*. George, the most unfortunate of us all – he had had the devil's own luck and not even one really fast lap of Monza – then said, 'I regard this as "unfinished business". I, for one, will return again next year or the year after.' Don said he was sure he could make his 3-litre do the 100 in the hour. It was as if the underlying enthusiasm which had made the whole thing possible in the first place had risen like a phoenix from the table and, though not yet home from the current venture, possible dates for the next attempt were being mentioned before we went to bed that night.

The journey from Paris to the Channel coast was uneventful; damned cold, but uneventful. It is ironical to record that Bob Gregory, after having driven with Fred Hofmann in the Commer all the way from Monza with the 4½ on tow, was warned for speeding near Leatherhead. The boys in blue must have wondered if they were having their legs pulled when told that the van had towed the Bentley all the way from Italy in three days!

The party disbanded at my house as the clock neared midnight, the Burtons cheerfully facing the last 25 miles of their 860-mile tow. Monza to Maidenhead ten feet behind a Commer van. Is this a record? Incidentally, even after this George couldn't tell us the number of the van!

We had not achieved what we set out to do – over 100 miles in the hour with each car – but we had proved to ourselves that each of the cars was indeed capable of such a performance. We learned a lot, mostly the hard way. George confirmed he would go again; the magic '100' was within Don's grasp and he, too, could not resist having another go. It was taken for granted that the Speed Six would be there again, and it was assumed that I would once again undertake the organization and administration.

And so we retired to lick our financial wounds and to let the boffins solve the valve trouble before returning to the fray. (We took our problem to Terrys – the spring people. They set up a bench rig and ran tests which confirmed the diagnosis. A spring with different characteristics was specified and, as an additional safeguard, stronger valves were made and fitted.)

Flying Kilometres and a reconnaisance of Montlhéry

During the winter we discussed the possibility of using the Montlhéry track, just outside Paris, for the next sixty-minute 'blinds'. We had chosen Monza the previous year because it was a relatively new circuit and we reckoned it would, therefore, be much smoother than the old Montlhéry piste. The Monza track, however, was quite bumpy and subsequent enquiries led us to believe that the French track might be no worse, although it was a much 'tighter' circuit with a lap distance of about $1\frac{1}{2}$ miles compared with the $3\frac{1}{2}$ miles of Monza. The advantages of being able to play at record breakers so much nearer home were apparent, but we did not feel happy about mounting another full-scale 'Monza-type' operation on hearsay alone; some sort of reconnaisance at racing speeds seemed advisable. I was arranging for a party of enthusiasts to be timed in their Bentleys over a measured mile, and kilometre, in Belgium – myself in the Speed Six included – and decided to go on afterwards to try out the Montlhéry track. This coincided with Gordon McDonald's avowed intention of improving upon Tom Plowman's 30/98 Vauxhall performance in his $4\frac{1}{2}$-litre Bentley. Thus, I found myself organizing a two-pronged foray to the continent in 1959.

The idea entered my head sometime before Christmas that it might be possible to arrange for the well-known Jabbeke-Aeltre stretch of the Ostend-Brussels autoroute to be closed for the purpose of timed runs over a measured kilometre and a measured mile. The late Forrest Lycett had been there in 1950 by courtesy of 'Goldie' Gardner – making record-breaking attempts there with his MG – and set up new National Class 'B' Records for the Flying Kilometre and Flying Mile of 134.755 mph and 133.828 mph respectively in his famous 8-litre now in the Sears family collection. That Forrest Lycett joined us was, in his words, '. . . solely due to the benevolent yet persistent importunity of Stanley Sedgwick, President and Good Shepherd of the Bentley Drivers Club for, truth to tell, I had been but lukewarm at best.' We were anxious to see the 8-litre take back the honours from Maurice Trintignant, who had improved on the 8-litre's 1950 speeds in a Facel Vega, achieving 139.895 mph and 140.186 mph for the kilometre and mile respectively.

Forrest's last defences were breached when I secured from Dunlops an undertaking to build special tyres for the 8-litre and to guarantee them up to 150 mph, so he 'phoned Don McKenzie, son of 'Mac' who had built the car, and gave him carte blanche to go through it from end to end with a view to making it faster than it had ever been before.

Permission was sought from the Belgian Government to close the Jabbeke road, but this was not forthcoming as it was now part of the completed and very busy autoroute joining the capital with the coast. Through the good offices of Mr. de Harlez of the RAC Belgium, the Government agreed to place at our disposal a completed stretch of a new motor-road in the course of construction between Antwerp and Liège.

It was an optimistic and dedicated band of Vintage Bentley enthusiasts that gathered on Sunday morning, 24 May 1959, to drive their cars on to the ferry at Dover. They comprised at least one Vintage Bentley of each model except the 4-litre. David Llewellyn was to uphold the honour of the 3-litres, Don McKenzie having a full-time job ministering to the Lycett 8; Harold Pounds and the late Harry Rose took their $4\frac{1}{2}$-litres and George Burton again appeared in his $4\frac{1}{2}$; Stanley Sears, accompanied by son Jack and Tony Townshend, was giving an airing to his 'Birkin Blower'; the Speed Six (ferried by Hugh Young) was mine, and Oliver Batten's 8-litre was company for its distinguished fellow. Eight competing Bentleys, plus a back-up of helpers. I took my Mk VI as a maid of all work. The spares van, was driven on this occasion by Fred Hofmann and Peter Corney. Bill and Marion Cook came along in their Phantom III Rolls-Royce, which also did its share of 'to-ing and fro-ing'. Dunlop produced the necessary tyres and honoured us by sending D.J. MacDonald (Dunlop Mac) to keep an eye on them; and Esso provided petrol and oil.

At Ostend the cars were lined up and various petrol tanks were drained of their Golden Esso (unobtainable in Belgium) to be reserved for Forrest Lycett's 8-litre which pinked badly on petrols of lower octane. This completed, the journey to Antwerp began, the Mk VI leading with the P III bringing up the rear, Bill Cook thus resuming his Monza role of 'tail-end Charlie'. The van was left to pursue its own leisurely course.

On the Monday morning at 10.30 am the the convoy set off to explore the stretch of road which was to be our testing ground. It will not be difficult to imagine the amazement of the townsfolk to see a line of Bentleys rumbling and roaring over the pavé, down narrow streets, twisting round trams and in and out of the traffic. Ten kilometres later we had reached the Autoroute, stretching as far as one could see with only one very slight curve, and a gentle gradient at one end. I led the way in the Mk VI at between 95 and 100 mph and a never-to-be-forgotten sight in the rear-view mirror was a column of flying Vintage Bentleys in pursuit, their spinning locking rings sparkling in the bright sunlight. Soon after, I made a run in the Speed Six and managed a sustained 125 mph, a gratifying come-back after the disappointment of Monza.

The party then adjourned for lunch and spent the afternoon removing wings, lamps and screens in readiness for the following day. This was a safety precaution but would also make quite an appreciable difference to maximum speed. Tyre sizes were varied and pressures checked regularly, Dunlop Mac unobtrusively picking his way from car to car armed with the biggest tyre gauge under the sun. By this time, a number of passing motorists had pulled up to admire these gleaming monsters from a foreign land. Harry Rose expressed himself well satisfied with just under 110 mph. David Llewellyn, however, was overgeared and went into a further huddle over the tyre sizes. There was some concern, too, for Forrest Lycett who found the 8-litre to be decidedly faster than it had been for years, but taking too long to reach 130 mph. Don McKenzie worked late that night and happily rounded up the missing horses, as the results of the next day proved beyond doubt.

THE day started with a 5.30 breakfast in Trappist-like silence and a procession to arrive at the motor-road at 6.45 am. Our side of the twin-track highway was closed to public traffic from about 8 am. The cars were parked in echelon at the roadside, and it looked as if a Le Mans start was the order of the day! The weather was ideal: cloudy, bright, cool and a slight breeze. The RAC of Belgium were on duty to record the times electrically; the Belgian police were there to direct traffic and generally control matters.

The rules governing records require the distance to be covered in both directions within an hour, and it must be the same piece of road. Thus, when a mile and kilometre are being timed it is usual to measure off the mile and then place the kilometre at one end of, and within the mile. Flying runs can thus be timed over both the mile and the kilometre on a single run; this is so in both directions. There are strict limitations as to permitted gradients at each end of the measured distances which themselves have to be level within very small tolerances. At Herentals – the village nearest to the stretch of road we were using – there was a 3 kilometres run-in at one end of the measured mile and 5 kilometres at the other, and so everyone had ample opportunity to wind up their Bentley to maximum speed before entering the timed distances – and ample distance for slowing down on completing the mile.

Most of the entrants were pleased with the outcome of their endeavours, with the exception of George Burton, who seems only to have to cross the Channel with 'NPA 83' to take aboard unsuspected gremlins. The 4½ could run week-end after week-end in competitions in England, but after Monza – Antwerp! With characteristic zeal George tackled the job of dismantling his engine – lifting the block at the roadside – when he clattered to the end of his very first run over the mile. The evidence was all too damning; the cylinder liner had dropped on No. 3 and lay in fragments in the sump. Nothing could be done to enable further competition driving, and once again George Burton was cheated of the opportunity to show the paces of his car under controlled conditions. Let it be said that the failure in the engine was no part of the work done by George himself. The block which failed on the way to Monza had been sold for 6d (2½p) and a replacement block – which had appeared to be 100 per cent – was used instead.

Stanley Sears' blower car looked and sounded magnificent and did just about what its owner and Tony expected – 125.304 mph for the mile and 125.599 mph over the kilometre. It was refreshing to find that this car (and Harry Rose's 4½) which habitually won Concours d'Elegance was expected to provide continental transport for its owner and also to acquit itself commendably in competitive motoring – a welcome contrast to some of the cotton-wool concours-only cars of all makes with which we are all familiar.

Harold Pounds' speed over the mile so exceeded his expectations – over 119 mph with an unblown 4½ – that he called it a day. His unbridled pleasure at his car's performance delighted everyone, not least Dunlop Mac who said that in all his experience he had never seen anyone so enthusiastically overjoyed over the performance of a car.

David Llewellyn's efforts to achieve an average speed of 100 mph using Don McKenzie's 'Monza' 3-litre engine borrowed for the occasion, were unsuccessful but 98½ mph was no mean performance.

Oliver Batten's 8-litre, with its home-made body in one of its characteristically ugly forms, averaged 123.587 mph over the kilometre despite an unintended air-brake. As soon as he took off on his first flying run the boot lid of his car – about 4 ft square – came unlocked. Hinged at the top behind the seats, it flapped up and down all the way, rather like a rapidly reversing hungry whale. Oliver was completely unaware of the sheet metal jive going on just behind but was surprised that he was several hundred revs down on his expected performance.

I was delighted with the Speed Six and with my average speed over the two-way mile of 127.818 mph. It reflected great credit on Fred Hofmann and George Burton and their merry men at Henley that this car, which is not greatly modified, should have been made to go so fast. Its 128 mph was within striking distance of the speed attained by Forrest Lycett's 8-litre at Jabbeke in 1950. To me, driving at that speed in the ideal conditions of the day was out of this world. The car felt very steady and it was exhilarating in the extreme. It brought home to me the vast difference between 100 mph and 125 mph in a Vintage car.

I had planned to borrow George's 700 × 17 tyres for the standing start runs, but when I went to get them off his disabled car – feeling rather like a corpse-robber – someone else had been there first. The 4½ was jacked-up on the roadside minus engine and front wheels. I used the next best size available, 700 × 18, but the overall ratio thus obtained was hopelessly high for sprints.

The cynosure of all eyes was, of course, Forrest Lycett's 8-litre. During a 15-mile warm up he found that Don had indeed breathed effectively upon the works and the car had been transformed overnight.

The time of his first run went unrecorded, but the 8-litre made several runs through the measured distances. The lack of a communication system between the timekeeper and competitors meant that such times as reached the drivers did so spasmodically and were, to say the least, unofficial. We had heard that the 8-litre had improved on the Facel Vega's time, but did not know by how much, and, in view of the limited time available and the number of cars to be timed it was not possible to hold up proceedings to find out. I asked Forrest Lycett if he would like to have one more pair of runs over the flying mile before we started the standing runs for the other cars. He decided to do this, but expressed a doubt as to whether he had enough petrol for a flying distance, although he had sufficient for a standing start attempt. But off he went. I had not seen any of the Bentleys flat out on the measured mile, so Bill Cook took me down the parallel track in the PIII to see the 8-litre on the return run.

This was not to be as the engine blew up on the first run. Our alarm at the rush of police and officials towards a cloud of smoke in the distance was relieved when we perceived the 8-litre at rest on the grass verge Forrest Lycett surveying the scene. Thus did the 8-litre experience its first ever blow-up through fuel starvation, the resultant weakened mixture burning a hole in a piston crown. Poor Don had spent the morning driving up and down the parallel track with a supply of fuel, only to be passed by the 8-litre going the other way, or to arrive at the turning-point just as Forrest Lycett took off in the other direction. It was unfortunate that the car became hors de combat before covering a standing kilometre in both directions. Equally unfortunate was it that the timing apparatus failed to record the 8-litre's first pair of runs over the mile for, as the rev counter clearly showed, the first of these was marginally the best run of the day.

The average speeds of the two pairs of runs which counted for the flying kilometre and mile Belgian National Class 'B' Records were 141.131 mph and 140.845 mph respectively; (these comparing with 139.895 mph and 140.186 mph by Maurice Trintignant on the Facel Vega the previous November and with Forrest Lycett's own speeds of 134.755 mph and 133.828 mph in 1950 at Jabbeke). The best recorded run was 141.667 mph over the kilometre.

Forrest Lycett had been an enthusiastic owner of Bentleys for over thirty-five years and during that time devoted much thought and not a little money to improving his Bentleys. The fruits of such experimental work thus carried out by 'Mac' have benefitted all owners of Vintage Bentleys. I had known Forrest Lycett personally only since the war, but my impression of his agelessness was borne out by those who had known him much longer than I. That Forrest Lycett continued to enjoy driving his 8-litre in competitions – in which success can be made or marred by fractions of a second gained or lost in gear changes – in spite of the physical discomfort caused by arthritis in his hands was illustrative of the courage of the man. It was characteristic of him that he said nothing at Antwerp of the pain he was suffering whilst driving. Forrest Lycett's performance in his 8-litre would have called for the highest praise if he had been young and in robust health; as it was, it was magnificent. There is not a member of the Bentley Drivers Club who would not count himself fortunate indeed to be able to drive nearly as well at an age many years his junior. Outside immediate Club circles the fact that an elderly gentleman could drive an elderly car at such a speed was considered little short of miraculous and evoked the highest admiration. (It was not generally known that he bore a substantial part of the cost of closing and policing the road for the benefit of all.) Forrest Lycett not only owned the fastest vintage Bentley in the world, but could justly have claimed to be the only septuagenarian in the world to have been timed at over 140 mph.

At the end of the morning's proceedings I towed Forrest Lycett's 8-litre, with my Mk VI, back to the garage in Antwerp. I decided to leave it on the ground floor, as I was not keen on towing it up two steep ramps to the second floor where we had a large garage to ourselves. Imagine my surprise, on returning to the garage after a brief visit to the hotel, to find that Hugh Young had leapt into the Mk VI, romped up the ramps with the 8-litre on tow and thought nothing of it.

By 1.15 pm the Government were given back their road and we returned to lunch, followed by a post-mortem of the morning's activities conducted concurrently with the mounting of wings, etc. Forrest was mobile again by early evening, Don having removed the valve gear from No. 2 cylinder to relieve the compression, the 8 motoring home quite happily on five cylinders. By now, George had removed No. 3 piston, con rod and valve gear (not forgetting to seal off the oil hole in the crank journal); and had the sump replaced before sunset. After a little persuasion and some hearty pushing the 4½ came to life again. Inevitably she was hardly smooth on three cylinders, and the general effect on George was that of undergoing vibro-massage treatment. However, it was decided that she was fit to run to Paris on the following day, for George was going to drive the reconnaisance laps in the Speed Six at Montlhéry in place of Gerry Crozier, who had not been well enough to accompany us.

Perhaps the most noteworthy feature of this effort was the wonderful spirit of co-operation and sportsmanship that characterized the whole venture. The way in which a number of chaps of widely differing temperaments, ages and means worked together as a team without any ructions is a tribute to the single-mindedness imbued in enthusiasts by the Vintage Bentleys. An outsider would never have known, for instance, that the cars had been prepared by three different firms specializing in Vintage Bentleys and that the proprietors and brains of all three firms were in the party. Their knowledge, effort and tools were pooled for the good of all and the owners of all the participating cars were the first to give credit to the chaps concerned: Burton, Hofmann, McKenzie and Townshend.

On Wednesday morning the party split up, the 'mile and kilometre only' contingent returning home whilst the Montlhéry party, comprising my two Bentleys, the spares van and the lame 4½ of George Burton set off for Paris. The van crew, who had left Antwerp well in advance, were held up at the frontier for an hour-and-a-half explaining how they came to have one more spare tyre on board than listed in the inventory.

13 *George Burton in the Speed Six passing the pits at 120 mph plus, Montlhéry 1959*
14 *The Speed Six engine after the fire at Montlhéry, May 1959*

The sight of the Speed Six in my rear-view mirror was a stirring one and the driver, Hugh Young – owner himself of a very nice Speed Six of more pedestrian aspect – was thoroughly enjoying himself. As darkness fell, he discovered that the Speed Six rear lights were not operative and, being somewhat fatigued stopped at 10.20 pm and booked a room in an all-night café 60 miles north of Paris. No sooner had he registered than in walked George to book another room, with the news that a second liner had gone and he was leaving the 4½ to the tender mercies of the AA for shipment back to England. Hugh and luggage were transferred from the Speed Six to the Mk VI which then continued to Paris,

BENTLEY

15 *Bill Cook in his 300 SL Mercedes and the faithful Mk VI at Montlhéry, 1960*
16 *Gordon McDonald arriving at Montlhéry en famille*
17 *Don McKenzie arriving at Montlhéry in the 3-litre*

leaving George and family to follow on the next morning in the Speed Six.

The following morning we set off for Montlhéry, some 15 miles south of Paris, first calling at Orly to pick up Geoffrey Kramer who had flown from England to assist with lap-scoring and time-keeping. Gordon McDonald and family were already at the track, his 4½-litre stripped down to racing trim. No serious attempts were contemplated until the following day, but Mac put in several trial laps at between 105 and 112 mph before lunch, to familiarize himself with the steeply banked concrete circuit, and made the rather disconcerting announcement that he had felt something 'pick-up' – the compression was down on No. 4. It sounded like a piston ring playing up, but oil applied through the carburettor air intakes appeared to ease the situation.

The afternoon was sunny with a slight breeze blowing when Mac took off again, but the over-cooled engine (58° C) was not giving its best performance. Part of the radiator was blanked off, and a fair quantity of summer grade oil drained from the sump and replaced with SAE 30 in the search for higher working temperature, better upper-cylinder lubrication, and another 200 rpm.

Three more laps were then reeled off, two of them at over 110 mph but the 4½ was still running cool, and was brought into the pits for further blanking off. It was now time for the Speed Six to have a run and Fred Hofmann introduced it and himself to the circuit with four laps, gradually increasing the lap speed from 110 mph to 118.75 mph on the fourth circuit. Returning to the pits, Fred announced that the throttle had been nowhere near fully open. When asked by Geoffrey Kramer, 'Why not?' the answer was, 'I'm not a bloody racing driver.'

The visit to Montlhéry had a two-fold objective as far as George and I were concerned: to see if the valve trouble experienced at Monza had been overcome, and to compare the tracks from a speed potential point of view. It was not

18 *Gerry Crozier prepares for his first run at Montlhéry, Easter Monday 1960*

intended to attempt an hour's run with the Speed Six. It was only when Fred's reconnaisance produced a lap within one mile per hour of the best lap at Monza the previous year that our fear that the roughness of the track might not permit the Bentleys to be driven at their maximum speed was dispelled and, as the Speed Six was going like a train, it was decided to run it for an hour next day.

Friday, The Day, was cool and cloudy with a slight breeze, ideal conditions for the work in hand. Speed Six and 4½ both had their final goings over, petrol pumps, distributor caps and ignition leads being taped up, and were then driven round the circuit for a few check laps to ensure that all was well. George put in one lap at 123.9 mph (3,550 rpm) on 700 × 19's and pronounced both car and driver to be very happy. An extra turn was given to the shockers to cope with the petrol load for one hour, the tyres checked by Dunlop Mac for the *n*th time, and all was ready. Like Fred, George's hoof was not right down on the floorboards, but he was going 'almost as fast as I can drive it'. Mac had reached 114 mph at 3,700 rpm with an occasional 3,800 on 700 × 17's against the 19's of the previous day. There was now no more to be done to either car.

Accordingly, the Speed Six set off at noon, followed after several laps by the 4½. The two made a handsome high-speed couple, Mac dropping down the banking to allow George to pass when necessary. For about 35 minutes the Speed Six circulated steadily, lap after lap, running very sweetly and going like hell. Then for four or five laps it had a tendency to misfire and George eased back from the 122 mph mark down to 116 mph thinking, as we all did, that it was a spot of plug trouble. For three or four laps after that she picked up again and everyone heaved a sigh of relief. However, Fate was to be agin us again, and the misfiring recurred. As George came past we could see a lick of flame from the left side of the bonnet. We did not

19 *When a Speed Six swallows a valve! Portrait of Geoffrey Kramer through a piston.*

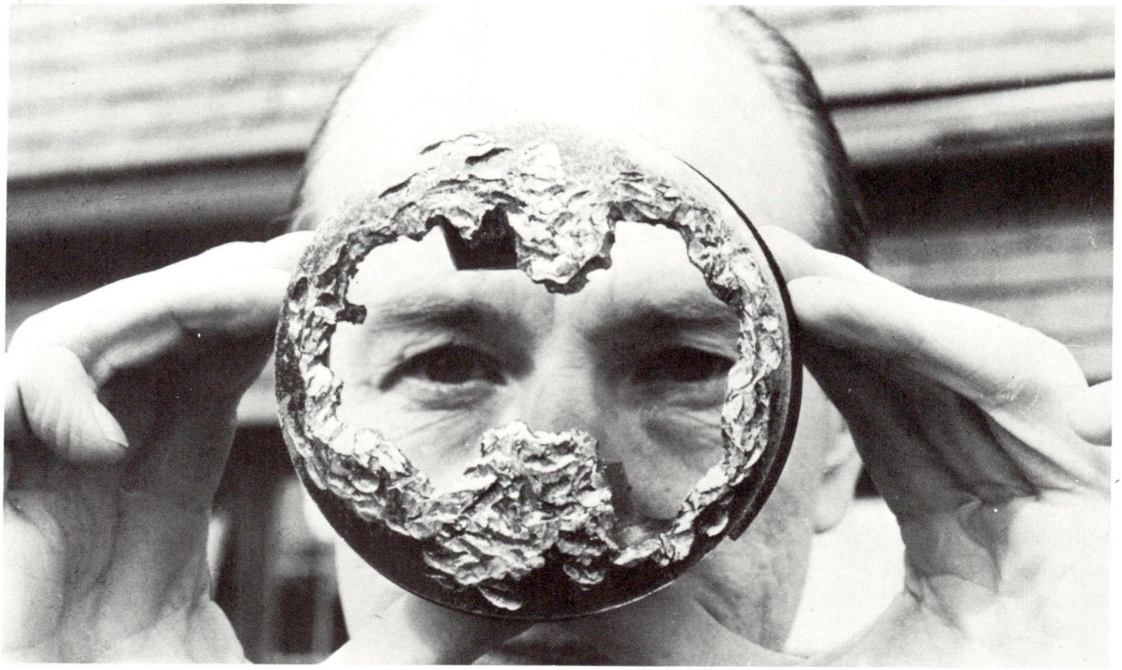

know whether he knew the car was on fire and stood by with fire extinguishers ready to signal him to stop. George had seen the flames and maintained speed in the hope that the rush of air would subdue them until he reached the pits. Once at a standstill, the flames leapt up round both sides of the bonnet and down into the under-tray. The sight of a gallant Bentley in flames is one which would grip the heart of the most hardened individual. The fire was soon extinguished, thanks to prompt attention and quick thinking, and no serious damage was done except to petrol connections, plug leads, and the paint work on the bonnet. The main thing was that George was OK and unharmed, having abandoned ship with some agility.

It did not take long to discover the cause of the trouble: a carburettor float chamber had worked loose due to the rough surface of the track, the loss of petrol resulting in a lean mixture which caused flames to spit back through the air intake and so start the fire. Another carburettor float chamber was also found to be loose, yet the securing nuts had been checked and tightened only a short time before the start of the run. Here I think we should pause to pay tribute to W.O. for designing all his Bentleys with the exhaust system on the opposite side of the engine to the carburettors. Petrol streaming from a carburettor on to a hot exhaust manifold would have produced effects ten times more serious. Some strong elbow grease by Geoffrey Kramer during the remaining hours restored the blackened engine to its former condition and, with new connections and leads fitted, there was very little to show what had happened, especially as no mechanical defects had been incurred.

Meanwhile, Mac had been pushing steadily on round the track averaging about 110 mph (21 laps at over 114 mph and a best lap at 116.8 mph) but again cruel Fate stepped in after 40 minutes of magnificent driving. As Mac came off the banking and into the pits, I think his worries of the previous day were in everyone's mind. A nasty metallic sound and loss of compression on one cylinder had caused the pit stop and it was unpleasantly obvious from the engine note that the trouble was serious. The block was lifted and examination revealed that the gudgeon pin on No. 4 had failed, probably due to the piston seizing, and the 'blower' con rod was twisted and bent. The piston crown was wedged hard up against the valve heads, the skirt being in pieces down in the crankcase.

McDonald had failed to complete the planned one-hour high speed run. Nevertheless, out of adversity came not despair, but determination to tackle the problem with renewed vigour the following year and to put into practice many lessons learnt the hard way. In the outcome, the temporary repairs effected to the 4½ did not survive another week's holiday-making and this car, too, returned to England by train.

As for the Speed Six, the reconnaisance turned out to be an attempt to run for the hour which terminated after 45 minutes. Its performance had, nevertheless, exceeded all expectations and demonstrated that it was capable of lapping Montlhéry at a sustained average speed in excess of 120 mph, its best lap being 123.38 mph. Not only did the reconnaisance satisfy us of the suitability of Montlhéry for these high speed runs in Vintage Bentleys, but it proved conclusively that the Monza valve troubles had been solved, no tappet on the Speed Six having varied by more than one thou. after 45 minutes of hard thrashing at Montlhéry and several miles flat out at Antwerp, which would have played hell with the Monza valves.

So ended our dual-purpose venture into high-speed motoring for 1959. Could we leave it at that – 'No.' All were agreed that our seeking after the 'Elusive Hour' must be continued the following year.

That elusive hour – the third attempt

And so once again the convoy of would-be record-breakers and their support group crossed the Channel and headed for Montlhéry where the track had been booked for part of the day on Easter Monday, 1960.

Esso and Dunlop were again playing their full part and RR had again lent us their Commer van for the transportation of spares.

The cars to be driven in anger at Montlhéry were the three which had been to Monza two years earlier – my Speed Six, George Burton's 4½ and Don McKenzie's 3-litre – plus McDonald's 4½ which had shown such promise at Montlhéry the previous year. The support team had been augmented by Michael Ford, an official RAC timekeeper, and several other willing helpers. The faithful Mk VI was again in attendance as was Bill Cook in his 300 SL Mercedes, specifically adding pit signalling to his role of 'tail-end Charlie'. Optimists all, we had raised our sights considerably for the larger cars. It was no longer 100 miles in an hour, but 120 miles for the Speed Six, 114 or thereabouts for the 4½s, and still 100 for the 3-litre. Our high spirits were damped on the Sunday by the sad news of Forrest Lycett's death – knocked down by a taxi near his home in Kensington.

A certain amount of preparatory work was done on the cars on Sunday. George Burton's 4½ had a new body, still a family-carrying four-seater, but all accessories being quickly detachable to meet the needs of competition motoring. McDonald's 4½ was in good shape, with lowered compression ratio and 700 × 18 tyres. His run from the coast had been interrupted when, cruising along at 80–85 mph, a hub race broke up and rather surprisingly locked the offside rear wheel. Thinking a tyre had burst, Mac refrained from using the brakes; and a brand new racing cover was worn down to the canvas before the 4½ came to rest. The skid mark, as spotted clearly by us on the way to Beauvais, several days later, was surely the longest in history.

A glance under the bonnet of the Speed Six revealed that everything which could be wired up had been so dealt with. This time Hofmann and Burton had made up special flanges which had been brazed to the float chambers of the two large carburettors and shaped round the air intakes, being secured thereto with jubilee clips. This idea proved very successful in the ensuing runs and is a very positive method of combining immobility with detachability. The three smaller carburettors were amongst the numerous other parts which were well and truly wired on. Happily, Gerry Crozier was fit again and looking forward to putting the 6½ through its paces on this new (to him) track.

Mercifully, the weatherman produced a sunny, dry day on Easter Monday, but there was, nevertheless, a fairly fresh wind blowing. Slowly the minutes ticked away until at midday Gerry took out the Six for a few preliminary laps to check plugs and generally warm up the oil. There was a very slight leak from one of the rivets on the petrol tank, not serious enough to worry about at this stage. Gerry pronounced himself quite happy with the car and the uneven track, which he preferred to Monza, as it 'has a different kind of bump!'

He was then despatched upon his attempt to complete an hour's run flat out. It really was flat out. The lap times varied scarcely one-fifth of a second as the Bentley raced round – a never-to-be-forgotten sight and sound – at over 120 mph. The circuit measured 1.583 miles, so that a car lapping at 120 mph came past about every 47 seconds. The minutes (surely the longest minutes in the world) dragged by: 15 minutes and still going like a train, 30 minutes and all's well, 45 minutes, then 100 miles completed. Dare we uncross our fingers? No; the engine makes an odd noise and the car comes low off the banking next time round to stop at the pits. A gallant effort, during which the speed of the car for 50 minutes never dropped below 120 mph, had ended. It was soon found that the centre of an inlet valve cap had broken off, but fortunately the valve hadn't dropped in and there was no further damage. Geoffrey Kramer and Fred Hofmann started work at once to replace the valve cap in readiness for another go later in the day.

Meanwhile, Don McKenzie had started his run and was circulating consistently at around 97 mph. The aim of 100 miles in an hour for a 3-litre Bentley was indeed an ambitious one and would have daunted lesser mortals than Don. He was not one to under-estimate the task and had gone to great lengths in matters of weight saving, wind cheating and friction-reducing to attain his ends. It was one of these 'modifications' which was to prove his undoing – he had fitted only two rings on each piston and had assembled the engine with generous clearances. The outcome was a voracious appetite for oil which proved beyond the capacity of the comparatively small sump to supply. Thus, after 40 minutes of very creditable motoring indeed, Don had to give up with non-existent oil-pressure, there being no oil to pump. Slide rules and mental agility showed that if he stopped during the course of an hour's run to replenish his sump then, on his previous showing, he could not hope to improve upon his performance at Monza. With the best possible good nature Don called it a day, in the sad realization that his gamble had availed little – and had certainly not brought the elusive 'ton' within his reach.

Neither Gordon McDonald nor George Burton were ready to commence their runs in time to complete them within the allotted spell during the lunch break, and had to wait until 6 pm before tackling the job. Gordon, having made a few practice runs in the middle of the day, was sent off to start his hour at 6 o'clock. George Burton was not immediately ready to start, his carburation not being au point – of which more anon. McDonald's 4½-litre was surely the most versatile of cars. He had left home for France with his wife in the front seat and two of his children in the back – goodness knows where he put the luggage – and was combining a fortnight's holiday in the Château country with his run at Montlhéry. On arrival at the circuit, the family debouched from the car, the wings and other bits were stripped off and he was ready for the 'Hour'. The hands of the clock went never more slowly as the 4½-litre covered lap after lap and the nearer the end of the hour approached the greater became the suspense. At last Michael Ford told me that the hour was up and I unfurled the chequered flag for the first time. As McDonald crossed the line there was a most un-Bentley-like noise under the bonnet; fortunately it was only two exhaust pipes which had broken away at the manifold. The car had survived its hour without any harm and had covered 111.18 miles. And so the Famille McDonald put on the wings and went off to resume their holiday. A truly remarkable performance.

Whilst McDonald was doing his stuff, George Burton was endeavouring to get his carburation right. He, and the resident mechanic Repain tried everything, but each time the car went out for a practice spin it was clear that there were a lot of horses missing. Now this 4½ had a very much raised compression ratio and was always run on 100-octane fuel in England. In France the Octane value of fuel was Government controlled, and the Esso Super available in France was 94 Research Method. We had taken some Golden Esso in cans from England and this was used to lace the local brew. However, the Burton gremlin was still in attendance and after the first few laps of the attempt at the hour the car 'blew-up' and came to rest followed by a cloud of blue smoke. There was a hole in a piston and that was that. George had not succeeded in 'avenging' the Monza misfortune, but he removed the rockers from the offending cylinder, fixed the valves in the closed position, and continued his holiday with Margaret and his two children on three cylinders, returning home a week later with no further damage.

About 6 pm Gerry took out the repaired Speed Six and soon got going at her morning speed of 121 mph. The McDonald 4½ and the Speed Six circulating together again created a memorable sight and sound, especially when Gerry went high on the banking to overtake the smaller car. This happy situation prevailed for some time and slowly the minutes passed. After 32 laps Gerry gave his now familiar thumbs up sign, but he was not to experience the onlookers' growing concern for the petrol tank leak, which appeared to be growing worse. After 30 minutes I was considering flagging him in as by then there was a definite increase in the amount of petrol spraying from the leak and one backfire from the exhaust might have started a blaze. At that moment, however, there came a crackling noise from the engine and the Speed Six came slowly back to the pits. Possible petrol shortage came to mind, but two steady streams on to the concrete from the leaking tank dispelled this theory.

Examination of the engine revealed that the gaps had closed on one magneto, but that otherwise everything was in order for another go. It was by then too late for further operations at Montlhéry that day and arrangements were made to use the track for a short time the following day. Then we came upon a real snag.

Sid West of Dunlops had to tell us that there was now insufficient tread left on the big (7.00 × 19) tyres for another hour – and to think of all that lovely tread buffed-off at Fort Dunlop! I had to decide whether to give up the attempt or to fit smaller wheels (6.50 × 19) and allow Gerry to use more revs. Knowing that this was to be our last visit to Montlhéry, I decided to take the calculated risk of blowing up the engine in an attempt to cover the 120 miles in an hour. Off went Gerry and succeeded in lapping at just over 120 mph, but not ten minutes had passed before the engine swallowed a valve and the Speed Six's indigestion became acute. A valve had broken and gone through the crown of a piston after dancing a tattoo in the combustion chamber to no mean effect. The car was attached to the Commer with a bar and returned to England with Fred Hofmann and Peter Corney taking turns in the warm comfort

20 *Charles Mortimer drives away in his new acquisition, the Speed Six*

of the lorry cab and in the unheated cockpit of the Bentley.

Looking back upon our venture I feel that the performances recorded were praiseworthy indeed. We had not achieved all we had set out to do, but I think Con summed up the situation when she said, 'When you first started this business you wanted to do 100 miles in an hour. Now you have done it in fifty minutes and you are disappointed.' As Fred Hofmann said, a sustained speed of 120 mph for a prolonged period such as 50 minutes, in a Bentley which was not by any means an out-and-out track car, would have been an achievement worthy of note some 30 years previously when the car was new. I felt that, having chalked up a measured mile at 127.818 mph and 100 miles at 120.62 mph, AC 260 had really done more than one could reasonably expect and had earned its retirement from such strenuous activities – a prospect which also appealed to my pocket, for there is a limit to which one can indulge one's hobby.

It seemed likely that the thunder of Vintage Bentley exhausts had been heard for the last time on the pistes of Europe, but our regret was tempered by the tremendous amount of enjoyment all concerned derived from those efforts to record yet more meritorious achievements in the annals of Bentleys, undertaken by enthusiasts just for the hell of it.

In due course the Speed Six was once more sorted out at Henley and had a less demanding life for another 18 months before I decided to part with it – or 'her', as I prefer to say, for she had become a personality in the Sedgwick family – and to venture for the first time into Veteran car ownership.

After a short spell in Charles Mortimer's ownership it was bought by Lord Weir, rarely to be seen outside of his Scottish home.

We were very sad to see the Speed Six go; this particular car was – and still is – Con's favourite of the Vintage Bentleys we have owned. Nearly ten years were to elapse before another 'W.O.' Bentley graced our garage. It was, and still is, the 8-litre 'UL 7'.

21 *Although the 8-litre radiator is five inches lower than standard, the bonnet is just level with the roof of a Daytona Ferrari. Alongside Jack Durlacher's car at Eze*

One in a hundred – the 8-litre

Although the first production model 8-litre was delivered in October 1930 and thus fell within the accepted definition of a Vintage Car as one manufactured before 31 December 1930, not all the hundred 8-litres built were finished by that date. Nevertheless, the Vintage Sports-Car Club has granted a dispensation whereby all 8-litre Bentleys, including those completed in 1931 and 1932, are classified as Vintage cars on the grounds that the component parts were probably manufactured in the relevant period.

I first saw my 8-litre in 1946 at a meeting of the Bentley Drivers Club in Kensington Gardens and at once rated it the car I would most like to own. A pipe-dream then, even though prices at the time were expressed in hundreds rather than thousands of pounds, and I little thought that UL 7 would become my very own 25 years later.

The chassis, a long wheelbase one (13 ft), with a 3.78 axle ratio, left the Bentley Works on 4 February 1932 for the Northampton coachworks of Arthur Mulliner where a Sedanca de Ville was mounted for its first owner, who took delivery of the completed car at the end of April, 1932.

A year later, having covered only 5,000 miles, it passed into the ownership of Mr Willie Evans of Hendon who kept it over three years before it was bought by Mrs Nea Vivien Flemmich of Grosvenor Square. The Service Department record shows a mileage of 64,014 on 4 March 1935, indicating that Mr Evans was a 30,000 miles-a-year man. It seems likely, therefore, that the mileage was approaching 100,000 when Mrs Flemmich acquired it in mid-1936. Anyway, this lady sent the car back to Bentleys for a complete overhaul and a new body. The wheelbase was shortened to 12 ft and practically every part replaced with new parts. A Barker Sedanca de Ville was built on the car – described by McKenzie as '. . . the most terrible body I have ever seen, the back consisting mostly of a glass box to carry two large

22 *The 8-litre Bentley – handsome from any angle*

23 *The 8-litre Bentley – the rounded tail a tribute to the panel-beater's craft*

dogs.' (A strange contrast this to its present owner who won't have any dog in any of his cars!) The total bill is said to have been about £4,000, an almost unbelieveable sum in those days, and this seems to have impressed the Works sufficiently to justify an entry in the Service Record to the effect that the car was *re-delivered* on 31 December 1936.

Twelve months later the 8-litre was obtained by 'Mac' for Mr A.C. Clark, of Sherborne, with only about 4,000 miles on the clock since the rebuild. On Mr Clark's instructions the 'High Priest' then went to work and, in his own words, '. . . altered nearly everything to produce the nicest one I ever built intended for fast and comfortable Continental touring.' The modifications included the lowering of the scuttle and radiator by 5″. Three SU carburettors and two Autopulse electric petrol pumps were installed – the Autovac being retained as a stand-by – and a complicated set of pipes, junctions and taps devised to change over from one fuel feed system to the other. The coil was dispensed with and two magnetos running at three-quarters engine speed installed, as were pistons of 'Mac's' own design, weighing 6 ounces less than the standard ones, raising the compression ratio to about 6 to 1. A 3-in diameter exhaust pipe was used with the object of recouping some of the 28 bhp said to be absorbed at 3,000 rpm by the standard 2-in system. The fitting of 19″ wheels with 7.00 × 19 Dunlop 90 Fort tyres lowered the whole car another inch. (Even so, the bonnet line is just about level with the roof of a Daytona Ferrari.) New hypoid bevels were made to raise the axle ratio to 3.3 to 1 which gave 110 mph at the now permissible 4,000 rpm. Large black-dialled AT speedometer and rev-counter directly in front of the driver convey the message in this respect.

The relatively new body was discarded and replaced by an open four-seater tourer built by Corsica. Well, there are certainly four comfortable seats, but I sometimes wonder if this wasn't the original 2 plus 2, for the foot-wells in the rear compartment were certainly not meant to take normal adult male feet. There are raised wind-deflectors on the scuttle – rather like the TC MG – and a single fold-flat screen. The rounded tail is as good an example of the panel-beater's craft as I have ever seen; it conceals a first-class hood which is comparatively easily raised by sliding forward the whole frame and fixing the hood-iron pivots in this new position.

Mr Clark drove the reconstructed 8-litre about 16,000 miles, the intervention of World War II doubtless curtailing his plans. Oliver Goodwin bought the car in April 1945, in memory of his son who had introduced him to the Vintage Bentley cult before being killed in a Services flying accident. 'Bertha' – as Oliver and his wife, Helen, called the 8-litre – was their pride and joy for many years and they put in a big touring mileage before Oliver's failing health severely limited its use. They took part in the Swedish Rally to the Midnight Sun in 1950 which involved vast distances in quite a short time, and there is a plaque on the side of the bonnet marking this venture.

I was not the only one to approach Oliver during his lifetime with a view to staking a claim to consideration should he ever decide to sell the car, but it was not until two years after his death that I wrote to Helen enquiring if she still had the 8-litre and, if so would she consider selling it. After conversations in which it was apparent that the finding of a good home for the cherished Bentley took precedence over seeking the highest price in the open market, I bought the car in April 1971 and counted myself privileged to have become the owner, even though the price had 'grown another nought' since I was first captivated by its functional beauty.

After a once-over at Hofmann & Mountfort to remedy the obvious deterioration during 2 years of standing and a look-round to ensure that the car was a safe and efficient means of transport, Con and I set off for a short holiday in the South of France to include the Monaco Grand Prix. At the southern end of the Autoroute du Sud oil spray on the passenger's windscreen foretold of internal troubles which had not earlier manifested themselves. The oil pressure was normal, but the engine and nearly everything under the bonnet was covered with oil. It seemed to be coming from the front end where the water pump shaft emerges from the cam cover. I tightened a few nuts and continued at reduced speed with one eye glued to the oil pressure gauge. The leakage persisted and it was a case of adding oil at frequent intervals until we reached our hotel where I parked the car under the trees, but not before depositing an appreciable pool of black oil on the pink forecourt before the eyes of an unappreciative management. (On subsequent arrivals at this hotel I have been met laughingly with a bucket of sawdust, shovel and broom!)

I contacted local Bentley Drivers Club member, Michael Glass, who very kindly asked his mechanic, John Sands, to work on my car and, with the aid of several telephone conversations with Basil Mountfort back in Henley, proceeded to diagnose and cure the trouble. Investigation showed that at some time in its life the inside of the rocker-box and cam-cover had been treated with a red anti-corrosive paint. During the period of lay-up, the treated parts had been high and dry and this, combined with the 'action' of the Elektron alloy, caused the paint to flake off when the engine came to life again. The resultant 'goo' progressively blocked the drain tubes from the rocker chest to the sump, until the surplus oil up top found its way out of a relief hole designed into the system, and thence everywhere under and around the bonnet. After a thorough clean-up and refill of fresh oil – 5 gallons at French prices! – the journey home through Italy and Switzerland was trouble-free and we enjoyed many miles of cruising at about 85 mph, in company with Bill and Marion Cook in their 300 SL Mercedes-Benz convertible. On my return home H. & M. examined the engine and made sure that any remaining paint was removed from the system. My oil leak problems were by no means over, however, as a good deal of oil was getting out of the joint between the iron cylinder block and the Elektron crankcase – a constant niggle to most 8-litre owners. It wasn't the cost of keeping the sump full which worried me, but the unsightly oil-streaked engine on display whenever the bonnet was raised and the tell tale drips in the car park which did not exactly 'go with the car.'

Eventually, after the 1,000 mile run described elsewhere, I accepted the need to lift the block if any real improvement was to be achieved and again headed in the direction of Henley-on-Thames. It did not take long to discover a slight lack of flatness in one of the mating faces. This was hand-polished appropriately, restoring oil-tightness so far as was humanly possible, but still leaving a trace of weep. But the story doesn't end there . . .

Whilst the car was on test, following reassembly of the engine, two rear pistons 'picked up', with consequent loss of compression. The reason for the 'pick-up' was inexplicable, as everything appeared normal and the engine was not unduly tight. Time was important, so Basil doctored the affected pistons to the best of his, or anyone else's, ability and reassembled the engine after checking one or two possible causes. However, as was expected, the piston slap on the two rear cylinders was excessive. Acceptable on a racing engine, but not for a touring car such as UL 7.

A serious problem now had to be faced. New pistons were definitely called for, but virtually unobtainable, being of a special type. The alternative was a complete engine strip, rebore and the manufacture of new pistons, a very expensive procedure merely to cure a bit of piston slap! By a tremendous stroke of luck, Don McKenzie whose father had built the car, unearthed a pair of pistons identical to those

24 *The 8-litre on a typical French road – with the extension of the autoroute system one sees fewer and fewer stretches like this*

required. So once again the block was off and this time, while he was at it, Basil decided to strip thoroughly the whole block to ensure no further trouble ensued. Fortunately so, as the reason for the 'pick-up' came to light. The front alloy water jacket plate had badly corroded and broken up, and – possibly whilst the block was on end during the hand scraping operation on the base – the broken-up bits had found their way down the internal water gallery, effectively blocking the feed to the two rear cylinders and causing serious overheating. A few other matters were attended to and the whole lot reassembled.

The moral of this cautionary tale is that with the very best of intentions all round, a job which started as an oil leak ran into four figures, and without drastic operation of the 'Old Pal's Act', and the sheer luck in finding the two pistons, it would have been very considerably more.

I am inclined to think that probably it would have been better in the long run – and not much more expensive – to have faced up to a complete engine overhaul at the start. It is a good thing that appreciating values nowadays absorb the high cost of maintaining these cars in the manner to which they are accustomed, for make no mistake, it is an increasingly costly pastime. Not only is it necessary to manufacture specially more and more replacement parts, but not nearly enough youngsters are learning to follow in the footsteps of the decreasing number of skilled and experienced craftsmen to whom we owners of old cars owe so much.

Thus the 8-litre went back into service, hopefully with many thousands of trouble free miles before it. But it was not to be; 'Lady Luck' was not riding on my radiator cap.

In June 1974, Con and I spent a most enjoyable week in the car accompanying the tour of the UK organized by the Bentley Drivers Club for visiting Overseas Members, which included, among other diversions, visits to the National Motor Museum at Beaulieu; the Concorde factory at Filton; the restoration job to end all restoration jobs, the SS 'Great Britain', at Bristol; and a foray into Snowdonia to witness a spectacular start-up of the restored World Speed Record car, 'Babs', in which Parry Thomas had been killed on Pendine Sands. We decided to leave the Scotland-bound tourists after the Vintage Sports-Car Club race meeting at Oulton Park and to spend a few hours at the International Balloon meeting at Cirencester on the way home after an overnight stop at Bourton-on-the-Water. We bowled happily southwards on M5 in glorious sunshine, the combination of sustained speed – well, 70 mph – and high ambient temperature keeping the rather tired radiator busy. (From time to time since I had bought the car, it had been neces-

25 *The piston looked as if an angry giant had taken a bite out of it and then gnashed his teeth on the top!*

sary to discourage leaks with that most effective preparation known as 'Barsleaks'.) However, the needle – which for some time used to pass the 100° Centigrade mark and start going round the dial again when crawling along in heavy traffic – kept the right side of 90; the 8-litre was going in the manner to which it had been designed to become accustomed. With a final burst of speed, a mite over the limit, I signalled a left turn for the Cheltenham Exit and lifted my foot, when it happened! A loud bang and clouds of smoke from under the bonnet. Not again, I thought, as I switched off and coasted to a standstill off the motorway. A peek underneath revealed no pool of oil on the road; a stare under the bonnet showed the crankcase to be intact; turning the engine (switched off) with the starter did not result in any abnormal noises, but the tell tale puffs of smoke from the oil filler indicated a holed piston. That put paid to the plan to visit the Balloon Club gathering and after arranging for the Bentley to be collected by the Car Recovery Service Club and transported to its second home at Henley-on-Thames, we repaired to the Queen's Hotel for the night. We returned to London by the scheduled motor coach service and finished the last lap home in a borrowed Silver Shadow.

The prospect of more expensive repair work was not pleasing, but was overshadowed by anxiety lest the job should not be completed in time to participate in the Monte-Carlo Rally for Old Cars, which started two weeks later and to which I had been looking forward immensely. Hofmann & Mountfort pulled out all the stops and lifted the block to ascertain the extent of the damage. Sure enough, the rear piston looked as if an angry giant had taken a bite out of it and then gnashed his teeth on the top for good measure. The reciprocating remains had scored the bore but not to the extent that it required machining. Again there was no obvious single cause for the collapse of this piston. It seemed that the clearance had been, perhaps, a little less than it might have been in the quest for silence, and that the continuous running in the heat had contributed to the seizure. In the course of the work it was discovered that the petrol tank was bone dry – shades of Forrest Lycett's spectacular blow-up at Antwerp – an oversight which almost certainly weakened the mixture with disastrous results. Fortunately, Don McKenzie again turned up trumps and produced a replacement piston which was fitted with a greater than standard clearance, all concerned counselling the acceptance of a bit of slap in the interests of longevity. By dint of assiduous labour, the work was completed and the 8-litre brought over to Cobham the day before I was due to leave for my chosen starting-point of John o'Groats. The only problem I expected to encounter was possible boiling of the less than perfect radiator in the mountains, but a large bidon of water and some reserve tins of Barsleaks would cope with any difficulties which might arise.

Now about this rally. The announcement of a Monte-Carlo Rally for Old Cars in July in connection with the 25th Anniversary of the Accession of Prince Rainier whetted my appetite for a midsummer Continental run of a mildly competitive nature.

The Automobile Club de Monaco invited entries from owners of cars built between 1923 and 1939 and offered a choice of seventeen starting points ranging from Oporto to Athens, and Stockholm to Palermo. I was delighted when my 8-litre Bentley was accepted as a starter from John o'Groats and pleased that Hugh Young agreed to accompany me as co-driver.

In the event, indisposition prevented me from driving the 700-odd miles to the John o'Groats starting point, and I was allowed to join the London starters two days later. Thus, at five o'clock of a July morning we reported to the RAC in Belgrave Square where our fellow-competitors were gathering. Peter Rae and Douglas Macfarlane in the former's 1925 3-litre Bentley and Anthony Heathcote in his 1938 25/30 Rolls-Royce with 'Skit' Poulter, arrived on time with over 700 miles already to their credit after a foul-weather drive from John o'Groats. The other London starters were Nicholas Harley (1926 H6B Hispano-Suiza), Peter Bone in the Craven Foundation (of Canada) 1930 Model 'A' Ford and Peter Kendall-Torry's 1937 $4\frac{1}{4}$-litre Bentley.

The regulations called for an average speed of only 25 kph as far as Annecy, where all the routes from the various starting-points converged, and thereafter it was increased to 35 kph over the hills to the Riviera. Our route took us to Dover; across the Channel to Calais; thence via Time Controls at Reims and Besançon to Annecy. The regulations indicated that there would be Controls of Passage in Rouen, Chalon-sur-Saône and Bourg, but these did not materialize and the choice of route between Time Controls was entirely free, despite contrary instructions emanating from Officials en route.

I realized that quite unhurried driving would take us from Calais to Reims in less than 5 hours, so I reserved a room at the Novotel just outside Reims to secure some rest. The skies looked threatening as we disembarked at Calais, and we erected the hood and a couple of side-screens. On arrival in the 'Champagne Capital' we drove round the disused Grand Prix circuit – rather a depressing experience this – and checked into the hotel at 6 pm. We were due to check in (and out of) the Control at the Automobile Club at 10.54 pm, so we had a meal and went to bed for a couple of hours. On the way to the Control we filled up with petrol and, after a welcoming glass of champagne, checked out. Much to the surprise of fellow competitors setting off through the night for Besançon, we went back to the hotel to bed, registering a wake-up call for 1 am. At this time the sky was clear and the moon shining brightly, so the hood was furled and at half-past one we set out for a leisurely drive on deserted roads. After a

26 *Hugh Young securing the hood for the wet run across northern France on the first day of the Rallye Monte-Carlo des Voitures Anciennes*

couple of hours the first streaks of dawn appeared and we switched off the lights just after 4 am in Chaumont, a short night's motoring indeed. The water temperature was steady at 70° and oil pressure, at 2,000 rpm, was 60 psi. Arriving in Besançon in time for an early breakfast we became aware of strange old cars appearing from different directions. In the Control we found starters from Sweden, Denmark, Germany and Austria gathered in the sunshine. It was a fine cross-section of desirable pre-war cars – Bugattis, Hispano-Suizas, Rolls-Royces, Bentleys, Mercedes, Alfa Romeos and several examples of makes not frequently encountered. The next Time Control was at Annecy where competitors from the remaining starting-points would join us. The misinformed Officials at Besançon were telling competitors to follow the circuitous route via Chalon-sur-Saône and Bourg, possibly to fulfil advance indications for publicity purposes. I decided to rely on a telex message sent by the Automobile Club de Monaco to the RAC in London stating that the choice of route between Controls was at the competitors' option. We pursued a leisurely course by the shortest route through Lausanne and Geneva. My insistence on turning left on leaving the Control car park, when everyone else turned right, caused some confusion among the marshals and gendarmerie. We stopped in Pontarlier to replenish the petrol tank and seized the opportunity to have the car washed using a do-it-yourself installation of Swiss manufacture called 'Hypromat', in which device each franc inserted produced a sequence of high-powered sprays of hot water, soapy water, steam, rinsing water, etc. through a fish-tailed hose. It was a hot, sunny day and motoring along the Autoroute from Lausanne to Geneva above the lake in the sparkling open Bentley was very pleasant. At 3 pm we drove into the parc fermé on the lakeside in Annecy. I counted 99 Rally cars including now some classic American cars – Packard, Pierce-Arrow, Marmon. The Bugattis, of which there were 28 in the Rally, belied their reputation for unreliability, all reaching this point without penalty. Especially creditable, in my view, was the performance of the four Bugattistes who had started from Athens, led by Philippe Vernholes in his Type 44 and shepherded by a tender vehicle of the French Bugatti Club. (Some competitors thought this set-up rather like a 'works' operation, but I considered it a praiseworthy Club effort.)

We enjoyed a full night's rest at Annecy before tackling the mountain route to the south. This common route took us over the Col de Leschaux and Col du Frêne, through Grenoble to a Time Control at Aspres-sur-Buech; thence by Sisteron and Digne to Grasse. This was effectively the end of the controlled road section, for the run-in to Monte-Carlo had been neutralised. A good job, too, for the traffic congestion was terrible.

The Automobile Club de Monaco, assisted by the sponsors of the Rally (the manufacturers of Chesterfield cigarettes) did everything possible to make it an enjoyable experience from the moment competitors entered the Principality. The Finishing Control outside the Casino was similar to that set up each year for the 'real' Monte-Carlo Rally. A large crowd lined the approach to the Control, and there were the customary official greetings, photographs and a loudspeaker commentary. We walked across to our prepaid lodgings – in l'Hermitage, if you please – and from then on enjoyed a lavish social round of lunches and dinners culminating in a Gala affair at the recently opened New Sporting Club.

The day after our arrival in Monte-Carlo was to include a highlight of the event: a speed hill-climb in the centre of the town! The course was about a kilometre long and one's climb started in the Avenue Princesse Grace facing west. After a hundred metres or so one turned sharp right up the hill towards the old station hairpin, now driving on the Grand Prix circuit but in the opposite direction to the race. After negotiating the hairpin one continued climbing, sweeping to the right, then left up the hill below the Metropole Hôtel. A straw bale chicane stuck out into the road from the left-hand side just outside the Wagons-Lit office. One then turned left in front of the Café de Paris negotiating another chicane before streaking round the gardens in front of the Casino to the Finish line below the terrace of the Hôtel de Paris. All this on a Saturday afternoon in July! The road was closed to traffic, but crowd control and protection were at a minimum – a few straw bales which spectators used as grandstands; no crash helmets required, and passengers carried. Arrangements conceived no doubt as fitting for a lot of old cars grinding up a hill but, in practice· exciting in the extreme for drivers, passengers and spectators alike in the case of the more potent Vintage sports-cars. I enjoyed the climb in the 8-litre immensely, made more demanding by the presence of a chicane which had not been there in the morning when I had walked the course. Hugh had been enjoined to brace himself in the passenger seat with the ciné camera set to run continuously, to glue his eye to the view-finder and to film the road ahead from start to finish. This he did with satisfactory results, except for a momentary lapse when the unexpected chicane appeared from nowhere calling for a sharp tack to port when he had expected to proceed straight for the Casino. The Bugattis raced round the Casino gardens with élan to the accompaniment of screeching tyres, and the sight and sound of Von Raffay's supercharged 'S' Mercedes completing the climb is something I will never forget. Fastest time was set up, not surprisingly, by a 1937 Type 328 BMW.

The next day's activities included a procession of all the competing cars to the Palace in Monaco, in front of which the prize-giving was to take place. The square, full of beautiful 'classic' cars, was a sight to behold. The outright winner was a 1926 Hispano-Suiza H6B saloon which had started from Athens. The owner, Modeste Trehin, collected some impressive silver-ware and a cheque for 10,000 francs for his pains. Second, third and fourth places were filled by Bugattis, Types 37, 44 and 57, respectively, the highest placed British (Scottish) entry being Peter Rae's 3-litre Bentley in 9th position.

The method of marking penalized the relative youth of the 8-litre and the relatively short distance from London, and we were unplaced. The Rally was a great success and we greatly enjoyed it.

The 8-litre had run beautifully and overheating had been experienced only occasionally in traffic, and not at all in the mountains. Oil consumption had been nil and petrol consumption had worked out at 9.9 mpg overall for the 1,000-mile trip.

Hugh readily agreed to my suggestion that we should start the return journey early on the day after the Rally ended and follow the A8, A7 and A6 autoroutes without commitment as to the journey's end that evening.

We left Monte-Carlo at 7 am and stopped after 90 miles at Brignoles for breakfast. The radiator was seen to be leaking rather badly and in went a couple of tins of Barsleaks which did the trick. The weather was fine, but a very strong cross wind was blowing. The mileage recorder was checked against kilometre markers and found it to be accurate within 1/10th of a mile over a distance of 125 miles! We refuelled at Montélimar and continued our leisurely progress – about 70–75 mph – pleased to find that the autoroute now went past Vienne on the opposite bank of the Rhône, avoiding the single track overpass in the town. After lunch at the International Motel at Dardilly, north of Lyon, we set off again at 1.42 pm. Ten hours actual driving time saw 500 miles behind us and as we reached the Paris end of the autoroute just before 6 pm I said to Hugh, who was driving at the time, 'How about going straight through to Dunkerque?' He responded with a laconic 'It's OK by me.' We negotiated the Boulevard Périphérique to the accompaniment of Gallic gestures from fellow motorists at the steam issuing from below, and ate just north of Paris at 7 o'clock; truly a leisurely progress this, for the day's stops had reached the unprecedented total (for me) of 2 hours 44 minutes. We reached the Motellerie at Dunkerque – which had seen the start and finish of our run across France and back in a day in the Rolls the previous year – at 11.10 pm, the day's distance being 773.7 miles (point-to-point average 47.8 mph; and driving average speed 57.6 mph).

By the time I reached home at Cobham the round trip mileage amounted to 1,889.7; 190¾ gallons of petrol had been converted into energy and exhaust gases at the rate of 1 gallon every 9.9 miles. A couple of pints of oil restored the oil level to the full mark and the radiator leaked no longer.

Altogether a most enjoyable expedition and one I hope to have the opportunity of repeating on a future occasion. For my part, the 8-litre provides Vintage motoring at its best. Despite the troubles I have experienced I cannot see myself parting with it in the foreseeable future. As a well-known motoring scribe put it, writing for an American readership, 'UL 7 . . . is a princely possession, a source of that special satisfaction that comes with the knowledge that one's car has no exact counterpart anywhere in the world. With its gleaming black panelwork, beautifully contoured helmet-type wings, becomingly bulbous tail surmounting a fuel tank with a capacity of slightly over 30 gallons, twin side-mounted spare wheels . . . and the Savile Row fit of its tonneau cover, it is a stand-out in any internal-combustive company, even at gatherings exclusive to Bentleys.'

I know that the car has lived up to my highest expectations and when at the wheel I feel ten feet tall.

Post-War Bentleys – Mk VI

My Mk VI Bentley, mentioned many times in the telling of the exploits of AC 260, rendered sterling service both at home and abroad.

I had driven many miles in various Mk VIs since its introduction in September 1946, including the run across France from Le Havre to Cannes in a day – recounted later in this book – sufficient to confirm that it was an admirable means of transport. So that when, in March 1956, I judged the time had come to replace my Phantom III Rolls-Royce with a more modern and handier car, it was natural that my choice should fall upon the Mk VI Bentley. It did not take long to find 'KDN 373', which had been very well looked after by its owner, and for the first time I found myself with a modern car at my disposal.

It was delivered new in August 1952 and had done just over 50,000 miles when I acquired it.

27 *The Mk VI Bentley in March 1956, with over 50,000 miles on the clock*

The body was the Standard Steel Saloon but the engine was the $4\frac{1}{2}$-litre version put into production in May 1951. This model was referred to colloquially as the 'Big Bore/Small Boot' to distinguish it from its predecessors with the $3\frac{1}{2}''$ bore ($4\frac{1}{4}$-litre) engine and from its successors (the R-Type) with the lengthened rear end giving an enlarged luggage boot with the lid hinged at the top.

We had several most enjoyable trips in a dozen countries, in addition to the 'nursemaid' trips to Monza, Antwerp and Montlhéry. Four particular touring holidays stand out in my mind – three in summer and one in the depths of winter.

France, Italy, Switzerland, Germany & Belgium
Our enjoyment of the first of these, in August 1957, was enhanced by the vicarious pleasure we derived from the wide-eyed interest of our daughter Carol (then 14 years old) and a schoolfriend, in everything and everybody, for it was their first touring holiday in Europe. Our friends, Derek and Mary Waller accompanied us in their open Sunbeam-Talbot. Four up, with luggage stowed on a roof-rack as well as in the 'small boot', we trickled (well, for me anyway!) across France, unashamedly rubber-necking on the way. In Paris, the gigantic tricolour flag filling the Arc de Triomphe on Liberation Day was particularly moving. We went southwards via Geneva where we interviewed possible au pair girls in our room at the Hôtel du Rhône – not without a few raised eyebrows from the management who seemed to suspect a white slave deal under their very eyes.

After spending a few days at Nice we drove eastwards along the Riviera Ligure, through Genoa, and by the spectacular coastal road over the Bracco Pass to La Spezia and Viareggio. It was on arrival there that I realized my document case was missing and a phone call confirmed that it had been left in the restaurant in La Spezia where we had lunched. I rose early next morning and drove 35 miles to Spezia to retrieve the missing treasure and back again to Viareggio before the rest of the party had made it down to breakfast. The leaning Tower at Pisa was the highlight of that morning, and all of us 'did' Rome with gusto the following day – St Peter's, Colosseum, Trevi Fountain, Forum, the lot.

Then we drove along the coast road to Naples savouring to the full the warm Italian sunshine, and lunched in the open air at a restaurant overlooking the Bay of Naples. We then drove as far as possible up the slopes of Vesuvius, completing the climb to the crater's edge by chair lift. We reached our destination, the Miramare Hotel, in Positano, that evening and met up with Bill and Marion Cook in their 220 S Mercedes saloon. They had their daughter, Jacquie, with them and the three schoolgirls formed a happy, if noisy, group from then on.

We all went on a launch trip to Capri, against the better judgment of Bill Cook who didn't like the look of the weather, the sea, the craft or its crew. Bill's forebodings proved to be well founded when, on the return trip to Positano, fog came down and the engine stopped. There were no navigational aids aboard, the crew were trying to restart the engine with lighted cigarettes hanging from their lips in the resulting petrol fumes, and we knew we were drifting towards some rugged cliffs. After a period of anxiety, the fog cleared, the motor started, we were still afloat and not on fire, and reached our destination safely, Bill vowing 'Never again, etc. . . .'

We started our homeward journey after visiting the ruins at Pompei and spending a day in Florence, and chose to follow the mountain road used in the Mille Miglia over the Futa and Raticosa passes to Bologna.

An unscheduled stop was made at the top of the Raticosa Pass to replace a lost fan belt on the Mk VI. We arrived at the Grand Hotel Fasano, a modest Walkerley-recommended establishment at Cannero on Lake Maggiore, for the night. The next day Bill and I went in the Mercedes to Monza to see the practice for the Italian Grand Prix and afterwards to Johnny Lurani's nearby villa at Cernusco where we were to be house guests over-night. Johnny's house is very large and beautiful and stands in very attractive grounds. The interior is vast and the casual visitor can get lost without difficulty. The bedrooms are large, the corridors long and even the 'usual offices' are housed in rooms which could serve as living-rooms in more modest houses. Bill Cook found a 'loo' in which the meaningful appliance was situated in the far corner of a longish chamber, the door to which had no lock or bolt. Needs must when the devil drives so he ignored the vulnerability of the position in which he found himself – and I mean that, for it was not long before the Contessa entered unaware of its occupancy. With such dignity as he could muster from the throne, Bill exchanged greetings and Nelly gracefully withdrew unabashed by the encounter.

We enjoyed the Grand Prix. It was stimulating to see three Vanwalls in British Racing Green on the front row of the grid (Moss, Brooks and Lewis-Evans) with Fangio (Maserati), and very gratifying to witness Stirling's win.

The homeward trek continued up into the Alps. The Cooks left us after lunch in Andermatt to take a more direct route home and we went over the Furka and Grimsel passes to Interlaken to stay at the Krebs Hotel – the much-loved hostelry of previous holidays in the $4\frac{1}{2}$. It was whilst we were there that the Mk VI was savaged by a Swiss Army lorry which scraped its solid metal frame along the side of the Bentley which was stationary with its nearside wheels on the grass. Front and rear wings were badly dented and the knowledge that I was driving a creased car took some pleasure out of the rest of the trip.

We returned to Ostend via the Rhine Valley and spent an interesting half day at the Daimler-Benz works and museum outside Stuttgart.

Altogether a very nice holiday.

(At this juncture I should mention for the record that I had a reconditioned engine fitted in June 1958, at 85,000 miles.)

St Moritz in Winter

We decided to sample the joys of a winter holiday at St Moritz in 1958 and left home just after Christmas in the Mk VI with Carol and yet another schoolfriend. The sun shone on dry roads all the way to Switzerland, and we made the most of New Year's Eve in Zurich. It was not until the foot of the Julier Pass that we encountered snow-covered roads, and chains were recommended (or compulsory, I can't remember which) for vehicles crossing the pass. The weather was deteriorating fast and it was getting dark, so I sent my passengers on to St Moritz by one of the regular Alpine coaches whilst I waited to purchase a set of chains and have them fitted. This done, I followed and arrived not far behind.

At first I left the car outside the hotel, covered accommodation being scarce and expensive. The Mk VI looked so neglected and forlorn – snow-covered and door locks frozen – that I swallowed hard and paid a high rent for space in a heated garage. We did little motoring whilst in St Moritz, enjoying ourselves on the nursery slopes and watching others skiing, tobogganing, bob-sleighing, curling, skating, etc., taking hot chocolate in Hanselmann's, sleigh-riding and so on. Little did we suspect the nightmare journey that faced us on the way home.

When we left St Moritz it was snowing hard and the roads were snow-covered or glazed with black ice all the way to the Channel coast! I drove confidently with my newly acquired snow-chains and crossed the Julier with no trouble – until there was a loud bang. A chain had broken and was flailing round under the mudguard. It was one of the transverse chains which act as a tread and, after securing it temporarily – it needed welding – I drove slowly into the next village to find a garage. As I entered the workshop the car stopped with a jerk and wouldn't budge. The brakes seemed to be hard on and I could see no reason for it. Then I had a brainwave. Could the chain flailing round under the car, have caught one of the lugs of the brake adjusting wheel and tightened the brakes solid? A look under the car revealed that this was in fact what had happened, so it was soon rectified. We resumed our journey, but the chains broke again on several occasions, calling for first-aid fixing at the roadside, followed by welding at the next garage. The cause of the breaking was a mystery to me. The chains were the right size, of Swiss manufacture and properly fitted. It was not until some time later that I came to the conclusion it was a mistake to fit chains at all on the Michelin X tyres which I was using on the Mk VI at the time. I imagine that the relatively unyielding tread put a strain on the chains for which they were not designed. The breakages caused cumulative delays and it was late afternoon by the time we passed through Chur. Approaching Sargans I was motoring along with care in the snow – no Monte-Carlo Rally 'special stage' dicing for me – when I saw a tractor come out of a field ahead on the left and turn to follow the road in the same direction as me. It was towing a makeshift snow-plough made of timber, rather like railway sleepers, joined to form a 'V', and an old man was perched on this device. I moved over to the left to overtake and suddenly saw that, in turning left into the road, the snow-plough had deposited a curved wall of snow about 18″ high in my path. I braked gently, took avoiding action, moving back to my own side of the road behind the agricultural equipage, but just failed to stop before touching the corner of the snow-plough – scarcely above walking pace – tipping the old boy off into the snow. Fortunately he sustained only a sprained ankle. Nevertheless, we were much delayed whilst he was carried into the farmhouse, and police were called to take particulars. He should not have been riding on the plough, which had no provision for passengers and his mate driving the tractor had thoughtlessly dropped a chicane into my path.

We ate a late dinner at the railway-station in Zurich before braving the snowstorm again to reach a motel on the outskirts. Driving into the car park through snow a foot deep, very tired and cold, we found the motel a welcoming haven in an unfriendly world.

Next morning we resumed our journey homewards. I was disgusted with the troublesome chains and discarded them at the border at Basle to be sent back to the makers for a rebuild. I had made reservations in Paris for our overnight stop and was determined to reach there despite the bad weather. The last 150 miles into the capital were covered in darkness. Heavy snow reduced visibility almost to nil and there was so much of it on the road, and so little traffic, that at times it was like driving across a ploughed field. It was a weary party that retired to bed that night, after a very trying 350-mile drive and knowing the journey to the coast the next day would be quite hazardous, the snow having given way to ice.

I was pleased to arrive home safely with my charges and I question the sense of using a car for journeys to and from a winter sports resort unless it is to be used a lot during the stay there. Even then, a comfortable jet flight to the nearest airport and a rented self-drive car could save a lot of trouble and strife, unless one is exceptionally blessed by good weather or aspires to be another Erik Carlsson.

Portugal, Spain and Morocco

That we chose the North African desert as the focal point of our 1959 holiday was not a conscious rebellion against the winter weather we had endured in Switzerland at the turn of the year, but we certainly were intent on finding warm sunshine.

It is nearly 1,400 miles from a Channel port to Gibraltar, the obvious jumping-off point for Morocco. As I wished to avoid driving out and home by more or less the same route, I decided to go by sea to Lisbon and start the motoring from there. Accordingly, we boarded the P. & O. liner 'Stratheden' at Tilbury on Tuesday, 18 August, the Mk VI having been stowed deep in the hold the previous day. The voyage to Portugal imbued us with the holiday spirit – fortunately 'the Bay' was in friendly mood – and it was in a relaxed frame of mind that we disembarked at Lisbon 2½ days later. The sight of the Mk VI being unloaded by crane and slings, swinging high in the air, did nothing to further our sense of well-being, but all was well and we drove the short distance down the estuary to the Monte Estoril Hotel where we stayed a day or two.

We saw quite a lot during our very short say – Cascais, Sintra, the giant Atlantic rollers on Guincho beach and the wonderful museum of Royal carriages and coaches at Belém. Being inclined to collect 'mosts', I perceived that this trip would enable me to touch the *most* westerly and the *most* southerly points of Europe. The most westerly is a cape (Cabo da Roca) 30 miles west of Lisbon where we visited the lighthouse on the headland. From Lisbon we headed for Gibraltar 450 miles away, spending a pleasant evening in Seville and, the following day, visiting the Gonzalez, Byass cellars – home of 'Tio Pepe' – at Jerez de la Frontera. The southernmost point of Europe is Punta Marroqui (Moroccan Point) on Isla de las Palomas (Isle of Doves) rising in the straits, and we went as near to it as possible on the mainland at Tarifa before driving round the Bay of Algeciras to Gibraltar.

The ferry crossing to Tangier was pleasant enough and we felt a thrill of adventure as the Mk VI wheels first turned on African soil. Based at the El Minzah Hotel, we savoured the strangeness of our first landfall in Morocco. By the time we left for Rabat the following day we were becoming accustomed to being in an Arab-speaking world, but we certainly felt very adventurous to be leaving the city for the hinterland. We knew that if we had a breakdown, the language barrier would be almost impenetrable. In the villages we would have been surrounded by an inquisitive, babbling crowd – between them we would be as lonely as the bedouin whose tents we saw at intervals. We made for Rabat, 180 miles away on the Atlantic coast, and after seeing something of this capital city, turned inland to Meknes and on to Fès for the night. We found these two Moroccan towns fascinating and the native quarter unspoilt – squalid by European standards, but full of interest. It was an astounding experience to stand on the high ground outside the walled city of Fès and to hear a murmuring coming up from the Medina, for it was the accumulated chatter of the inhabitants rising upon the air!

Our return to Tangier was made via Chaouen, a beautiful town of fountains and mosques on the hillside, which was a sight for sore eyes after driving 200 miles on a dusty, desert secondary road north from Meknes. We completed our 600-mile-plus drive in North Africa on schedule and without incident.

Back in Spain we drove up the Mediterranean coast to spend a few days at Torremolinos, at that time a little-known place. We stayed at the newly-opened Pez Espada Hotel, then isolated on a deserted stretch of beach. I have not revisited Torremolinos since, and I doubt if I would recognize it today. We turned inland at Malaga for Granada where we stayed at the Alhambra Hotel adjacent to the famous building from which it has taken its name.

When planning this holiday I discovered that the highest road in Europe was just outside Granada and I was determined to drive up it. This mountain road in the Sierra Nevada was little known to motorists, presumably because it wasn't a pass; it led nowhere except to the top of the mountain ridge from which there was a breath-taking view over the surrounding Sierra. The road started at Pinos Genil, 3 miles outside Granada, and climbed to a height of over 11,000 feet in a distance of about 22 miles. The upper section of the road resembled a causeway, one car wide, built up of sharp stones chipped out of the mountain side. As we passed the Residencia Universitaria at 8,400 feet we were stopped by a monk who asked us to keep an eye open for two climbers who had left the previous day and had not yet returned. We did meet one of them higher up; he was quite all right and said his companion was following. They had made an unscheduled night stop in the mountains. I was conscious of the engine power falling off as the altitude increased (by no less than 25% at 8,000 feet). The road became increasingly rough and difficult. I gave up, reluctantly, about half a kilometre from the summit, having scraped a rear wing when negotiating a tight hairpin corner between rocks, but was delighted to have made the climb. My passengers' appreciation of the wonderful scenery was tempered by the 'scariness' of the climb! The road has since been continued beyond the summit down the Mediterranean side of the range, to join the road from Granada to the coast. The Col de Restefond (La Bonette) in France – a mere 9,193 feet – hitherto acknowledged as being the highest pass in Europe, must yield pride of place to Spain with this 11,247 ft road. I would certainly make a return visit if I were to find myself in the area again.

From Granada I drove almost due north nearly 600 miles right across Spain, through Madrid and Bilbao to San Sebastian. We did a round of the sights in Madrid and then drove 30-odd miles out into the Guadarrama Range to visit Valle de los Caidos (Valley of the Fallen) especially to see the underground basilica of Santa Cruz. This is like a cathedral, 850 feet long, carved out of (or rather into) the solid rock of a hill, the latter surmounted by a gigantic granite cross 500 feet high and 150 feet across the arms. The whole of this was constructed as a monument to the dead of the Civil War, whose remains are buried in the valley.

The drive across France through Biarritz, Bordeaux, Le Mans – an inevitable lap or two of the 24-Hour Race circuit – Chartres and Paris was followed by a cross-channel flight from Le Touquet to Lydd. On reaching home the trip recorder registered 3,127 miles and the overall petrol consumption had been slightly more than 17 mpg.

Scandinavia

It is human nature which drives the Englishman south in search of sunshine whenever an opportunity arises to get away for a week or two from the daily round in this unpredictable climate of ours. Thus, Northern Europe – Scandinavia in particular – does not figure high on his list of possible holiday areas.

Nevertheless, in 1960 we decided to see something of the Scandinavian countries and hoped the sun would follow us. We chose August as the month most likely to be favoured with good weather and so it turned out, for we had glorious sunshine nearly all the time.

Con, Carol and I motored northwards to Newcastle-upon-Tyne during August Bank Holiday weekend to board the car-carrying boat (rudely referred to by experienced travellers as the 'Vomiting Venus') for Bergen via Stavanger. From Bergen there was really only one obvious road northwards, but it tacked backwards and forwards in order to cross or circumnavigate the deep fjords. The road was twisty and, in places, very narrow with bays to permit vehicles approaching from opposite directions to pass one another. Much of the surface comprised loose stones, and several ferries had to be taken to cross fjords. All these features added interest to this journey through magnificent scenery, but only relatively small distances could be encompassed in a day's motoring – about 80 miles was the daily average on the northward leg.

We drove eastwards from Bergen to meet the Hardangerfjord near Norheimsund and spent the night at Granvin. We had entered a mountainous land of rugged beauty and were never far from running water, waterfalls and rushing streams abounding. The sparseness of traffic was a joy and we meandered northwards through Stalheim to Gudvangen, then by a couple of ferries – one taking 3 hours and the other 10 minutes – across the Sognefjord to Balestrand, our next overnight stopping place. The next two days took us through Olden to Grotli, where we doubled back to Geiranger, after deviating to climb the then new Dalsnibba road just for the breath-taking view; that's why it was built, it led nowhere. From Geiranger we took the impressive 'Eagle Road' up the cliff-like side of the fjord and the Trollstigveien (Witches' Road) on to Andalsnes, the most northerly point on our trip. We were now 250 miles north of John o'Groats and felt pretty adventurous, until I looked at the map and found that North Cape at the 'top' of Norway was about 800 miles further north as the crow flies, and goodness knows how much further by road. The daylight hours were so long it was difficult to sleep at night and I remember reading a newspaper outdoors at about midnight.

We retraced our route to Grotli and headed eastwards into the Jotunheimen Mountains, making a pincer movement to reach Elveseter after pausing to admire one of the famous timber built stave churches at Lom. We were just about as high up in Norway as you can go by road, and the following morning went by Jeep up to a nearby glacier in very barren terrain indeed, before leaving for Oslo.

We stayed at the Royal Norwegian Automobile Club (KNA) Hotel and were shown the sights of Oslo by a keen Vintage Bentley enthusiast, Halvor Haneborg. (He managed to conceal his 3-litre from prying German eyes during the Occupation by walling-up part of his garage – and still drives the same car today!) I am not a 'museum man' myself, but I was fascinated with the display of Viking ships; being able to walk aboard Nansen's famous polar exploration

28 *Kreuger's 8-litre Bentley in the Technical Museum, Stockholm*

ship, 'Fram'; and to inspect the Kon-Tiki balsa-wood raft on which Thor Heyerdahl had drifted across the Pacific in 101 days. Possibly the most unusual experience was a walk round Frogner Park to see the Vigelund statues – well worth a visit. We left Norway regretfully, having enjoyed every minute of our stay in this delightful, unspoiled country and beat it eastwards to Stockholm. At that time the Swedes drove on the left-hand side of the road and we had to change sides through a chicane when crossing the border. I was fascinated by the large rafts of logs being floated down by river from the forests. They were tied together and towed by one boat whilst another had hold of the rear end, more than 100 yards away, to nudge it round the bends. A compulsive scenario, this, for the amateur film-maker.

We stayed outside Stockholm at Saltsjöbaden and, frankly, found little to interest us in the city except Kreuger's 8-litre Bentley on show in the Technical Museum. From here we turned southwards along the Baltic coast to commence our circuitous journey home. The craftsmen at work in the glass factories at Kosta and Orrefors held us spellbound for a while, then we streaked across to the west coast to spend the night at Bastad before going south to cross on the ferry from Helsingborg to Helsingør (Elsinore) in Denmark. As was so often the case, all the hotels in Copenhagen were full and we had to stay outside the city.

Our guides in Copenhagen were Ditlev and Else Scheel who had made us so welcome on our first Continental motoring holiday when living in Bern. We really enjoyed our rubber-necking and must have seen everything worth seeing in and around Copenhagen during the few days we spent there; of course, it wasn't the 'porn' capital of Europe in those days. We left with some reluctance to drive to Korsør to catch the ferry to Nyborg. On the way I had a blow-out in one of my Michelin 'X's whilst travelling at 75 mph, but came to no harm and reached the boat before it sailed.

That night we reached Hamburg and stayed at the 'Vier Jahreszeiten' Hotel for a couple of nights. We went to the famous Zoo and drove along the Reeperbahn in St Pauli – though not to linger on this occasion – but the thing which Con and I will never forget occurred just as we were leaving. We were in our bedroom on an upper floor at the front of the hotel packing up the last of our belongings prior to checking out. Carol had gone downstairs to put something in the car which was parked across the road. Suddenly, we heard the screech of brakes and skidding tyres. We dashed to the window and were relieved to see Carol was safe. She had, in fact, stepped into the road momentarily forgetting that the traffic kept to the right in Germany and had caused a motorist to make an emergency stop, fortunately without physical harm to anyone, but with a fairly disturbing mental effect on all concerned.

Motoring through northern Holland, I enjoyed a fast run across the dyke enclosing the Zuider Zee; this is a level road running dead straight for about 12 miles. And so down to Rotterdam. Here we saw what I think was the first 'people only' shopping precinct, which the forward-looking Dutch had built on the ruins of their bombed city. I do not profess to understand modern art, but I must admit that the giant Zadkine statue, 'The Devastated City', conveyed vividly to me its portrayal of the city of Rotterdam having its heart torn out in May 1940 by the German bombers. We stopped overnight at Scheveningen on the Dutch coast; a fantastic firework display on the foreshore was thrown in. It was here I saw the Dutch mounted police in action. A group of youths were walking noisily and defiantly along a part of the promenade which was being kept clear for passing traffic, spectators being kept on the pavements, when a mountie took one of the gang by the shoulder of his jacket and cantered off so fast that the offender's feet were scarcely touching the ground. He deposited his charge some distance away, by which time his chums had melted away!

We arrived home having done 3,715 miles in three weeks with a petrol consumption of 17.8 mpg. We have never regretted that we 'went up' instead of 'down' for our holiday that year.

In retrospect

My Mk VI Bentley proved itself to be a first-class means of transport. It was fast, safe, comfortable and a joy to drive; versatile, equally at home shopping, commuting, towing, touring; and all-in-all just about the best compromise one could wish for. I wrote at the time, 'We all have our own ideas as to which is the fastest car available; which has the best cornering and road-holding; which gives the best ride; which is the most economical; most comfortable; best value for money; easiest to drive; cosiest; best in acceleration; best braked; etc.; but no one car can possess the ultimate in all these features.

'The man who seeks the best of everything without demanding the ultimate in anything will find the mixture served up at Crewe in the shape of a 4½-litre Standard Steel Saloon.

I would go further in the light of subsequent experience: I am firmly of the opinion that the continued success of the post-war products of the Crewe factory stems largely from the fact that the Rolls-Royce and Bentley cars have given 'the mostest of the bestest.' When I parted with the car in August 1961, a necessary step to enable me to acquire that unique Bentley, 'Olga', I had driven the Mk VI about 90,000 miles, thousands of them in a dozen Continental countries, and enjoyed every one of them – so had all my passengers.

Prototype Continental – 'Olga'

I am not keen on the practice of giving names to cars, but I bow to the tradition of calling the prototype 'R' Continental Bentley by the soubriquet *Olga*, a name derived from its registration letters long before the car came into my hands.

Encouraged – perhaps goaded would be a more appropriate word – by Walter Sleator, their distributor in Paris, Rolls-Royce took up the concept of a 'Continental' Bentley using the R-Type chassis and engine as the basis for the new car. The aim was to secure a 20% increase in maximum speed, 120 mph compared with the 100 mph of the Standard model; the two main ways of achieving this were by designing an aerodynamic body and reducing the overall weight. At that time it was considered that the best tyres available would not permit sustained speeds around 115 mph unless the kerb weight was kept down to 34 cwt.

H.J. Mulliner built a light alloy body to a form decided upon only after exhaustive wind tunnel tests, and that body is still on my car. In August 1951 the dream became the reality. Initial tests in this country gave a maximum speed of 114 mph using Dunlop Medium Distance Track tyres at 3,750 rpm. As the permitted engine speed was 4,250 rpm it was apparent that the overall axle-ratio of 2.79:1 was too high and a lower one (3.07:1) was substituted.

Then 'Olga' was sent to France for testing at Montlhéry under the supervision of Walter Sleator. Tests on the track showed that the change had in no way spoiled the car's maximum performance whilst, because the acceleration had been improved thereby, it was more quickly reached. Official timing by the Automobile Club de France gave 'Olga' an average lap speed of 118¾ mph taken over five laps, with a best lap speed of 119¾ mph. This test was conducted using Dunlop MDT tyres, inflated to 50 lbs sq in. Using India Shallow Tread Road Tyres, the maximum speed recorded was 115.5 mph.

Although very little tyre trouble was experienced during the high speed tests when using the tyres which had been designed for the purpose, a normal 6-ply tyre used under the same conditions survived for only 20 miles.

'Olga' was used by Charles Faroux as his Course Car during the 1952 Le Mans 24-Hour Race and then embarked upon a very busy life as the Works Demonstrator. It was made available to the Press for road-testing – the first Road Test report was published in the 'Autocar' on 12 September 1952 – and driven by the Sales Staff, distributors, dealers and potential customers all over Europe. At the time, the new Continental Bentley was the fastest 4-seater production saloon in the world; the best mean speed recorded by the 'Autocar' was 115.4 mph. One run, with the driver only, was timed at 120 mph. For the first time the 'Autocar' had to extend its acceleration tables to 100 mph for both third and top gears. This Road Test report concluded thus: 'This Bentley is a modern magic carpet which annihilates distance and delivers the occupants well-nigh as fresh as when they started. It is a car Britain may well be proud of, and it is sure to add new lustre to the name it bears.'

Production of the R-Type Continental continued until May 1955, but only 208 were made. Of these, the most sought after today are those similar to 'Olga', having right-hand drive, manual gearbox, and two-door H.J. Mulliner coachwork, of which 75 were delivered to UK customers. During the production run I was to drive 'Olga' on several occasions, each time enhancing my liking for the car. When no longer required as a demonstrator, 'Olga' was used as a Company car, at first at Director level and then in the hands of several senior employees. I had said to 'Doc' (F. Llewellyn Smith, then Managing Director of the Motor Car Division), that, if he ever decided to sell 'Olga', I would like first refusal. He reminded me that it was RR

29 *'Olga' reborn in June 1961 – note the rear-wheel spats in position*

policy to break up prototypes and I cringed. It was something of a surprise, therefore, when Jack Scott, the Sales Director, called me in November 1960 to say that the Company had finished with 'Olga' and was I still interested in buying it? He said it was in pretty poor shape and, if he sold it to me, he didn't want me complaining and coming back with the car, so whatever work was necessary would have to be done on delivery at my expense. I asked him to lend it to me for a week-end to enable me to make up my mind. When I drove 'Olga' that week-end I was frankly shocked at its condition – it was down on the back springs and sounded like an Underground train – which is not, perhaps, surprising as it had covered nearly 250,000 miles by then. Despite its superficial tattiness and the obvious need for mechanical attention, its underlying charm and qualities came through and I knew I was hooked. Actually, I was somewhat apprehensive that the purchase price of the car plus the cost of the necessary reconditioning, would prove too much for me. I was biting my nails in a sweat of indecision. I felt that if I couldn't own 'Olga' myself she should go to a good home and telephoned Peter Hampton to say that if he was interested, maybe RR could be talked into letting him have the car if I turned her down. I took Peter for a ride in 'Olga', and he drove it himself in a manner and at a speed which would have done credit to an experienced driver not handicapped by the loss of use of one arm. Peter was favourably impressed and said he would give me a firm answer the next day. I returned home in torment at the thought of 'Olga' slipping through my fingers and called Peter to say 'Forget it, I have decided to take the plunge.' He said, 'Pity, I was just going to telephone you to say I would buy if it could be arranged.' It was my gain and Peter's loss – and we are still speaking to each other! For my part I have never regretted for one moment this big decision.

30 *Bentleys at a cocktail party in Antwerp on the eve of the speed trials – note the absence of mudguards and lamps*

I asked Roney Messervy (Service Director of RR) to quote for the mechanical work necessary to make the car as new and requested the same from H.J. Mulliner for the coachwork. With these quotations before me, I deducted the total from what I considered to be the (then!) market value of a similar model in 'as new' condition and offered Jack Scott the difference, which was little enough, in all conscience. I was delighted when he said 'Done', and my motoring life entered a new era. The desirable heap was delivered to Hythe Road in December 1960 and work on the mechanical side commenced. Replacement $3\frac{3}{4}$-in bore engine, gearbox and radiator matrix were fitted. The chassis and running-gear were overhauled – front suspension, propeller shaft, rear axle and half-shafts, rear springs, rear dampers, steering, electrics – brakes were relined and hose connections replaced. A new set of Dunlop RS 5 tyres was fitted and two months later 'Olga' was handed over to H.J. Mulliner at their Putney works. Whilst at Hythe Road 'Olga' had acquired a new chassis number. The chassis number on the car when I bought it was 9 B6, presumably an experimental number, and Roney Messervy thought it should have a number more in keep-with the series allocated to production Continentals. He chose BC 26A, i.e. one number beyond those issued to the first batch of 25 cars. Many enthusiasts have wondered how 'Olga' could be the first Continental when 25 others had 'lower' chassis numbers; now they know.

Mulliners were to restore the car to new condition. This involved repainting, re-upholstering, re-trimming, replating all chromium, new head lining, repolishing woodwork, new carpets – in fact, the lot. I made frequent calls to see 'how it was getting along' and could scarcely contain my impatience to gain possession of the reborn 'Olga'. In the event, the paintwork was sub-contracted to Hooper Motor Services and the retrimming to Wood & Pickett; both firms did a first-class job. Incidentally, I changed the colour of the body from the original darkish grey to 'Shell Grey', and had the 'orange' woodwork darkened to a rich brown. The interior of the car was fairly spartan in the interests of weight-saving, so I added a radio, a rear-window de-mister, headlight flashers, and an ashtray (!); and moved the turn indicator from the centre of the fascia to the steering column. I put the car on a weighbridge and found that the car weighed 33¾ cwt with some petrol in the tank.

I was anxious that 'Olga' should be ready in time for the Bentley Drivers Club meeting in Kensington Gardens on 1 July 1961, and the target date was achieved. It was indeed a proud Sedgwick who re-possessed 'Olga' looking like new and with a new speedometer set at 00000.

In the middle of September I took 'Olga' across the Channel for the first time – though goodness knows how many times she had been abroad in her previous life. I drove across Holland and down the Rhine Valley to Wetzlar where I had arranged to take a 4-day course in photography for Leica owners at the factory. Afterwards I drove south through Basle, over the St Bernard Pass to Turin and via the Col de Tende to Eze-sur-mer, to join, unexpectedly, Con and Carol who had flown there for a short holiday. For the life of me I cannot recall anything about the journey home, so on this occasion you will be spared a detailed itinerary and timetable.

In May 1962, I once again led a party of Bentley Drivers Club Members to take part in the Belgian Day of Records organized by the Antwerp Motor Union on the same stretch of the Antwerp-Liege motorway which we had used three years previously. This time I was driving 'Olga' which not only took over the role of maid-of-all-work, hitherto fulfilled by the Mk VI, but was to take part in the competition. Tuning for the run through the measured kilometre was limited to increasing tyre pressures and turning the wing mirrors through 90 degrees. My speed for the Flying Kilometre was 111.234 mph on the outward run, and 108.326 mph on the return, giving a mean speed of 109.760 mph. The standing kilometre time was 34.92 seconds at the first attempt and one-hundredth-of-a-second longer on the second run. (Some owners of R-Type Continentals kid themselves about the maximum speed of their cars; it is my considered view that a production car has rarely exceeded 115 mph.)

Later in the year (July) we embarked on another motoring holiday, this time taking 'Olga' into Czechoslovakia. My passengers were again Con and Carol and we were looking forward to this excursion into Eastern Europe – this was, of course, before the Russian invasion of Czechoslovakia.

After a night at Wurzburg and lunch in Nuremburg we crossed the border at Waldhaus/Rozvadov. The 'Welcome to Czechoslovakia' banners contrasted strangely with the thoroughness with which the armed guards frisked 'Olga' before we were allowed to proceed through Pilsen to Prague, 110 miles away. I found the atmosphere rather sad. The city was a mixture of beautiful old buildings – many in a state of neglect – and drab modern buildings. There was a delightful corner reminiscent of Venice; the famous astronomical clock, dating from 1460, in the old Town Hall, which we managed to reach on the hour to see the action; Wenceslas Square (the Piccadilly of Prague); fantastic illuminated books in a one-time monastery; and – not so lovely – a great monolith of Soviet leaders headed by Stalin. (This statue weighed several thousand tons and must have posed quite a problem when Moscow decreed the removal of all likenesses of Stalin. Never did hear what, if anything, happened to it.) We drove through attractive countryside crossing into Austria north-west of Vienna; I must admit to feeling a renewed sense of liberty as we left Communist soil and drove towards the capital.

It was our first visit to the Austrian capital and in addition to seeing the well-known sights – the Schönbrunn Palace, the Prater amusement park with its great wheel, the Spanish Riding

31 *The 'Markus' in the Technical Museum in Vienna, claimed by some to be the first petrol motor car*

School – we went backstage at the Opera House, and sought out the Technical Museum to see the 'Markus', built in 1875 and claimed to be the first petrol-driven motor-car in the world – a claim strongly refuted by the historians of Daimler-Benz at Unterturkheim. The horses of the Spanish Riding School were at the stud farm at Piber near Graz and we were able to see them on the way to Venice. We stayed on the Lido and a launch trip across the lagoon proved rather costly as I dropped a cine lens overboard.

After a few days here we removed ourselves to Cap Estel, at Eze-sur-mer. I am a restless individual, rarely staying in any one place for more than three or four days, and the Lido Venice had provided me with enough sun, sea and sand for a bit, so I flew home for a week leaving 'Olga' with Con and Carol on the Riviera. I flew to Nice a week later, collected 'Olga' and family, driving home via Geneva and Paris.

May the following year (1963) saw 'Olga' once more with the Bentleys in Belgium for the spring meeting. Unfortunately, it was no longer possible to hold this competition on the new autoroute and it was transferred to another piece of road which was not long enough to give adequate acceleration and braking distances for flying runs at maximum speed over the measured distances. Only standing start times were recorded over a kilometre and a mile. 'Olga's' time (34.33 secs) over the kilometre was three-fifths of a second quicker than the previous year. Not many of the cars reached their maximum speed by the time they crossed the finishing line at the end of the kilometre, but it seemed like it for the road was tree-lined, comparatively narrow and lined with spectators!

The following month I took 'Olga' across the Channel again, this time to Le Mans to assist in Briggs Cunningham's pit, but returned home immediately afterwards as we were not planning to have a motoring holiday in Europe that year.

I was using 'Olga' daily for travelling to and from the office, until the coming of the 70 mph limit and increasing traffic took away what little pleasure there was in this 20 miles-in-an-hour journey. 'Olga' was also used on many Bentley Drivers Club occasions. During the first $2\frac{1}{2}$ years I covered 50,000 miles and reached 100,000 miles on 22 February 1972. This later milestone in the life of 'Olga' was marked in suitable fashion. I had been invited by the Chairman and Directors of Rolls-Royce Motors to dine at the Connaught Hotel for the purpose of accepting the Company's donation to the 'W.O. Bentley Memorial Fund' and I realized a few days before this engagement that 'Olga's' mileage was 99,900+. I invited David Plastow and John Craig to be aboard when the magic figure was reached. I left the office a few miles short of the target and drove out to St John's Wood and back, and around the West End to park outside the Connaught with the distance recorder reading 99,999 miles. I was joined by the above-mentioned Members of the Board and drove off round Grosvenor Square. The faces of the three occupants broke into boyish grins of delight as the five nines gave way to the five zeroes during the third lap.

Later in the year – on 20 August 1972 to be exact – 'Olga' came of age and I conceived the idea of celebrating her 21st Birthday by inviting owners of her progeny to drive to my home and drink the health of their prototype. Daft, you may think, giving a birthday party for a car, but none of the like-minded enthusiasts who arrived in the R-Type Continentals would agree. Fourteen of these cars turned up, coming from all quarters and some quite long distances. Several owners had an opportunity of driving 'Olga' and praised her mechanical condition, handling and light steering.

And 'Olga' – now more than 23 years old – is still going strong, enjoying a less busy life, but always ready and seemingly eager to get cracking when the occasion arises.

33 *Joseph Cugnot's second steam car of 1770 on exhibition in the Musée des Arts et Metiers in Paris, seen during a fleeting visit*

32 *'Olga' waiting for a run in regularity-speed tests at Pierre Bardinon's racing circuit at Mas du Clos, near Aubusson*

34 *A group of enthusiasts during a visit to the Mahy Collection in Ghent. Ghislain Mahy is at the wheel of his 1906 Fondu with his son Ivan. From left to right are Louis Giron, Evelyn Mawer, John Hampton, Ronald ('Steady') Barker, Bill Cook, the author, and Bob Gregory*

35 *'Olga's' 21st birthday party guests, August 1972*

36 *Bill Cook serves an appropriate toast on 'Olga's' coming-of-age*

My other cars

The 'Merc' in my life

Acquisition

By a stroke of good fortune an ambition of many years was realized when I acquired my Mercedes at the end of 1960. I was lunching with Lord Montagu at Beaulieu on the occasion of a Bentley Drivers Club gathering and was introduced to a fellow guest from South Africa, Count Luccio Labia, and learnt that two De Dietrich cars referred to by 'Peterborough' in the 'Daily Telegraph' a few days earlier were owned by his mother.

These two cars of 1903 and 1905 had been put into a furniture depository, together with other family possessions, by Luccio's grandfather, Sir Joseph Robinson, when he returned to his native South Africa before World War I, and had remained untouched ever since. Luccio's mother, Princess Labia, had taken the family's fabulous collection of pictures out of store and Luccio, already the proud owner of more than one Vintage car in South Africa, was set on restoring the cars and using them. He was, however, returning to his home in South Africa and wanted the restoration done here. Ronald ('Steady') Barker and I undertook the unenviable task of arranging and supervising the restorations. There were many pitfalls along this road, but both cars are now running and in beautiful condition. The 1905 De Dietrich is in Cape Town. The 1903 one, on loan to the Montagu Museum, was driven by its owner in the 1964 Brighton Run, and has taken part nearly every year since.

What has all this to do with the Merc? Well, on one of his visits to England Luccio mentioned that there was another car belonging to the family in a house near Brighton. My eyes lit up at news of a big Edwardian, and when the car was brought up to the depository in London 'Steady' and I, with Maurice Smith, then Editor of the 'Autocar', went to look at the Mercedes. It was extremely dusty, and a bit battered. The aluminium steering wheel was smashed and the wooden rim lay in pieces on the floor. The windscreen was broken and the tyres were flat and iron-hard. We could see that it was substantially all there and would make a wonderful car if restored properly. Luccio decided that he did not want to take on another restoration job and offered the car to 'Steady' and me jointly for a nominal price. 'Steady' was planning the restoration of a Napier and reluctantly opted out. I couldn't believe my luck when I found myself the owner of a 1910 Mercedes with large closed bodywork. It was a dream come true.

I went to work enthusiastically to learn all I could about the car and to plan its restoration. I had neither the knowledge nor the facilities to undertake the job myself, and count myself fortunate that Louis Giron agreed to deal with the mechanical side; Leslie Willis, who had been trying for years to retire from coachbuilding to farm quietly in Kent, was persuaded to do just one more job for me.

Whilst waiting for Louis to start work I wrote to Dr Schildberger, then Curator of the Daimler-Benz Museum at Stuttgart, giving the Serial number of the car and asking if he could identify the model and establish the date of manufacture from his records. He replied that the Mercedes was a type 28/50 PS and that it had been delivered to their agents in Düsseldorf on the 20 December 1910.

The specification of the car soon emerged from inspection and contemporary literature. Known as the 45/50 hp model in this country, it has a four-cylinder engine with a bore of 120 mm and stroke of 160 mm giving a capacity of 7,241 cc, the T-head cylinders being cast in pairs. The carburettor, of Mercedes manufacture, is fed from a pressurized tank at the rear. Before starting the engine one must work vigorously at a hand pump, air pressure thereafter being maintained by an exhaust-driven pump. The Bosch Dual Ignition comprises a trembler coil (used only for starting) and a magneto. Usually the engine will start from cold on the switch once the cylinders have been

37 *Twins – the 'tulip' back coachwork is by J.A. Lawton – a 1911 Silver Ghost Rolls-Royce in front of the author's 1910 Mercedes*

primed and the engine turned over a few compressions. I do this by exerting all my weight on the starting handle through my foot. Although not strong enough to swing the engine on full compression, I can do so without undue strain on half compression. This is arranged by pulling a handle conveniently located under the radiator, which lifts the exhaust valves.

Very unusual is the scroll-type clutch, which comprises a spring coiled around a drum, within a cylinder lubricated at will by the driver. When the clutch pedal is depressed, the spring is compressed and the resulting increase in diameter brings the spring away from the outer surface of the drum, thus disconnecting the engine from the gear-box. This works very well indeed, but after changing gear one must allow the clutch time to become fully engaged before pressing the accelerator again, otherwise there is juddering and slip. The only disadvantage of this type of clutch is that the engine cannot be started by towing the car in gear and engaging the clutch in the usual way; the coil is then tending to unwind and will not transmit the drive from road wheels to engine.

A contemporary catalogue gives the range of engine revolutions as 300 to 1,250 per minute.

The gate-change gear-box has four speeds, and this car must be one of the first Mercedes to have a propellor shaft drive instead of the sprockets and chains that were used at least up to the 1908 models. There is an arrangement for water-cooling the drum of the transmission foot-brake, but this was disconnected when the car came out of storage and has not been reconnected. The handbrake works internal expanding cast iron shoes (since relined with Ferodo) in the rear wheel drums. All wheels were fitted with 935 × 135 beaded edge tyres, although the catalogue refers to 915 × 105 for the front wheels.

The body is an elegant open-drive limousine by J.A. Lawton & Co. and is notable for the double-curved back – sometimes called the 'tulip' back. I know of only one other similar body, on a 1911 Silver Ghost, owned until recently by Fred Watson and built by the same firm. The Merc. is 7 ft 6 ins high and weighs 1 ton 19¼ cwt. The price of the Chassis was 16,500 Marks ex Works (about £825) which is some £160 less than the Rolls-Royce Silver Ghost of the period.

Restoration

The Mercedes bore the Registration No. 'XB 6193' on a crumpled number plate and an earlier number 'P 8462' painted on the radiator honeycomb, barely discernible. It was the latter number which Surrey Council agreed to revive for the car, despite all their records of that time having been destroyed. (On several occasions since then, when the sunlight has been falling on the radiator from a certain angle, I have

38 *The 1910 Mercedes arriving at Weybridge after being off the road for forty years*

convinced myself that the fading number is actually 'P 6462'!)

On the 4 March 1961, Adam Bros. of Kingston winched the car on to a low-loader and transported it to a garage at the back of the Oatlands Park Hotel, Weybridge, where Louis set to work, the doors of his own workshop nearby not being high enough to admit it.

Our first attack was on the tyres, which had to be removed from the rims with a hacksaw. It proved impossible to obtain 935 × 135 covers; the 880 × 120 cover fits the same rim and I decided to use this size on the front wheels. The informed consensus suggested that these tyres would be too narrow in section for the rear wheels and that it would be better to use 895 × 135, which are still in the Dunlop range. To implement this decision the two rear wheels had to be reduced in diameter, and the work was entrusted to Thomas Tingley, Limited of 92, Brandon Street, Walworth, London, S.E.17, one of the few wheelwrights still around who would undertake this sort of job. Once the new dimensions were calculated it was a simple matter to cut a piece out of the detachable rims, re-roll them to the new circle, and then to weld the ends together.

The wheels themselves were quite another matter. They were wooden-spoked and the iron rim had one side bent up at right angles and the other side down. Thus, they could not be rolled to a new contour when cut and shortened, and they had to be cut into two semi-circles and reshaped to a template before being welded into a circle again. New felloes were made and fitted to the shortened spokes. The detachable rims were originally secured to the wheels by eight bolts and wedges. One of these disappeared when the rims were cut down, and to respace the remaining bolts, with or without the insertion of another one, was really out of the question. So the rear wheels now have seven securing bolts, two of them more widely-spaced than the rest; this arrangement has given no trouble whatsoever.

I could not afford to have the chassis and engine stripped down to the last nut and bolt and then rebuilt from the ground up. The compromise I decided upon was to make sure that the mechanical side was superficially clean and working safely and efficiently, and to give the coachwork the full treatment inside and out.

Louis Giron, with characteristic thoroughness and painstaking care, began the long task of examining and restoring to full working order every mechanical part of the car without, if possible, dismantling the engine. This had seized solid, but yielded to a soaking in Redex and after a few days could be turned freely by hand. We were pleased to find that the radiator was neither blocked nor leaking. Work proceeded slowly but surely. Every oil pipe was cleaned out and its function ascertained; petrol and air lines and the petrol tank cleaned and tested, and so on. The magneto was sent away to be overhauled and re-magnetized, but the Bosch coil presented more difficulty. I could find no one who would re-wind it and wrote to Stuttgart in despair. Imagine my surprise when Dr Schildberger wrote to say that Bosch were sending me a replacement, but pointed out that '. . . they could not say in advance how long a product that was manufactured about fifty years ago will continue to work satisfactorily.' They also sent a wiring diagram and made no charge. The coil was fitted, and is still working perfectly.

The radiator cap was missing, so a new one was manufactured from brass and 'Woodite', based on photographs of Bill Cook's 1908 Mercedes radiator cap and an impression in dental wax of the internal thread of the radiator filler. I must digress here to refer to the radiator badge. This was in the form of a circular medallion bearing the name 'Daimler Motoren Gesellschaft' round the periphery and 'Mercedes' across the centre. Dr Schildberger could not understand why the car did not bear the three-pointed star which came into use in 1909, and we did not discover the reason until a knowledgeable member of the Mercedes-Benz Club said to me, 'I see your car is an English delivery.' He then explained that he knew this by the circular radiator badge, which was fitted to all Mercedes delivered in this country at that time, because the Star Motor Company objected to the use of the three-pointed star. My informant went on to say that if I prised off the badge I would find the three-pointed star underneath. Not wishing to do any damage to satisfy my curiosity, I removed the radiator cap, and peered hopefully into the radiator. Sure enough, the star was embossed on the radiator just where the medallion covered it. I spent quite a time after this examining files and letters at the Patent Office and, although finding nothing to show that anyone had objected to the use of the three-pointed star on cars in England, I feel sure that the covering up of the manufacturer's trade mark must have resulted from something of the sort.

Then one day Louis said to me 'I am going to start her up tomorrow morning.' And he did – just like that. The exhaust manifold was off and the noise of the engine, running on its 40-year-old plugs, was music to our ears.

Soon after – on Remembrance Day 1961 to be exact – the car was driven for the first time, a trouble-free run of 50 miles from Weybridge to Leslie Willis' farm near Gravesend. The body had not been touched, except for repairing the steering wheel and replacing the broken plate glass windscreen with laminated glass. The car looked very shabby indeed, but its performance belied its appearance. It was to spend the winter at Leslie's for coachwork restoration.

The old finish was removed to the bare metal and coat after coat of paint was applied, the final one being varnished three or four times. The colour used for most of the body was ruby with the upper part black, and yellow lining added where appropriate.

The cloth upholstery and head linings in the rear compartment were stripped out and redone in similar material. Blinds, cords, window straps, etc. were all renewed as near to the original as possible; the silk tassels and buttons were made by an old lady of eighty. A new carpet was made for the back, and white ribbed rubber matting found for the front floor. Interior fittings were re-nickelled, the windows replaced with toughened glass, and the front seats recovered in black leather. This work went on through the winter and each visit to see the progress being made heightened the anticipation of the day when the Merc. would take the road again, as good as new.

Meantime, I conducted a search for lamps and a horn, for none of these were with the car when it was brought out of its resting place. Louis Holland found for me a beautiful pair of 'Rushmore' Searchlights and 'King of the Road' side and tail lamps. The headlamps could have been connected up to the acetylene cylinder in the polished wooden box on the running-board, and the oil lamps made to work. As I had no plans for after-dark driving in the Merc. I decided not to use the old lamps for lighting, but merely for appearance. The car had a small battery to operate the coil and Louis ran hidden wires to almost invisible sockets at the foot of the bulkhead and to the bottom of the body at the rear. If I am inadvertently caught out on the road after dark, I put four rubber diver's helmet lamps, two white and two red, on the side and tail lamp brackets, plug them in and I have legal get-you-home lighting.

'Steady' Barker let me have one of a pair of flat trumpet horns which had come with his Napier. I spent a long time trying to locate a suitable speaking tube and mouthpiece to connect to the brass earpiece behind the driver's head. I eventually found a firm which supplied tubing and fittings for ambulances. Their colour range was limited, but Leslie removed the woven outer covering and recovered it with the material used for the upholstery, and he even found an authentic mouthpiece with a tiny bulb-horn to attract the driver's attention.

At last, on 8 April 1962, I went down to Meopham to collect the finished car. It looked magnificent and was a credit to Leslie. It was a proud cortege that accompanied the Merc. back to Cobham.

Realization

All old cars interest me from a historical point of view, but I would not want to own a veteran car which had no other merit than its technical or historical interest. I had always wanted a big Edwardian which would be powerful enough and reliable enough to take its place as a means of transport in modern traffic conditions. And now I was the proud owner of such a car.

Today, the Merc. always stands ready for the road at any time and I use it as the spirit moves. I would drive it anywhere I would drive a modern car; it would take longer and manoeuvring would be more difficult, but everything else would be taken in its stride. Strangely enough, I find it less frustrating driving the Merc. in quite heavy traffic on the open road than modern cars, for the reason that the Merc. runs right along with the traffic, which always seems to be travelling between 40 and 50 mph, and the repeated desire to overtake does not arise. The only real hazard arises from the lack of front wheel brakes. One leaves a greater space, between oneself and the car in front, than would normally be the case and all goes well until some selfish driver overtakes and crowds in front, halving the braking distance.

After several shakedown trips I decided to enter some Concours d'Elégance – and I mean just that – competitions in which the elegance of the car was to be judged. If the rules called for the occupants being in contemporary costume, so much the better. I admire Veteran and Vintage car owners who are able to maintain (or have someone else maintain) their cars in immaculate condition outside, inside, underneath and everywhere else, but this is not for me. I endeavour to present the Merc. in a bodily clean condition, with the engine only super-

39 *The Mercedes in a Concours d'Elégance at Crystal Palace, with Con, Carol and Amanda – three generations – and the author in Edwardian costume*

40 *The engine of the 1910 Mercedes, superficially clean and working safely and efficiently*

ficially clean – but both in perfect working order.

As to the wearing of costume, I strongly disagree with the policy of the Veteran Car Club of Great Britain which discourages 'dressing-up'. I think that one of the gratifying things about owning a veteran car is the obvious pleasure it gives to other motorists and passers-by. If the fear is that costume will manifest the onlookers' enjoyment in the laughter of ridicule, then I have seen more evidence of this on the Brighton Run at some of the all-weather kit worn by some participants which might be more appropriate if they were skin diving or inspecting sewers. By all means keep dry, but don't decry those who go to the trouble to find or make authentic period costume. In my view it is just as meritorious to seek contemporary apparel as it is to seek contemporary accessories. It has also struck me that some of the veteran motorists who decry the wearing of costume are *still* wearing the costume they were wearing in those days anyway, without apparently being aware of it!

I am fortunate in having a wife who enjoys dressing-up, and am quite prepared to don a period chauffeur's uniform to match, when the occasion arises. Our first competition for an elegant combination of car and lady was on the occasion of the Silver Jubilee of the British Automobile Racing Club at Goodwood in July 1962. I entered the 'Day at the Races' class with my daughter, and was placed second, and in 'Motoring in Grandfather's Day' with Con as passenger. The latter combination won this class, also the Prix d'Honneur for the best turn-out of the day.

It had been in my mind from the moment I acquired the Merc. that the best way to fulfil my particular enjoyment of veteran car ownership would be to drive the car back to its birthplace in Stuttgart. And so in May 1963 I took the Merc. to Germany, accompanied by Con, Louis and Barbara Giron and three other friends, with two other cars. Louis took the car via the Dover/Ostend ferry to meet us after the Speed Trials in Antwerp. The next morning we set off about 9 am and drove via Liège, Aachen, Cologne and Bonn to Linz-am-Rhein. The Merc. had covered 180 miles in the day as a matter of course, and on the following day we drove the remaining 215 miles to Stuttgart, the Merc. cruising happily enough at 50 mph for mile after mile.

It was our misfortune to visit Daimler-Benz AG during their only strike for fifty years and this made the promised tour of the Works impractical. We were, however, welcomed by Dr Schildberger, Prince von Urach and Artur Keser who were delighted that we had made the pilgrimage and admired the Merc. very much indeed. There is no example of this model in the museum and the Merc. was garaged for the night in the museum in a place of honour.

We drove on the test track – eyes straying to a prototype '600' undergoing development – and many photographs were taken.

On the next day, Thursday, we covered 200 miles to Luxembourg. We had only one spot of bother, when the fuel-pump ceased functioning in the centre of Saarbrücken in the evening rush-hour. Some dirt had lodged in the valve and was eventually removed by squirting petrol on it and jiggling it up and down. This is one of the very few troubles which stops me on the road occasionally – we call it doing a 'Saarbrücken' – and the same cure is always effective. It happened as I was leaving the last Time Control in a Rally the following year and led to some spirited motoring along the Guildford Bypass to reach the Final Control dead on time.

The journey to Ostend on the Friday (205 miles) was notable for very wet weather. The Merc. bowled along regardless and on the Autoroute between Brussels and Ostend covered 49 miles in the hour.

We arrived home safely on Saturday evening, having covered a most enjoyable 1,100 miles in a week. Apart from routine lubrication and adjustment of brakes, the car required no atten-

41 *Louis Giron demonstrating the fruits of his labours to Dr Schildberger, Curator of the Daimler-Benz Museum, on the test track at the factory in Stuttgart*

tion, but Louis did one or two things as a result of experience gained on the Continental journey. These included the dynamic balancing of the flywheel in situ by the addition of weights, and the fitting of a pressure release valve in the radiator overflow to prevent an excessive quantity of water being expelled unnecessarily by the powerful water pump.

Berlin bound

When I learnt that the Allgemeiner Schnauferl*-Club was to hold its 11th Deutsche Schnauferl-Rallye in West Berlin I seized the opportunity to combine a visit to a city on my 'must-be-seen-sometime' list with another sortie with my 1910 Mercedes into the land of its origin.

And so, after giving the Mercedes a thorough checking-over and the cleaning of a lifetime, we left Dover for Ostend on a Belgian ferry during the seamen's strike on Monday, 6 June 1966. I was accompanied by Con, niece Anthea, and Louis Giron, and took my R-Type Continental Bentley along as a tender car. Disembarking at 4 pm we made for Antwerp where we were to spend the night.

The distance to Berlin was divided into three daily stages of approximately 170 miles each. These stages were dictated partly by the need to cover the autobahn across East Germany from Helmstedt to West Berlin more or less non-stop, and partly by the wish to confine our motoring to daylight hours. I knew from experience that the Mercedes could be relied upon to cover between 35 and 40 miles in an hour and thus planned on five to six hours' driving each day on the outward journey. Louis and I took turns driving the Merc. and the Bentley, rarely doing less than 50 miles at a stretch.

Not long after leaving Antwerp, Louis, driving the Merc. around the 50 mph mark felt the engine getting tight and stopped before it had time to seize up. The engine was tight when turned by hand, but after removing the compression taps and injecting a quantity of oil

* From the verb 'schnaufen': to breathe hard; to snort.

42 *Paul-Heinz Rohll's 1925 Mercedes once owned by Richard Tauber*

into each cylinder, it ran freely and we moved off cautiously into nearby Aachen, giving liberal supplementary squirts of oil into the engine by means of the hand-pump on the dashboard. The engine was now misfiring and this was attributed to the magneto not functioning properly. During lunch the engine cooled sufficiently to enable an investigation to be made. The magneto presented no problem to Louis who whipped it off and removed the carbon dust which was causing arcing. The tightening-up of the engine, however, caused us some concern.

We soon saw that No. 3 cylinder was the culprit by the newly-applied paint on the lower uncooled part of the block becoming discoloured with the excessive heat. The engine is lubricated by a mechanical pump which feeds oil to the bearings and cylinder walls. The two rear cylinders are served by a common supply and it was apparent that somehow or other the internal feed to No. 3 cylinder must have become obstructed. Gloom descended on the party, figuratively speaking, as we worked for a couple of hours in blazing sunshine in a not-so-back street amid a keenly interested and pressing crowd of Aachen citizenry. Would we have to abandon the trip and return home or should we go on for a bit and see what happened? Louis decided that the starved cylinder might receive sufficient lubrication if the manual supply of oil to the crankcase gallery was operated at frequent intervals; this would use a lot of oil, as the other three cylinders would be receiving more than they needed in order to ensure that No. 3 was sufficiently lubricated.

We decided to go on and left Aachen at 5 pm bound for Solingen, near Düsseldorf, 70 miles away. The magneto was now working properly and when we regained the autobahn we resumed motoring on the basis of not much exceeding 40 mph and giving three shots of oil on the hand-pump every mile, with additional shots when going up hills. The engine ran freely and, although we were aware of a non-standard

43 *Spectators on the Kurfurstendam lining the route of the parade which concluded the Deutsche Schnauferl-Rallye in Berlin*

knock at low revs and a weak compression in one cylinder, there was no lack of power at our cruising speed. Our confidence in the Merc. returned as the miles went by and we were to complete the round trip to Berlin and back without any aggravation of the trouble.

We reached our night stop – the delightful Burg Hohenscheid Hotel near Solingen – well before dark despite a further delay when the Merc. ran out of petrol after 162.7 miles. The tank had been filled, that morning, in Antwerp, but I had over-estimated the distance which it could cover on a tankful and paid for my optimism by having to drive 17 miles up and down the autobahn in the Bentley to fetch 10 litres of petrol from a filling-station barely more than a mile away! Topping up at the next garage took another 78 litres, so I now know that my tank holds 20 gallons.

We were now well into Germany, and the passage of the Mercedes attracted a great deal of attention from passing motorists and lorry drivers. Our arms grew tired from acknowledging waves of appreciation, and we were amazed at the amount of motoring done by overtaking drivers whilst they were looking backwards at us. On one occasion a fast-moving car travelling towards us on the other carriage-way ran smartly into the back of a truck for no apparent reason, and it was not for some time that the thought occurred to us that the driver might have been looking at the Merc., instead of where he was going.

Veteran and Vintage cars are a rare sight on the roads of Germany, there being no exemptions for old cars from the ever-changing legal requirements as to direction indicators, etc. In the matter of being able to use our Veteran and Vintage cars without let or hindrance on the roads of Britain we are more fortunate than our fellow enthusiasts on the Continent, who find it difficult to drive their cars except on special occasions and often (seemingly) under police supervision. Now that we have entered the Common Market vigilance is being exercized by all concerned to see that the owners of old vehicles in the UK are not 'harmonized' off the road.

The next day we settled down to a steady progress at the rate of one kilometre in one minute (37½ mph) and put 170 uneventful miles of autobahn motoring behind us, arriving at the comfortable Parkhotel Motel at Hanover in good time for dinner. We made an early start next morning on the last leg of our journey as we did not know what delay might be encountered at the East German border and we wanted to report at Rally HQ in Berlin in mid-afternoon. On arrival at the Helmstedt Control we found many other Veteran, Vintage and Classic cars on their way to Berlin. The tedious form-filling and queueing at one desk after another, to obtain visas and make currency declarations, occupied an hour. Going through the Iron Curtain by road is always a sobering experience and one's enjoyment is damped by the implication of armed guards in watch-towers and barbed-wire fences patrolled by dogs. I could not conceal a smile when I observed the East German officials carrying out their mandatory search of the boots and bonnets of the cars on trailers; even the owners themselves were hard put to it on some occasions to find any luggage compartment on their cars capable of holding concealed contraband. The rear seat cushions of the Mercedes came in for a severe pummelling before the last barrier was raised to permit us to embark on the 100-mile stretch of road through East Germany to West Berlin. Our expectations of finding somewhere to eat were not fulfilled and, as foreigners were not allowed to leave the autobahn, we arrived very hungry at the West Berlin border at 3.15 pm. Formalities here took only 35 minutes and we arrived at the end of the Avus just before 4 o'clock, where we were greeted at the Rally HQ by Wolfgang Möller, Secretary of the Rally. The Merc. had travelled 654 miles and we had enjoyed hot, sunny weather all the way. We checked in at the nearby new hotel Europäischer Hof, which had been taken over for the Rally, and then set about cleaning the car before rushing off to a civic reception at the Kongresshalle.

The cars competing in the Rally were housed in a colossal exhibition hall; it must have been 60 ft high and about the size of a football field. The 143 entries were divided into six classes: pre-1900; 1901–1908; 1909–1918; 1919–1925; 1926–1930; and 1931–1940. There were 41 Veteran and Edwardian cars; 82 Vintage cars; and 20 Post-Vintage Thoroughbreds. The vast majority of the entries (91) were from Germany; the largest foreign entry (13) came from Holland, closely followed by Czechoslovakia with 12. There were seven entries from Great Britain besides myself. The cars themselves were a mixed bag. Many of them were of makes and models rarely seen on this side of the Channel. Their condition varied from the immaculate to the indifferent and their appearance from elegant to hideous. On the whole, however, they were a credit to their owners, and certain cars stand out in my memory – for example, the Brescia Bugatti of Fritz Hintermuller from Switzerland; the ex-Richard Tauber 1925 Mercedes of Paul-Heinz Rohll, President of the Berlin Section of the ASC; and the 1893 Benz of Kurt Krannich.

I turned my attention to the Rally Regulations, which Charles Meisl had helped me to translate from the German before I left home. When I told friends in Berlin that some points were obscure, I was told not to worry as they were obscure to the Germans too. Anyway, the route and speeds had been altered and after an hour or so with Wolfgang Möller I had a pretty good idea of what was expected. On this occasion the organizers were faced with the job of planning a 60-mile route within the confines of their beleaguered city. Understandably, the police did not want route-finding and regularity tests in the city centre, and a good deal of ingenuity was needed to work out a route in the suburbs which scarcely ever left pleasant woodland and lakeside scenery.

During this run there were three short Regularity sections, two of them of unknown length, which had to be traversed at the very low average speed of 20 kph – a second-gear pace for the Merc. and many other cars! An arbitrary penalty of 60 marks on all cars fitted with speedometers seemed less fair than the practice adopted in England of covering up speedometers and thus placing all competitors on the same footing. As luck would have it, my speedometer chose the middle of the morning to cease functioning altogether and I suffered the double disadvantage of having no instrument and collecting the penalty points as well.

Enthusiastic crowds greeted the cars on their return to the Exhibition Hall, more like the finish of Pekin to Paris than a jaunt in the woods. In the evening the entrants and their passengers – seemingly hundreds of them – were taken on a 'beer and bangers' trip in a large pleasure boat on the Wannsee. This lasted until nearly midnight and, to one standing on the upper deck in the gathering dusk, the lusty German drinking songs emanating from the portholes below contrasted strangely with the unlit armed East German police boats patrolling menacingly beyond a line of buoys marking the edge of freedom.

The next morning, Saturday, was devoted to a complicated driving test devised to reveal the dexterity of the driver and the manoeuvrability of the car. It necessitated starting the engine – those fortunate enough to have a self-starter were allowed to use it – driving a slalom course through pylons into a garage and stopping within 20 cm of the end wall; reversing similarly into another garage; driving forward up quite a steep ramp, stopping and restarting without running back; reversing off the ramp and driving forwards to stop with the front wheel opposite to the driver's side on a white rectangle painted on the ground. There was the usual mixture of extremely skilful and completely clueless performances, but, generally speaking, the drivers did wonders with vehicles often totally unsuited to the exercise. For my part, the accolade went to Kurt Krannick driving the 1893 Benz, whose performance throughout the Rally commanded the admiration of all.

This is no place for a political dissertation, but one cannot write of a visit to Berlin without some reference to the situation there. Having driven the length of the umbilical cord through East Germany one experienced a sense of relief on perceiving the familiar trappings of the Western World on reaching West Berlin. The knowledge that an excursion in any direction would lead one into the barbed wire before long, although always present in the subconscious mind, did not inhibit our enjoyment of the Rally – and did not appear to permeate the minds of the Berliners themselves. Nevertheless, to stand looking over 'The Wall', or through the wire, is an experience which administers a mental shock quite beyond anything gained from the written word or the television screen. I found it difficult to credit that such a division could exist in an adult world, but any tendency to ridicule the situation in one's mind was instantly suppressed by the thought that a false step in the wrong direction would invite a lethal fusillade. I certainly left Berlin with a better realization and fuller understanding of the position in which the Berliners find themselves.

Saturday evening saw the Prize-giving Dinner in the Kongressehalle, and the fierce thunderstorm raging outside provided a Wagnerian background to the speeches of visiting dignitaries from the Veteran Car Clubs of other countries. In the absence of any such personage from the UK, I was prevailed upon by the British competitors to say a word of thanks to the organizers.

I have never seen a more lavish array of prizes at any motoring 'do', and it looked as if everyone was to receive something. In the event, the allocation of awards seemed quixotic, to say the least. My seventh place out of 15 in the class did not merit – and did not get – an award, but Major Collings confessed his surprise at receiving a prize for his 26th place in an admittedly very large class. Garrett seemed as surprised as anyone else when he collected two jolly good items for having been the first person to enter the Rally and for having a German-born wife: A very nice gesture was the presentation to 'England' of an engraved silver tray. (It seems that Veteran Car rallies were not known in Germany until the early '50s when a member of the ASC returned from a visit to England and started the series of Schnauferl Rallies, of which this year's was the 11th.) The oldest member of the ASC – both in age (80) and in membership (50 years) – Richard Lüders, gave this award in recognition of the tremendous amount of enjoyment which Veteran car enthusiasts in Germany had derived from what was, as far as they were concerned, an idea from England. I accepted this silver tray and handed it to the President of the VCC of GB on my return.

The Rally concluded on the Sunday morning with a parade of all the competing cars through the centre of Berlin. As far as we were concerned, this turned out to be the highlight of the Rally. The sun shone and the crowds lined the route in 'Brighton' fashion. I have not seen more enthusiastic spectators at a Veteran event, and the keen interest displayed had to be seen to be believed.

When the parade arrived back at the TV Tower we reluctantly bade farewell to friends old and new, and turned the Merc. westwards along the old Avus track towards home. We cleared the tiresome frontier formalities at 12.45 pm and retraced our path to Hanover. Next day we continued along the autobahn, but made a southerly detour near Köln to spend the night at the Burg Ockenfels Hotel overlooking the Rhine at Linz.

The following day we left Linz-am-Rhein at 8.15 am for Ostend planning to keep a 6 o'clock appointment in Ghent to see Ghislain Mahy's private collection of cars. We were, in fact, 10 minutes late after covering 216.4 miles, surely a tribute to the reliability of the Mercedes.

We found it difficult to drag ourselves away from the fabulous collection of several hundred cars, but we wanted to reach our destination before dark and did so, arriving at Ostend just before nine after a day's journey of 255 miles. We had left Berlin at noon on Sunday and completed the 658 miles to the Belgian coast by Tuesday evening without any trouble whatsoever.

The following day when passing through Sevenoaks, only 30 miles from home, we had a puncture – the first one during my ownership of the Merc. – and changed the tyre and rim, counting ourselves fortunate that we should encounter such little tyre trouble after hearing the dire tales of others. An examination of notes made during the trip reveals that the total mileage covered during the 10 days was 1,535 and the overall petrol consumption was 8.36 mpg (Phew!!).

Edinburgh to London in daylight

In 1968 the advance publicity for the Veteran Car Club London-Edinburgh Rally threw out the challenge of 400 miles in four days as being designed to sort the men from the boys. From the point of view of an Edwardian owner this seemed to me to be rather overstating the case, and I lightheartedly added to my 'declaration of intent to enter' a postscript in the words 'Why not sort out the giants from the men by organizing the return trip in one day instead of four?' I should have known better! The Competitions Committee took up my suggestion and I found myself lumbered with it, but not that much organizing was required.

Dawn breaks very early in Edinburgh in midsummer – lighting-up time ended at 4.16 am on the day in question – so it was decided that intending participants could start at any time of their own choice between 5 am and 6 am. To qualify for a certificate it was necessary to arrive at the Royal Automobile Club in London before lighting-up time at 9.31 pm. The choice of route was entirely free; two, but not more, persons could drive, and all persons travelling in the car were to act as observers on behalf of the Club to see that the car was not towed – except the minimum distance to reach a garage to effect repairs. (In the event, none of the cars was towed at all.) In every other respect the run was to be regarded as a normal pleasure drive for those who enjoy Veteran or Edwardian motoring in the grand manner.

Five members presented their cars and their Road Books to 'volunteer' Starting Official Brian Mawer, waiting in the grey dawn in the coal yard behind the ice rink, where the cars had spent the night. They were, in addition to myself – R. Lewis (1907 Napier), G.E. Dorrington (1913 Renault), L.B. White (1913 Rover), and S.A. Smith (1914 Vauxhall). All except the Napier left Edinburgh impatiently on the dot of 5 am of a dry Sabbath, while Lewis left a quarter-of-an-hour later.

Accompanied by Louis Giron who shared the driving, I opted to follow A1 as far as the Doncaster Bypass, then to turn off on to the recently opened M18 motorway connecting with M1 at Rotherham. This route measured 405 miles and was the longest of the various alternatives. It was, however, relatively level and included some 240 miles of dual carriageway. The first two hours saw 77½ miles behind us on dry roads, but when I then handed over to Louis the heavens opened. For the next 50 miles conditions were appalling. There was continuous, heavy, driving rain; several miles of flooded road which rendered the brakes useless for a spell; some fog, and all this laced with a cold east wind blowing off the sea. We passed quickly into Newcastle (3¼ hours/118 miles) and out again. The rain ceased and the car was going like a train until the outskirts of Durham when the engine just stopped without any warning. There was air pressure in the petrol tank, but the carburettor was dry. Householders appeared in their doorways and proffered tea and help – it was barely 8.30 am. A few strokes on a foot-pump applied at the carburettor end of the fuel line cleared whatever unaccountable foreign matter had caused the obstruction. Nothing of the kind had occurred since the tank was thoroughly cleaned when the car was reconditioned seven years previously, and there has been no recurrence since. This stop, and replenishment of the tank at a nearby garage, occupied 42 minutes and my voiced hopes of reaching London in well under 12 hours dwindled.

We pressed on, aiming to breakfast at Scotch Corner, which we reached at 10.02 am, only to be told that breakfasts finished at 10 am. On to the motel at Leeming, 12 miles further, where we found the restaurant closed until lunchtime.

The Merc. was cruising consistently at 50 mph and five hours later we were 218 miles nearer London, having averaged 43.6 mph, including two stops for petrol. Our average speed for this 218 miles, excluding stops, was 45.9 mph – this without exceeding 50 mph. At 3.50 pm we reached the London end of M1 and 34 minutes later drew up outside the RAC in Pall Mall, where we found that the Prince Henry Vauxhall had clocked in 39 minutes earlier. (If only we hadn't had that 42-minute stop for the petrol stoppage . . .!) Our running time from Edinburgh to London (405 miles) was exactly 10 hours, an average speed of 40½ mph. The total time, including stops amounting to 84 minutes, was 11 hours 24 minutes, which meant a door-to-door average of 35½ mph.

I was delighted with the magnificent demonstration of reliable performance given by the Mercedes, and the credit for this goes to Louis Giron who is entirely responsible for overhauling and maintaining the mechanical side of the car. It was a great joy driving the Mercedes for mile after mile at a steady 50 and, even at this modest speed by modern standards, it was surprising how many cars we overtook on the motorways. Not quite so pleasing was the petrol consumption – 9 mpg! I know the car weighs over 39 cwt, but a penny a furlong in

44 *The author and Louis Giron outside the RAC in Pall Mall after the run from Edinburgh*

those days – phew!

S.A. Smith, driving N.A. Ridley's ex-Pomeroy Prince Henry Vauxhall, had followed A1 all the way from Edinburgh to London and drove the entire distance himself. The car had no hood and the occupants were well soaked in the border country. Mrs Smith had to dig into her luggage for a skirt to replace her slacks before being allowed past the august portals of the RAC to take tea as a guest of Brian Dinsley, who had given up his Sunday afternoon and evening to verify the arrival times of the 'Edwardians'.

R. Lewis drove his 60 Napier the whole way himself and was unaccompanied – a creditable performance. He left Edinburgh at 5.15 am and checked in at the RAC at 7.33 pm – a very good solo effort.

G.E. Dorrington also turned in a solo performance in his 1913 Renault, but had a passenger to help him cope with a blow-out on M1, 50 miles from London. He followed the same route as the Mercedes and with a top cruising speed of about 40 mph achieved a door-to-door average of 27.3 mph.

L.B. White, in his 1913 Rover, also drove all of the way. He came up with the Napier at Swiss Cottage only to lose it in the traffic. As the Rover approached the RAC the Napier appeared out of a side turning, both cars arriving together at 7.33 pm. White had completed the 375 miles in 14 hours 33 minutes, thus averaging 25.8 mph.

Some may think that this venture might be called 'And Five Were Foolish', but it must surely be admitted that the Run served as a demonstration of the high standard of maintenance of these old cars and that, when it is demanded of them, they can put up a performance which would not disgrace a modern car. Perhaps it just shows that they really don't build them like that any more.

45 *Philip Mann and John Rowley in the former's 1914 Grand Prix Mercedes*

Mercedes 70th anniversary run – 1971

Always on the look-out for an excuse to undertake a long trip in the Merc., I accepted with alacrity an invitation from Erik Johnson, Marketing Manager of Mercedes-Benz (Great Britain) Ltd, to participate in a run to Stuttgart to mark the 70th Anniversary of the name 'Mercedes' and, co-incidentally, the 85th Anniversary of the birth of the first cars of Gottlieb Daimler and Karl Benz.

So it was that Louis Giron and I found ourselves on the quay at Harwich on Friday, April 23, waiting in pouring rain to embark on the 'Prins Oberon' with 15 other cars. The wet and cold weather, coming after nearly a week of warm sunny days, was most disappointing and set the pattern for the following five days. It had not been possible to persuade the owners of some of the best Mercedes in the country to join the run, and owners of other makes, mostly associated in some way with Daimler or Benz, were invited to make up a worthwhile contingent. There were, in fact (in addition to my 45/50), only three Veteran Mercedes taking part: Tom Lightfoot's 1902 Mercedes Simplex, Charles Howard's ex-Malartre 1913 37/95 tourer and – joining us on Sunday evening at Köln – Philip Mann's beautifully restored 1914 Grand Prix car. Other 'associated' cars were Ted Woolley's 1897 Daimler Phoenix, the tube ignition of which fascinated crowds wherever it was taken off its trailer to be driven in parades and processions; George Dorrington's Benz-engined 1900 English Mechanic; Tom Lightfoot's 1901 7 hp Daimler-engined Panhard, entered by Philip Sumner (these latter two cars were trailered on the road sections); Cecil Bendall's Prinz Heinrich Austro-Daimler driven by John Mitchell; and the two British-built Daimlers of Murcott (a 1908/9 22 hp open tourer once owned by King Edward VII) and Acock (1910 15 hp two-seater). Anachronistic accompanists were the 540K Mercedes-Benz of Charles Howard, a good-looking but out-of-character Freestone &

Webb semi-razor-edge saloon, and the 1937 Roadster of John Barley, Chairman-elect of the Mercedes-Benz Club. The total of 16 starters was made up of Bryan Firth's 1909 12 hp Adler; Cecil Bendall's 1911 Rolls-Royce Silver Ghost, known as 'Stripes' from its unusual paint treatment; the 1914 Hupmobile of near-octeganarian Tommy Johnson; and 'AA 1', the well-known 1904 Renault Park Phaeton of the Automobile Association, driven by George Thompson and David Tuckfield.

The Run commenced with a 'send-off' reception in the Council Chamber at Harwich and it was not long before all the cars were safely aboard, Brian Robins (Editor, Motoring Programmes, Television Outside Broadcasts) and his 'Wheelbase' team joined us, as did Clement Freud representing the 'Daily Telegraph' Magazine.

The overnight crossing to Bremerhaven lasted 16 hours and proved to be a very satisfactory way of making a landfall in Germany. We were met on the quayside at Bremerhaven by a contingent of personnel and vehicles sent from Stuttgart by Daimler-Benz AG to accompany us on the 1,100-mile round trip to Ostend. No words of praise can exaggerate the tremendous contribution which this party made to the well-being and peace of mind of all (well, nearly all) participants. The Stuttgart party comprised three young executives, Helmut Holstein, Klaus Sekol and Ranold Mjornell, each driving a red 350 SL Mercedes-Benz – the new model to be unveiled in showrooms all over Germany that very week-end; Mr Kern, engineer and mechanic responsible for the exhibits in the famous D.B. Museum at Unterturkheim driving a 280 SE 3.5 saloon with a boot full of every imaginable tool, material and piece of equipment which might be needed during the run (including an oxy-acetylene welding outfit); a low-loader breakdown vehicle of the ADAC to convey disabled cars to the next stop; and a petrol tanker from ARAL. At every stopping-place participating cars – and those pulling trailers – were tanked-up free of charge by the ever-willing tanker driver. (As my Mercedes does only 8/9 mpg it was a great joy to be 'towing' a tanker full of free petrol.)

Thus protected and provided for, the convoy of vehicles set off for lunch at Syke, near Breman. The drivers of the three 350 SLs were keeping in touch with each other by radio telephone. They did not always manage to keep us on the right route, but what they lacked in experience of organizing runs of this nature they made up for by a dedicated concern for the safety and comfort of all; they did not rest until their flock was safely coralled at each stopping place.

The Austro-Daimler was the one casualty and, after a ride on the low-loader, was abandoned by its crew, the sleeve in No. 4 cylinder having come loose. That night saw us in the unlikely stopping-place of Bielefeld and it was still raining on Sunday morning when we left for lunch in Düsseldorf. The cars arrived in a very travel-stained condition but attracted an enthusiastic and appreciative crowd. It was here that the Run (and Düsseldorf) were enlivened by the arrival by air of 'Denny' – one of the 'Young Generation' dancers – wearing hot pants beneath an ankle-length fur-trimmed coat.

After lunch, I made a personal pilgrimage to 63/65 Graf Adolf Strasse which, although now a Ford showroom, had been the premises of the General Agency for Daimler-Motoren-Gesellschaft for Rhineland and Westphalia to which my car was delivered when new 64 years ago. With Clement Freud busy writing in encapsulated seclusion in the back of my car and 'Denny' in the front, we made a police-escorted tour of the city and then set off for the night stop at Köln.

Next, the AA Renault broke a bolt on its universal joint and was administered to by Mr Kern, who fabricated a new one in the nearest Mercedes-Benz branch. (Incidentally, all the Mercedes-Benz branches on or near the route had been alerted to stand by in case any help or

46 *Clement Freud at the wheel of Charles Howard's ex-Malartre 1913 37/95 Mercedes*

47 *Louis Giron willingly acts as doorman for photographers attracted by Denny of the 'Young Generation' dancers*

facilities were required to keep the cars running.) Philip Mann and John Rowley, in the former's 1914 Grand Prix winner, joined us at the recently opened Esso Motel at Köln, having been at the Vintage Meeting at Silverstone the previous day. They had driven from Rotterdam in five hours and this historic car made a welcome addition to the convoy. Fitted with mudguards to comply with the law and a rudimentary luggage rack, it motored at 70–80 mph and was indeed an impressive sight. It sounded great, too, and was usually last to leave the starting point and first to arrive at the end of each section.

On Monday, the route took us up the Rhine Valley to Bingen for lunch and on to Heidelberg for the night.

At Mehlem, about 10 miles south of Bonn, we came upon Bryan Firth's Adler at the roadside; a cheerful enquiry as to whether everything was OK died on our lips as we perceived that the car had been severely damaged. It transpired that whilst his attention was momentarily distracted by acknowledging a 'straight-on' signal from a travelling marshal the traffic lights had changed to red and he was unable to avoid running into the back end of a suddenly very stationary truck. Bryan was able to steer to the right, thus avoiding damaging the radiator, chassis or engine, but the side of the body demolished itself against the heavy metal corner of the truck. The front wing crumpled; the windscreen pillar was swept away taking with it part of the dashboard; the main door pillar was fractured and the roof bent up; the windscreen and division shattered and the roof cracked. By great good fortune, daughter Henrietta who was sitting in the front seat was uninjured and her mother in the back sustained only slight cuts. At first glance the poor little Adler looked to be ready for shipment home for extensive rebuilding. In the event, Louis Giron produced copper wire and ingenuity and tied the car together, and buoyed up by the thought of the ever-present low-loader, Bryan elected to continue the Run, disposing of his passengers in sundry vehicles. Fully exposed to the elements, he drove his car safely to Stuttgart and the experts there, working under Mr Kern, proceeded to strengthen the body structurally with angle-iron, fabricate a new windscreen and generally screw the car together in a most commendable fashion for the journey home.

During the morning another incident involved George Dorrington who had braked to such effect on one occasion that his 1900 English Mechanic leapt out of its wheel slots in the trailer and crashed into the back of the towing

49 *Bryan Firth's Adler after colliding with the rear of a truck*

48 *Outside 63/65 Graf Adolf Strasse in Düsseldorf where the Mercedes was delivered to the (then) general agency of Daimler-Motor Gesellschaft in December 1910*

50 *An accident with the 1900 English Mechanic caused by hard braking – the moral: 'Never mind how safe it looks, tie it down!'*
51 *The emergency repair to the split detachable rim near Luxembourg*

Renault 16 Estate car, whose occupants were shocked to be run into by themselves. A dented rear panel and a broken window were sustained by the Renault but the Veteran received only a slightly bent track rod. (Moral: never mind how safe it looks – tie it down.)

After dinner we were taken out by the Regional Chief of the Schnauferl Club to the 'Red Ox' – an ancient students' pub in Heidelberg. Here, led by John Mitchell in lusty renderings of traditional English songs, we vied with singing German students. Philip Mann, who had said on arrival at Köln that he was 'only here for the beer', was put to the test when confronted by a glass boot containing 2.5 litres – over 4 pints – but he passed with flying colours, not only consuming the entire contents but also mastering the technique of emptying the 'toe' without suffering a drenching.

The next day, Tuesday, culminated in our arrival in Stuttgart where we were greeted by Daimler-Benz and civic officials in the Killesberg Park. After lunch, during which our cars were washed by personnel thoughtfully provided by DB, we went through a lengthy driving test inside another part of the building. Unfortunately, the door through which the cars were driven into the building was not high enough to admit my car (7 ft 6 in high), nor Cecil Bendall's Rolls-Royce and one or two other cars. Meantime, judges had been inspecting the cars for quality and turn-out. It says much for the enthusiasm and skill of Bryan Firth that, despite his unfortunate accident, his Adler won the Concours and was placed second in the Driving Tests behind Tom Lightfoot.

Leaving the cars locked up for the night at Killesberg we made a rapid sightseeing tour of the city by coach and checked into our hotels before walking over to the Graf Zeppelin Hotel for the reception and banquet to be given by Daimler-Benz. Awards and mementoes were presented; speeches of welcome, appreciation and thanks were made. The Renault was again in trouble and the untiring Mr Emil Kern was busy in the Museum workshop making new bushes for the front universal joint on the propshaft.

Both Adler and Renault were ready for the road next morning when we presented ourselves and our cars at the factory at Unterturkheim. We spent some time in the museum and in the afternoon we made a tour of a small part of the huge plant at Sindelfingen and were able to appreciate something of the investment, planning, organization and techniques which go into the production of Mercedes-Benz cars. The convoy then left for Karlsruhe, where the night was spent at the Schwarzwald Hotel.

Friday dawned bright and sunny and was to be the first day without any rain. Cecil Bendall suffered the first of a series of punctures in 'Stripes' before arriving at the lunch stop at Saarbrücken, while a flat tyre on the Renault was dealt with in the car park amid an interested audience. There followed an uneventful run through attractive scenery to the Luxembourg border. Whilst waiting for the stragglers, I was chatting with John Rowley when he noticed by chance a slight bulge on the inside of one of my front tyres. Further examination revealed that the detachable rim had split circumferentially for a distance of about eight inches. We drove slowly into Luxembourg and, when caught up by 'the support team', had the rim and tyre bandaged with wide adhesive tape by Mr Kern. We crawled into the city and, after a brief appearance in the Market Square for publicity purposes, drove to the local Mercedes-Benz branch, where Louis and Mr Kern had the rim off, welded up and refitted in a very short time – and so to dinner and to bed, in anticipation of a 5.30 am call for the pre-lunch run of 150 miles to Brussels.

It became evident that the organization had creaked a bit when we came down at 6 am to find that no arrangements had been made for breakfast to be served at this early hour. It was a bright sunny morning, so we took a taxi to the Mercedes-Benz garage to collect our cars and left philosophically planning to stop en route for breakfast. Louis and I drove 40 miles before breakfasting – incidentally the only meal we paid for during the entire eight-day trip, all the others (with wines), our hotel accommodation, and sea crossings, being provided by the organizers in return for the modest entry fee of £20 per person.

The 150 miles to Brussels passed swiftly under our wheels and midday saw us competing with residents and tourists for parking spaces in the Grande Place. We were sorry to see Howard's 'Ninety' Mercedes, which had gone so well, arrive on the low-loader, having stretched a chain to the point where driving at any speed produced the most alarming noises as the chain jumped the sprockets. After lunch in a nearby hotel, we proceeded to Ghent amid the Friday evening Bruxellois speeding coastwards along the autoroute. That enthusiastic collector, Ghislain Mahy and his son, Ivan, joined us at dinner and afterwards, despite the late hour, invited those interested to see some of his collection of nearly 600 cars. It was 1 am before the party returned to the hotel, still marvelling at this Aladdin's cave. Saturday morning – the last day. Farewells all round in anticipation of haste and confusion at the Ostend docks.

And so our Run came to an end. As we sailed, our three shepherds/nurses walked back to their 350 SLs to drive back to Stuttgart freed from their charges, as did Mr Kern and the low-loader driver.

We had enjoyed ourselves immensely. Our reception in Germany had been warm-hearted, not only at the official receptions, radio interviews, TV parades and processions, but from fellow-motorists all along the route.

As I put my faithful Mercedes back in the garage, ticking over as sweetly as she did when we started out nine days and 1,300 miles earlier, I could not help trying to think of an excuse for proposing a repeat performance in the not-too-distant future.

500 miles in a day

Most of the important rallies of the Veteran Car Club include a competition based on the distance travelled to the Rally. Entrants may select a single turning point between their home, or other starting place, and the Rally venue and may start their journey up to two days before Reporting Time at the Arrival Control. The award goes to the car which covers the greatest mileage measured in straight lines on a map.

In 1970 I declared Newcastle-upon-Tyne as my turning point on the way to Crystal Palace and, with co-driver Louis Giron, left Cobham on Saturday morning. We drove to Newcastle, asked an astonished AA scout in the Market Place to sign a statement that we had passed that way that day, and drove back to the Selby Fork Motel for the night. We resumed our journey early next morning in driving rain and checked in at the Crystal Palace a few minutes before 11 am to win the Distance Award by a considerable margin.

I have a liking for round numbers – being an accountant may have something to do with this idiosyncracy – and the idea of doing 500 miles in a day in the Mercedes appealed to me. Past performances indicated that, with reasonable luck, such a distance could be achieved in daylight if a substantial part of the trip were to be undertaken on motorways.

When the Regulations for the 1972 London Rally arrived I perceived an opportunity to fulfil this ambition and called Louis Giron to ask if he felt like another marathon run in the Mercedes. He said, 'Yes, when?' I told him the plot and declared my turning point to be Gretna Green.

We left my home at Cobham, Surrey, at 3 pm on Friday, 4 August, with 180 miles to go to reach our night-stop at the Saxon Cross Motel on the M6 near Sandbach. The location of the night stop had been chosen so as to leave a 500 mile journey for the Saturday, on to Gretna Green and back to Cobham, where we planned to spend the night before a leisurely trundle across the suburbs to Crystal Palace the following morning to check in by 11 am.

The drive to Sandbach was uneventful – Kingston/Chiswick/North Circular Road/M1 and M6 – and we arrived there at 8.30 pm. It had been a wet journey and already the August Bank Holiday traffic had commenced streaming northwards. The speedometer cable broke after 65.2 miles and subsequent mileage and speed calculations had to be done by 'dead reckoning'. Before turning in, we went to a nearby garage to replenish the petrol and oil tanks, the former being filled appropriately enough from an old-fashioned hand-operated pump, though the brand name on the surmounting globe was unknown to us – 'Globe', in fact.

An early start was necessary to cover the self-imposed distance in daylight, and after a 4.30 am call we turned on to M6 again at first light (5.20 am) for the 155 mile journey to the end of M6 beyond Carlisle and on to Gretna Green. We were astonished at the volume of traffic so early in the morning as holiday-makers made for the Lakes and Scotland – difficult to believe that so many caravans exist in the country.

I was driving and not hurrying on the cold engine. When I did try to bring it up to its usual brisk pace I met with little response and found it necessary to change down to third, and even second, on gradients which I would have expected to scale in top. We did not know the topography and thought that the grades might be steeper than they appeared, but soon stopped kidding ourselves and accepted the fact that the car lacked power. It was perhaps natural (but, as will be seen, entirely unjustifiable) that we put the blame on the strange fuel taken on the previous evening, and we resolved to perk up the mixture with some higher octane at our planned breakfast stop.

We topped up the tank at the West Burton Service Area and gave up the idea of breakfast when we saw the length of the queue in the cafeteria (at 7.40 am!). Confession is good for the soul, they say, and here comes a sizeable contribution to the well-being of mine: when I went to swing the engine on restarting I saw that the compression lever was already pulled out and, may the ghosts of Stuttgart forgive me, realized that I had driven 85 miles on half-compression averaging 38½ mph! (Apologies to the purveyor of petrol who might otherwise have remained unabsolved for life.)

We were soon on the road again in full song and with apparently unharmed exhaust valves, rejoicing in the regained vigour of the Merc. as we approached Shap Fell. A quick look into the cafeteria at Tebay revealed continued congestion at the counter, so we opted to continue to Gretna for breakfast. We arrived there at 9.30 am and got the AA Inspector on duty to verify the fact on my Rally number-plate, then we looked for breakfast. No luck at the Lovers' Leap Motel, but a very friendly reception at the Gretna Hall Hotel where sizzling bacon and eggs was prepared for us.

At 10.25 am I pulled out of the Hotel car park and now joined the Scots rushing southwards with boats and caravans. The traffic was heavy all the way to London, but presented no problems for us Edwardian motorists ambling along at 50 – mostly in the slow lane but overtaking quite a lot of cars for all that. We now had ahead of us the whole length of M6 from Junction 44 to Junction 1, and then M1 to London, the distance from Gretna Green to Cobham being 335 miles. We took on 14 gallons of petrol at Killington and at 2.08 pm passed the Saxon Cross Motel at Sandbach, from whence we had started nearly 9 hours previously, by then having covered 311 miles. We knew that we had 182 miles to go and I reckoned that, if we took the same driving time as on the outward trip the previous day, our ETA at Cobham would be exactly 7 pm.

The Mercedes was going beautifully and most of the time we were covering 48 miles in the hour. We shared the driving and progressed steadily towards London, and completed 400 miles just after joining M1. At 5.20 pm; after 12 hours on the road, 443 miles had been covered.

We arrived home at 7.10 pm, quite unfatigued with the Mercedes running as well as when we had started out 674 miles earlier. The day's run was 493 miles taking 13 hours 50 minutes = 35.6 mph. Deducting stops for petrol, oil and food totalling 1 hour 57 minutes, the driving time of 7 minutes under 12 hours showed an average speed of 41½ mph.

I see from my notes that the whole length of M6 and then M1, a total distance of 304 miles, took 7 hours 34 minutes (40.2 mph) and, deducting stops totalling 37 minutes, the running average speed was 43.7 mph.

Petrol consumption was as expected – between 8 and 9 mpg – 75 gallons having been burned – and not a single Green Shield Stamp collected!

This performance is a great tribute to the designers and engineers who built the car more than 60 years ago, and to the incomparable Louis Giron who keeps it in first-class condition. Apart from the broken speedometer cable, no harm befell the Mercedes – until Sunday morning when I drove out of my drive and caught an unclosed rear door on my own garden wall. This bent the handle and spindle, calling for some quick work by Louis so that the door could be opened and shut at Crystal Palace – an important matter this, as it was on the side from which Con would have to alight in the Fashion Competition after the Driving Tests.

As a postscript, I must record that during this journey of over 600 miles on motorways on the busiest week-end of the year, we saw only one accident – and that not serious – and were not held up by any congestion. The standard of driving was high despite the many holiday-makers with packed and (over)loaded cars. I estimate we saw about 50 cars in trouble with tyres or overheating and three broken wind-screens. This long run on our motorways served to confirm my view that they are among the best in the world.

52 *The would-be off-the-street parker's dilemma!*
53 *Many newly-weds have taken the first ride of their married lives in the Mercedes*

54 *The Phantom III Rolls-Royce acquired in December 1952*

Rolls-Royce Phantom III

Motoring in the grand manner

To own a P III is a unique experience for in truth one has a town carriage with a performance which until recent years would not have disgraced a sports car. I remember L.C. McKenzie saying to me about the P III: 'It has a maximum speed of 94 mph and a cruising speed of 93.' Certainly this great car is a stirring sight at speed, the only noise coming from the tyres and the exhaust gases fighting to reach the atmosphere. Many a time I have accelerated away from traffic lights overhauling 'boy racers' in sports cars, their faces betraying amazement as several yards of seemingly house-high automobile whooshed past.

I acquired my P III from Harold Radford just before Christmas 1952, with nearly 60,000 miles on the clock. It was a 1937 BU series chassis with solid tappets, not the earlier hydraulically-operated type, and the body was a semi-razor-edge Touring Limousine with division built by H.J. Mulliner. It had louvred bonnet sides, instead of the more usual three door vents, and was painted black. Beauty is very much a matter of personal taste and I consider this particular coachwork the most elegant to be seen on a closed Phantom III, perhaps because it looks right from every angle. From an owner-driver's point of view, the absence of a division would have been preferable, but the limited fore-and-aft adjustment of the front seats was sufficient for my longish legs and the division was scarcely visible from outside the car.

In the P III I found I could average 50 mph point-to-point almost anywhere in England; not much, perhaps, by today's standards, but quite creditable in those days before motorways. I took it to France once or twice – to Le Mans and Reims where I was timing Briggs Cunningham's cars in the long-distance races. At Reims I gave 'Bira' a lift to the circuit on Grand Prix day, and

55 *The Phantom III on the Mulsanne Straight at Le Mans, June 1954*

56 *A king among cars – the Phantom III in the car park at the Reims Circuit*
57 *On the way back to New York from the Classic Car Meet at Morristown, Pennsylvania, accompanied by another Phantom III*

he was quite perturbed because the petrol warning light was on and he thought I might run out of gas on the way. I reassured him and dropped him at his pit; and, although it was not funny at the time, we have laughed together since, because it was he, Bira, who ran out of fuel – in the race!

I drove the Rolls up to Town and back each day, an expensive pastime at 10 mpg. (Come to think of it, this is the sort of consumption I have been enjoying (!) in different cars on my lawful business these many years.) I do not regard the commuter grand prix in and out of London as a pleasure. In my case, it is marginally less inconvenient and time-consuming than the alternative car-train-taxi transport available to me. It is, of course, educational and, providing one curbs the competitive spirit and exercises restraint when provoked by aggressive and unmannerly drivers, commuter driving in the Metropolis does keep one's driving up to scratch. I doubt if there exists a more demanding 'university of the road' than 200 miles a week mixing it in the cut-and-thrust of commuter driving. No quarter is given – and none asked. Every driver knows what he is doing and what others are doing. Lane discipline is good and everyone is intent on getting along. There are black sheep and I could write a book on the 'back-doubles' and the degrees of gamesmanship permissible – and frowned upon. But I digress. . . .

When I was using the P III daily in London during the weeks preceding the Coronation period I benefitted from the regal aspect of my carriage, for there were many crowned heads and heads of state in Town. The appearance on the scene of a large Rolls-Royce, which might be carrying who-knows-who was spotted by bobbies who jumped to speed one's transit at the next intersection.

In March 1955 at 78,241 miles, I had a new back axle fitted with a higher ratio (3.9 to 1) than the standard 4.25 to 1. Less than a dozen

DXA 9

full-taste beer
Schmidt's

of these ratios, which gave 80 mph at 3,400 rpm, were fitted under the aegis of Roney Messervy in P IIIs belonging to enthusiastic owners. My speedometer was recalibrated and on one or two occasions in France I reached a sustained 100 mph. In August that year the P III was laid up whilst I was personally out of circulation with maintenance problems of my own. Not long after putting the car on the road again I was faced with the prospect of an engine overhaul, estimated to cost £1,250, and decided to change to more modern transport – the Mk VI already described. I had experienced nearly 30,000 miles of memorable motoring in the grand manner.

There was no difficulty in finding an owner for the P III who would do the necessary and thereafter provide a good home. Briggs Cunningham had often admired the car and had asked for first refusal if and when I decided to sell. He bought it in March 1956 and had it completely restored to new condition before adding it to his collection in the States. Whilst undergoing the mechanical overhaul at Hythe Road a new exhaust system, specially designed to absorb less horsepower and yet to achieve the same degree of silencing, was fitted. Mulliners removed the division and built additional strength into the door pillars and roof to make it into a real owner-driver car. That Briggs acquired the P III – and still has it – is my good fortune, because I can drive it whenever I visit his home. The first time I stayed with him (then in Connecticut) after the reborn Rolls had been delivered coincided with the Annual Concours d'Elegance of the Classic Car Club of America in Morristown, Pennsylvania, and I borrowed my beloved old car to take part. On arrival at the venue I was surprised to see more than one enthusiast prostrate himself on the pavement almost before my wheels stopped turning. I'd heard of the dedication of RR fans in the States, but this was ridiculous. It transpired that these enthusiasts had heard of my intended arrival in Briggs' new P III and they wanted to examine the new exhaust system! The Rolls was not judged to be the best one there, but it did take second place. This gives some idea of the high standard of perfection demanded, and attained, by our Transatlantic cousins. The P III now has an honoured place in Briggs' Automobile Museum at Costa Mesa in California.

250 GT Ferrari

Motoring in a new dimension

Surely it is the ambition of every true motorist to be the proud possessor some day of a thoroughbred from Maranello. I was no exception, but like so many others saw little prospect of having the wherewithal to realize my ambition. The price of a new Ferrari was quite beyond my means and I realized that the purchase of a used one was indeed a dicey business. Little did I think that I would ever have a Ferrari – and a unique one at that – but so it came to pass.

I have already mentioned Gerry Crozier, that motoring enthusiast par excellence. He had owned more cars in his time than anyone I knew. He was always changing them and he, too, aspired to owning a Ferrari. One Sunday he telephoned to see if we would be at home if he came over, his normal practice when he had acquired a new car, and I was not surprised when the blue nose of a Ferrari turned into the drive, Gerry at the wheel with an 'at last' expression on his face.

It was a 250 GT Berlinetta, recently imported from a private owner in Italy, and Gerry said it was thought to be the car which had won the 1961 Tourist Trophy Race at Goodwood. The colour was certainly 'Rob Walker' blue. He really enjoyed this car, but died not long afterwards and it was bought by Neil Corner.

I asked Neil, without any real expectation of being in a position to afford it, to let me know should he decide to sell it at any time. This he did in April 1967 and I fell, deciding to convert a holding of BP shares into the Ferrari. In a letter to Neil I wrote: 'I cannot tell you how

58 *The 250 GT SWB Lightweight Ferrari. (The figure in the designation of Ferrari models, with a few exceptions, indicates the capacity of one cylinder, thus 250 cc multiplied by twelve cylinders gives a total of 3,000 cc)*

excited I am at the prospect of owning this car. Its purchase is a deliberate Act of Folly and, instead of acknowledging that I am buying a car beyond my means, I am kidding myself that I am making a temporary investment in it, with a view to taking the dividend in pleasure instead of depreciated taxed currency!'

Driving a Ferrari for the first time introduced me to a new dimension in motoring. The instant performance at one's command and the sense of total stability and controllability at high speed has to be experienced to be believed. The turbine-like torque of the V-12 3-litre engine was exhilarating. One didn't overtake other cars, one squirted past. The vivid acceleration had to be used with restraint, lest other road users unaware of the capability of the Ferrari took avoiding action in anticipation of a collision which was never even a possibility. My Ferrari was not temperamental, as everyone assumes a Ferrari to be. It would poddle along slowly in traffic without boiling, oiling up or stalling; and would accelerate afterwards to high speed without any fluffing. And this was not an ordinary road-going Ferrari, it was a sports-racing car.

No sooner had the Ferrari arrived home than I began to delve into its history, which neither of its previous owners had done. I wrote to the factory – and Ronnie Hoare very kindly gave me access to his files at Maranello Concessionaires – which established that my car (Chassis No. 2119GT) had indeed won the Tourist Trophy, but in 1960, not 1961.

The car had been ordered from the Works by Maranello Concessionaires for Rob Walker on 13 July 1960, specifying right-hand drive; light alloy body; 600 × 16 Borrani wheels; engine to full competition specification, limited slip differential; 7/32 rear axle ratio; and painted Midnight Blue to sample provided. The letter concluded: 'The car will be collected from Modena on 10 August. This date is vital as the car is to be driven by Stirling Moss in the Tourist Trophy Race on Saturday, 20 August.'

59 *Stirling Moss winning the Tourist Trophy at Goodwood in 1960*

The car arrived in England in time for practice, and Stirling won the TT – 108 laps of Goodwood – at an average speed of 85.58 mph, his fastest lap being 89.44 mph. He won the Redex Trophy at Brands Hatch the following week at 80.35 mph, setting a new GT lap record at 82.09 mph. In December 1960 Stirling drove the car to victory in the 'Tourist Trophy' in Nassau, and then the Ferrari passed into the ownership of Équipe Endeavour.

Michael Parkes led from start to finish in the 12 lap Lombank Race for GT cars at Snetterton on 25 March 1961 winning at 89.51 mph – sharing the fastest lap at 91.18 mph with Graham Whitehead in another Ferrari. At the Goodwood Easter Monday Meeting Parkes won the 10 lap Fordwater Trophy Race at 83.22 mph, beating Innes Ireland (Aston Martin DB4 GT) and Stirling, who was 3rd, in an Aston Martin Zagato, and again achieving fastest lap (85.37 mph). At Oulton Park, Jack Sears drove it into 4th place, with E-type Jaguars making their debut and taking 1st and 3rd places. Michael Parkes spun-off twice in the BRSCC Norbury Trophy Race at Crystal Palace in May, and retired with a suspect rear wheel, but not before making fastest lap jointly with Roy Salvadori in an E-type at 77.70 mph – a new record for GT cars over 1,000 cc. The Ferrari's last appearance on a racing circuit was at Brands Hatch on 3 June, 1961 when Parkes won the 10-lap Peco Trophy Race at 82.30 mph, beating Salvadori and Graham Hill in E-types and again making fastest lap (83.39 mph).

The car then went back to Modena and in reply to an enquiry from Maranello Concessionaires in July 1961 the factory telegraphed 'EX MOSS BERLINETTA ALREADY SOLD REGARDS FERRARI.' And so the car went into limbo. I was delighted with the fruits of my researches and to learn what an excellent racing history lay behind my car. It is surprising how few Ferraris with racing histories are still extant, and I doubt whether any other can claim six first places.

Neil had repainted the car Ferrari Red, which pleased me. Perhaps, when I had it repainted again I should have gone back to the blue of its racing days, but Italian Racing Red looks right to me on a competition Ferrari. As a matter of interest, I put the car on a weighbridge to find that it turned the scale at 22 cwt with oil and water, but no petrol. I much enjoyed my initiation into Ferrari motoring that summer, driving off to distant places on the slightest pretext. The petrol consumption was a steady 17 mpg and the 25 gallon tank thus provided over 400 miles of motoring without the need to refuel. The only disadvantage of using this car was its very small ground clearance, about 3″ under the silencers. One had to be careful emerging from driveways with centre gate-stops; crossing gullies; surmounting bumps and ridges; negotiating rutted roads, etc. The scarred bottom of the sump told its own story, and it wasn't an idle whim that caused the exhaust system to be suspended on flexible hangers – with some spare ones in the tool-kit!

Clearly, the full potential of a Ferrari cannot be enjoyed in this country and I was determined to let her have her head on the Autostrade of her native land. Accordingly, I decided to combine a few days in the South of France with a visit to Monza for the Italian Grand Prix; a 'pilgrimage' to the Ferrari's birthplace and a thrash down the Autostrada del Sole just for the hell of it.

Con and I left home on 6 September 1967 with rather less luggage than usual. The already small boot was further reduced by the large petrol tank, but we made up partly for this by inserting two medium-sized suitcases behind the seats.

The Ferrari exhaust was smoking more than I liked. 'They' tell me that Ferraris always smoke, but I reckoned my car was burning more oil than it was designed to do.

We crossed on the 'Lord Warden' from Dover to Boulogne, made for Arras and joined the A1 Autoroute for Paris. At last, I could give the Ferrari her head and I had my first taste of

60 *On the starting grid (94) at Goodwood in the Fordwater Trophy Race in April 1961, won by Stirling Moss*

high speed motoring in this car. We stayed the night at Les Pléiades, at Barbizon and next morning resumed our journey south in beautiful, sunny weather. Miles and miles at over 100 mph. The race breeding of the Ferrari manifested itself in the ease with which it cruised at 120, 130 – with occasional bursts at 140 mph. Its roadholding and instant response to throttle, brakes and steering gave one confidence and a feeling of safety which, I think, puts Ferrari motoring into a different dimension.

We made more leisurely progress after leaving the Autoroute before Aix-en-Provence, and arrived at Eze-sur-mer in time for dinner. Con opted for a quiet stay at Cap Estel instead of flashing pointlessly up and down Autostrada and sampling the doubtful amenities of Monza on Grand Prix day, but our motor-minded niece, Anthea, jumped at the opportunity of flying down to Nice and accompanying me in the Ferrari on the planned 1,600-mile round trip. We left next morning for Turin to visit the Pinin Farina works. On the outskirts (or rather 'inskirts') of Turin I summoned a taxi to lead me to the obscure location of the famous coachworks, a ploy which saved much time and frustration. It was interesting to see Farina bodies being made by mass production methods. The body on my Ferrari was a Farina design but had been built by Scaglietti in Modena. Our destination was Como, where we spent a couple of nights to attend the Italian Grand Prix. Early next morning we went to Johnny Lurani's home on the way to Monza. Louis Chiron, who was staying at Cernusco, certainly appreciated the Ferrari, and when I came to a stop in the car park at Monza the car attracted – dare I say it? – more attention than the very latest creations from the Italian drawing-boards.

The next day, Grand Prix day, was bright and sunny. Jim Clark had been fastest in practice and we were delighted to be invited by Colin Chapman to be in the Lotus pit during the race. The start of the Grand Prix was a shambles.

61 *The Ferrari in good company: on the left, Heathcote-Drury's 1959 250 GT Berlinetta, and on the right, the 250 GT of the late Adrian Conan Doyle (note the unusual front end treatment)*

62 *The Ferrari on the Mulsanne Straight at the Hippodrome in company with Bill Cook's DB 6 Aston Martin during an exploratory visit to Le Mans*

The idea was that the cars would form up on a 'dummy' grid and, on a signal, move forward about 100 yards on to the proper grid to await the Starting Flag. In fact, most of the 18 starters 'mistook' (!) the first signal for the starting signal and streaked off with no regard to the proper grid; by the time the astonished Starter dropped his flag most of the field were braking for the first corner.

Jim Clark led the race, but on lap 13 came in with a flat tyre, punctured by a nail. When he went back into the race he was 1 lap and 20 seconds behind the leading car and set about catching him. Graham Hill in the other Lotus had to retire with a blown-up engine when leading the race after 55 laps. Jim was driving like the master he was, overtaking one car after another, and seven laps from the end regained the lead. The leading cars – Clark, Surtees and Brabham – went into the last lap, two seconds bracketing all these cars. We were preparing to celebrate another victory for Jim, but it was not to be, for he slowed down with fuel starvation and was passed by both Brabham and Surtees on the last corner, the former winning by one-fifth of a second! It was cruel luck for Jim Clark who had, I think, driven the race of his life. In effect, he had given all the other drivers a lap and 20 seconds start and overtaken them all in 48 laps. And as if to rub salt into the wounds of disappointment, it was found that the tank still contained 3 gallons of fuel, the trouble being something to do with the anti-surge material. After a brief visit to the BP Cocktail Party we pushed off to spend the night at the AGIP Motel outside Milan at the start of the Autostrada del Sole.

Next morning was The Day as far as I was concerned. Driving over 500 miles, the whole length of the Autostrada del Sole and back again, just for sheer enjoyment. It was, as I expected it to be, a most enjoyable day's motoring at fast cruising speeds on that delightful road of straight level stretches and sweeping bends through the mountains, over viaducts into cuttings, round the perimeter of towns and cities. In fact, a perfect testing-ground for the manufacturers of super sports cars located near Modena and Milan.

We left the Motel at 9.15 am; had 'elevenses' at Florence Sud; lunched at the toll-gate north of Rome; circumnavigated Rome on the Raccordo Anulare and continued on the Autostrada (A2 from Rome) reaching the toll gate at Naples at 4 pm (480 miles). The Autostrada south then became A3 and (at that time) terminated 5 kilometres before Salerno, where we turned off for Positano. Our day's motoring – the length of A1-A2-A3, 512½ miles – had taken 7 h 17 m including stops, a point-to-point average of 70.3 mph. Deducting the two stops totalling exactly an hour showed a driving average speed of 81.4 mph. Looking back, I think it should have been a good deal quicker, considering that I crossed France twice in the Rolls-Royce Corniche rather more quickly in 1973. It is true that we were slowed by single-lane working for road works near Piacenza, and again between Bologna Nord and Bologna Sud, but there were no more than the usual delays such as crawling uphill behind slow-moving vehicles in the over-taking lane.

The highest figure touched on the speedometer was 146 mph at 7,000 rpm; this I reckon is truly 140/141 mph. Timings over measured kilometres indicated that the instrument was exaggerating by 5 mph throughout the range. I was using Pirelli VR covers – (400 × 175) at 32 lbs psi – which give 793 road revolutions per mile with the 9/34 rear axle ratio equating to 20 mph per 1,000 rpm (i.e. 7,000 rpm = 140 mph).

Next morning we left Positano as a heavy thunderstorm turned itself off, retracing our path northwards at a more leisurely pace. We made a lightning tour of Pompei and then climbed to the top of Vesuvius. Unfortunately, I was directed up a road I did not recognize and, far from being the smooth surfaced road I had taken on a previous visit, it was a very rough road with a surface of lava rocks, 5 miles long. The journey up and down was more suited to a Land Rover than a Ferrari with 3″ ground clearance. The undertray and exhausts were scraping along every time a large lump or ridge of the volcano appeared in the road.

We resumed our journey and lunched at Caserta on the Autostrada. We ran in company with a new Maserati for many miles at 120+ mph, first one leading and then the other. Speed on this road is limited only by the capability of the car; 100 mph seems to be dawdling on some stretches and when getting along at 120 it is no uncommon thing to be passed by a Ferrari on 'Prova' plates as if one is standing still.

Our destination was Modena and as we pulled up at the Real-Fini Hotel, having driven 451.6 miles that day, we saw another 250 GT Berlinetta parked outside. It had an unusual pointed nose and belonged to Adrian Conan Doyle.

Early next morning we crossed the road to the Ferrari Service Department and saw more Ferraris gathered together than we had ever seen before in one place. We were taken to nearby Maranello and shown round the factory where Ferraris were taking shape in an atmosphere of clinical cleanliness. What impressed me most was seeing crankshafts for the V-12 engines being machined out of solid steel billets. Back at the Service Dept I swallowed hard and asked them to examine my engine and give me an opinion as to its condition. The chief technician attached an instrument to make a crankcase compression test, revved the engine straight up to 7,000 rpm and laconically said that it needed a complete overhaul! It was a bitter pill, but I was not really surprised as the oil consumption was by then phenomenal, no less than 7¾ gallons having been added since leaving home – 2,265 miles = 290 mpg.

Somewhat chastened I left Modena, but with no doubt in my mind about the car's continued ability to perform as hitherto, for it was going very well and the oil pressure was being maintained. It was clear, however, that some serious thought would have to be given to the need for a major job on the engine. The smoking exhaust was worse and it wasn't funny being overtaken by a cloud of blue smoke every time I came to a standstill! We had a very wet journey up the Autostrada to Milan and then on A7 to Genoa. The drive along the coast was particularly trying, what with heavy rain and heavy traffic, and we did not reach Eze until 10.50 pm, after stopping for a meal in San Remo.

We spent a few days at Cap Estel, during which I distinguished myself by falling backwards off an 8-foot wall trying to photograph a dolly bird sunbathing on the rocks below; a mishap which necessitated a taxi ride to the hospital in Monte-Carlo to stitch up a lacerated elbow, but which might have been much worse as I missed by inches an ugly tree stump before measuring my length on the ground. Anthea took a 'plane back to London and Con and I left for home in the Ferrari arriving the following day with the car still going like a bomb after the 3,494-mile trip, despite the gloomy verdict of Modena.

Considered in the home environment, it was clear that the engine overhaul could be postponed no longer. I wrote to Modena and received a quotation which compared favourably with the cost of having the work done here, even allowing for the cost of delivering the car to Italy and collecting it later, and for the Customs Duty of 25.2% payable on the bill. Since it also included a bench-test of the engine after rebuilding – a facility not available here – I decided to have the job done at Modena, together with some additional work of various sorts. I cannot pretend that the prospect of driving the Ferrari out to Italy and back was not a factor in reaching this decision.

For business reasons it was convenient for me to drive the Ferrari to Modena in January 1968, not the best month for a trans-European journey. On this occasion I was accompanied by my nephew Andrew, Anthea's brother, and I was more than pleased to have his aid and company in the adverse conditions we encountered. When we left home Europe was in the grip of ice and snow. It was quite an achievement to reach Dover where we spent the night. Cross-channel services were disorganized and when we arrived at Lydd the following morning, it looked more like Alaska than Kent. The airfield was icy and snow-covered and Le Touquet was also giving a realistic imitation of Greenland. It was 2.30 pm before we started off in the direction of Paris on ice and compacted snow. It took us five hours to reach Orly, and we ate a meal in the airport before continuing into the night at 8.50 pm for Avallon, where we stopped at the Hôtel du Chapeau Rouge at 11.15 pm.

We continued next morning in rain with the temperature at freezing point. We made good progress for the first 52 miles, then the roads became really icy. Lorries were crawling and so were we. In the hilly country near Chagny we came to a stop behind a queue of stationary traffic. To add to our difficulties my battery had become quite flat and the hand-brake would not hold the car. As we pushed the car to the brow of a hill it slid on the black ice to the opposite side of the road. Lorries were jack-knifed across the road and it was three-quarters of an hour before gritting enabled the traffic to move along. In the interval the battery recovered sufficiently to kick the engine into life. On towards Lyon; signposts had been knocked down and a number of trucks and cars were ditched, some overturned. We left the N6 at Tournus, turning east on N75 towards Geneva. Only half the width of the road was usable, the other half being occupied for mile after mile by telegraph posts and wires laid flat by the weight of snow. Lumps of ice dropped off the trees, some falling on the car roof with startling bangs. We stopped at Cuisery for lunch and were pleased to observe some vehicles coming through with Italian plates and assumed that the road to Geneva was passable, for no news was available because of the wires being down. At 2.20 pm we started again, drove through Bourg-en-Bresse and after Pont d'Ain came upon a roadside notice – 'CHAINES OBLIGATOIRE.' I had none, so proceeded with care on my naked Pirelli HS tyres without any dreaded sideslips! It was not until 7.30 pm that we pulled up outside the Hôtel du Rhône after negotiating the snow-covered streets of Geneva.

The next morning, a telephone call to the Touring Club of Switzerland enquiring about road conditions resulted in advice not to go to Italy at all that day; even the valley road to the Simplon train tunnel was under snow. Andrew was game and I decided to have a go rather than sit around waiting for who-knows-what. The ailing battery had been recharged during the night, and an inspection plate in the under-tray, which had been doubled back on frozen snow ridges and was acting as a sprag on the road when reversing, was hacked off. We left Geneva in good spirits, for the sky was blue and the sun was shining brightly. We headed for the Mont Blanc Tunnel and made satisfactory, if slow, progress enjoying to the full the wintry mountain scenery. I felt rather adventurous driving the Ferrari in these conditions, but it was a sobering thought that the driver of the huge petrol tanker and trailer in front of me was merely doing his ordinary day's work. It took us 2 hours 20 minutes to reach the entrance to the Tunnel, which I was seeing for the first time. It is a truly magnificent engineering achievement running straight through the mountains for over 11 kms at an altitude of 1,300 metres. I couldn't help remembering that a friend – who had better be nameless in this context – had reached over 100 mph in one traffic-free passage in his Lamborghini, the lights and bells installed in the tunnel to monitor the speed of vehicles 'doing their nut' at this unwonted intrusion. To digress even further, I know another Lamborghini owner resident in Hong Kong who exercised the privilege of part-proprietor of the Cross-Harbour Tunnel to drive his Miura through prior to the opening at a speed never before or since (nor ever again to be) equalled in the Colony! Is there an underground World Speed Record?

As we emerged on the southern slope and parked for refreshment, the Ferrari attracted interested enthusiasts as it always did, wherever it stopped in the land of its birth. The sun was shining brightly and the snow and ice on the road were melting. It was great to reach the plains below and to turn up the taps on the Autostrada near Aosta, getting along quickly again on relatively dry roads. We reached the Milan AGIP motel at teatime and thankfully discarded our fur-lined coats and snow boots. The Ferrari was filthy – I have never seen it dirtier. After a snack we sped down the Autostrada del Sole to Modena arriving at the Real-Fini at 6.20 pm, pleased that we had disregarded the advice of the TCS on this occasion, having completed 937 miles of Monte-Carlo Rally type motoring without mishap.

The Ferrari was handed over to the Service Department having covered 2,760 miles since she was last there for the drastic diagnosis leading to her present visit. Andrew and I returned home by train and plane looking down upon the snow-covered terrain which had done its best to hinder us. I wouldn't choose midwinter again for such a trip.

Peter Newens, another Ferrari owner, jumped at the opportunity to see the factory at Maranello and to ride back in my reborn car. We flew to Milan on 14 March and took a train to Modena. I collected the car and was told not to exceed 4,000 rpm (75/80 mph in top gear) for, I think, 1,000 kilometres, so we had a leisurely trip home via Geneva, where we looked in at the Motor Show and joined an enjoyable dinner party with visiting Brits. The Ferrari was running very sweetly and quietly. I felt somewhat naked without the familiar smoke-train, but it was a joy to know that the engine had been stripped down and rebuilt with new parts as

63 *Neil Corner approaching the pits at Le Mans in the 50th Anniversary Race for historic cars, June 1973*

necessary.

We arrived at Lydd on a Sunday evening, and there was no Customs staff on duty able to deal with assessing the duty payable on the cost of repairs which I declared. I paid a deposit of £180 and completed several forms. In the following weeks there followed a good deal of correspondence with the Customs people and I still feel aggrieved. They threw the book at me. Before leaving England to collect the car I had paid the bill for the work done on the car – about 1¼ million lire at an exchange rate of about 1,504¼ lire to the £ – but I arrived back in England with the car during a week-end when sterling was losing value and the authorities converted the cost in Italian currency at the estimated rate of 1,486 ruling on the day of re-importation, thus charging me on £10 which I had never paid. I asked them to deduct from the bill the cost of certain running repairs which had been done at the same time as the engine overhaul; the cost of petrol used in bench-testing the engine; and oil and anti-freeze put in after the rebuild. They refused and added insult to injury by adding a notional figure of £25 for getting the car to Italy and back! I have always been meticulous about declaring everything at Customs – and still am – but I am inclined to feel a bit 'Bolshie' when I think how I was treated on this occasion. Sure – the Customs could quote chapter and verse in support of their contentions and I could not refute them, but I certainly felt it was a case for an agreed settlement rather than the extortion of every penny which could be squeezed according to the letter of the law.

The rejuvenated Ferrari gave me much pleasure. I took it across the Channel again in the Spring of 1969 to make arrangements for the visit to Le Mans of the Bentley Drivers Club to celebrate the 50th Anniversary of the marque, and enjoyed a few blinds up and down the Mulsanne Straight in company with Bill Cook in his DB 6 Aston Martin.

In December 1972 Anthony Bamford, who knew about my Ferrari, expressed renewed interest in buying it for his collection. He drove it once round Hyde Park and gave me a cheque for the price I asked. I parted with the Ferrari because I was finding it more difficult (having no facilities of my own) and, therefore, more costly to maintain in the manner to which it was entitled to become accustomed. I had enjoyed to the full six years and 15,000 miles of motoring in this new dimension.

Anthony at once repainted the Ferrari in 'Rob Walker' Blue and I was delighted when he entered it in the 50th Anniversary Race for Historic Cars at Le Mans in June 1973, to be driven by Neil Corner. It gave me quite a kick to see it circulating on the famous circuit at racing speed. The race was for cars up to 1959, but with the quixotic facility one has come to expect from the French, the Ferrari of 1960 was allowed to compete in the 45-minute race with a penalty of 2 minutes. The result was that Neil was placed second to Willie Green in a 'D' type Jaguar at an average speed fractionally over 100 mph.

It's a strange world indeed. I replaced the Ferrari, fortuitously, with a V-12 Daimler, and I enjoyed just about the same performance, but with four passengers and luggage, air-conditioning and radio. That's what 12 years' progress and development in automobile engineering can do for us.

Thank you, Commendatore, for a great experience.

'Detroit Iron'

There will always be room for a luxury American car in my 'stable' as long as circumstances permit – an assertion which may seem to come oddly from one so keen on Edwardian cars, Vintage sports-cars and high-performance thoroughbred cars, but I know what I like when it comes to comfortable, safe and speedy transportation.

Come to think of it, the first car I ever drove (sitting on my school-cap before the days of driving tests) was an American one – my father's 1925 Chrysler '65' with an open touring body. It was quite an unusual car to see in England and I enjoyed being at the wheel.

The second American car in my life has been the subject of much badinage between Con and me, for it belonged to her father and the point at issue is whether it was Con or the Chrysler Imperial which inspired our first tryst! Anyway, it was a great car and would accelerate from standstill to 60 mph in 10 seconds, a performance, if I remember rightly, beaten only in prewar Road Tests by the Railton which took a fraction of a second less.

My next experience of an American car was in 1950 when Briggs Cunningham lent me his latest Cadillac, which was being used over here by Donald Healey. It was a revolution in transportation to me and I found its performance quite staggering. It was the first time I had driven a car with Hydramatic Drive and, as a result, came to the conclusion that two-pedal motoring would eventually oust the 'stick shift' for the average motorist buying a large or medium-sized car. I drove the Cadillac about 700 miles and could scarcely believe that all this could be had for the equivalent of £1,000 in the States.

Although I subsequently drove borrowed and rented cars for short distances during visits to the States, my first real taste of modern American automobile engineering came in March 1966, when I assisted my Chairman to ferry his new 1966 Lincoln Continental 4-door Sedan to Greece. We flew to Rotterdam and first set eyes on the car when the agent brought it round to the Hilton on the evening before our departure. I read the Owner's Manual, familiarized myself with the controls, filled up with petrol and put the car in the garage keenly anticipating the drive southwards on the morrow.

We cruised on the autobahn at 75/80 mph to Basle – a distance of 516 miles. A check against kilometre stones over a distance of 164 kms showed that the odometer was under-recording by 6.7%. Timing the Lincoln for 4

64 *The 1925 Chrysler '65' which belonged to the author's father*

65 *Briggs Cunningham's 1950 Cadillac at Eastbourne*

66 *1966 Lincoln Continental on the way to Naples. The car was registered in New York where front number plates are not required*

kms at a steady indicated speed of 90 mph later during the journey established that the speedometer was 6.9% slow at that speed, the true speed being 96.2 mph.

The next day was a pleasant Alpine drive of 356½ miles through the St Gotthard Tunnel to Milan and the following day took us the length of the Autostrada del Sole to Naples, 489 miles, where I left the Lincoln to fly back to London. The petrol consumption over more than 1,000 miles had been 12.45 mpg.

I really liked that Lincoln and as I bade 'Bon Voyage' to its owner, who was driving on to Athens, I said, 'If ever you decide to sell this car, please give me first refusal. I probably won't be able to afford it, but I'd like the opportunity to own it.'

Little did I think that the Lincoln would become mine in August 1969, 3½ years later. I collected it in Monte-Carlo with only 11,000 miles on the clock. It was unblemished, but one of the four silencers was leaking as a result of condensation. I had this temporarily repaired for the journey home and arranged for a replacement to be ordered for fitting on my return to England. The temporary repair failed, and so did another one, with the result that for most of the journey home the Lincoln sounded like a dragster! Acceleration in built-up areas called for delicate foot-work to avoid offending the ears of gendarmerie; and the blast of exhausts somewhat marred our otherwise dignified arrival at the Château de Saran of Moët et Chandon near Epernay for an overnight stay.

Although one reads a lot about driving British, European, and even Japanese cars in the British motoring press, little is written about American cars. This is understandable as only a relatively small, if growing, number of them are in use in this country. Unfortunately, there is a good deal of uninformed prejudice against them, even among experienced motorists who should know better than to condemn them without trial. The way I see it is this: it stands to reason that wealthy citizens of the United States, surely the most technologically advanced nation in the world, may be expected to demand a means of personal transport produced to the highest standards. That these standards are not those set by British motorists is not grounds for dismissing all American cars out of hand – often with derisory references to such things as gargantuan proportions, wallowing suspension, acres of chromium-plate, no brakes, etc., etc. The 'automobile' does not take the same place in the American home as the 'car' occupies in the Englishman's family. It is a utilitarian article – in the same sense as a refrigerator or a dishwasher – in that it has a job to do, and it is called upon to do it as efficiently and unobtrusively as possible. In the case of a car, the owner has perforce to be in constant attendance when it is in use, so additional criteria are that he should be made as comfortable as possible and called upon for as little effort and thought as is necessary to ensure its proper control. All this must be set against the background of conditions in the States, particularly the availability of cheap petrol, the vast system of motorways, countrywide strictly enforced speed limits, a love of things big, and space to indulge it. Accordingly, the present generation of top quality American cars, represented by Lincoln of Ford and Cadillac of General Motors (and, I imagine, the Chrysler Imperial), meet the requirements admirably. Beauty is in the eye of the beholder and I do not quarrel with those who find American cars in general vulgarly ornate, but I consider the Lincoln Continental to be elegant in its simplicity of line and freedom from embellishment.

During the 2½ years I owned the Lincoln I covered 23,531 miles, of which about 5,000 miles were on the Continent. (One of these European trips is described later in this book.) The remainder included 200 miles weekly, commuting from home in Surrey to office near Park Lane. I would be the last to suggest that such a large car (18 ft 5 in long and 6 ft 7¾ in wide) was designed with busy London streets

67 *The Continental boot is large by any standard, as Con and Anthea demonstrate*

68 *1974 Lincoln Continental Mark IV*

in mind, but it says a lot for the ease of control that neither the size nor the left-hand drive caused me any bother at all. The automatic transmission, power steering and power brakes called rather for the conveyance of wishes to the mechanism by a finger and a toe than any orthodox driving effort. Sitting on the near-side, one tended to drive closer to the kerb than with a right-hand drive car, and this compensated partly for the extra width. Visibility of the road ahead was sometimes enhanced when sitting on the extreme left and rarely was one inconvenienced by having to follow closely a slow-moving van.

My Lincoln Continental, which left the factory in August 1965, incorporated several features that have yet to appear in the best European cars. The parking brake was applied by foot and could then be forgotten, being automatically released when the selector lever was put into 'Drive' or 'Reverse' to move off again. Not only did the car have air-conditioning, but the heating and cooling systems were integrated and controlled thermostatically, the driver merely having to 'dial' the temperature which he wanted inside the car. Heated or cooled air was blown into the car as necessary to maintain the temperature at the selected level, and the atmosphere was dehumidified continuously. There was a vacuum-operated central locking system for the doors, controlled from the driving seat as were the controls for the electrically operated six-way front seat, the windows and the aerial. The car was strongly built and unfailing in its reliability, but had an appetite for silencers, of which there are four.

During the time I owned the Lincoln I became used to raised eyebrows, incredulous stares, gibes and worse, from my motoring friends on seeing me in the Continental. They could not reconcile my liking and ownership of Edwardian, Vintage and Sports cars with actually choosing an American 'barouche'. They did not know what they were missing – many of them didn't want to know! For my part, I derive differing pleasure from driving different types of cars, and count myself more fortunate than most in having had a Lincoln Continental at my disposal. (Peter Hampton is the only other Lincoln Continental 'fan' among my circle of friends, and few would question his judgment when it comes to cars.)

I had no plans to change the Lincoln, but a unique opportunity came my way in March 1972 to acquire a 1971 Cadillac Fleetwood Brougham at a sensible price. It was one of the other makes of car which Rolls-Royce Motors buy from time to time for evaluation. They had completed their examination, in the course of 6,346 miles, of the best that their transatlantic competitors could produce, and I took this opportunity to up-date and widen my experience of American cars, sold the Lincoln to a business associate who still has it, and became a Caddy-commuter.

The Cadillac had many of the 'luxury' features of the Lincoln, including automatic temperature control. The variable-ratio power steering was better; there was slightly less lean on corners; the luggage space was considerably less; the aerial built into the windscreen was an improvement; but I never liked the shape of the body. On balance it was an enjoyable means of transport and in it I made my one and only trip from home to the south of France in a day.

Con had preceded me by air to Eze. I left Cobham alone at 6 am on Monday, 25 September 1972 and arrived on the quay at Dover exactly 2 hours later (95.9 miles). It was 10.55 am when I pulled away from the Customs shed at Boulogne and I passed the Casino in Nice at 10.25 pm. The total elapsed time of 11½ hours for the 759 miles equated to a point-to-point average speed of 66.0 mph. My stops en route added up to 1 hour 10 minutes and the net driving time of 10 hours 20 minutes from Boulogne to Nice gave a running average speed of 73.5 mph. The total distance driven that day was 855 miles, accomplished in the air-conditioned, fatigue-free comfort characteristic of the

69 *1974 Lincoln Continental Mark IV at Moët et Chandon's Chateau de Sarans near Epernay*
70 *The Mark IV parked alongside a four-door sedan at Beaulieu*

best American cars. The overall petrol consumption was 11.2 mpg. Incidentally, during the journey I checked the odometer and speedometer with the aid of kilometre markers and stop-watch. The former was under-recording the mileage by 2% and the speedometer was $6\frac{1}{2}$% slow.

After a few days we left for Aubusson (collecting Peter and Jane Newens at Clermont Ferrand airport on the way) for the Ferrari and Bentley competition week-end at Pierre Bardinon's Mas du Clos circuit. The high street in Aubusson is very narrow and it is almost impossible to park outside the Hôtel de France, even to unload baggage. Con said, 'Wherever are you going to park this great car?' 'Outside the pub', I replied, hoping my serendipity in this regard would not let me down. As I drove down the road I could see cars parked nose-to-tail all the way past the hotel. It didn't look too promising, but just as I reached the hotel a car started to pull out from the kerb and, believe it or not, it was a Cadillac Fleetwood – the first I had seen since leaving London – and I swept into the vacated space amid cries of astonishment from my passengers, conscious that if it had been any smaller car I couldn't have got in!

Whilst enjoying the Cadillac, I was trying to decide which of the four 'top' American cars – the Cadillac Fleetwood or Eldorado, or Lincoln Continental or Mk IV – I would like to have when the time came to sell the Cadillac. I drove an 8.2 litre front wheel drive Cadillac Eldorado in California; another (a convertible) in Belgium and a third one for a week-end in England. I found little difference between the front- and rear-wheel drive in the kind of driving I was able to do, and I rejected the concept of a convertible in England. It would be used in the down position on relatively few days in the year, the temperature-controlled air-conditioning being preferable on really hot days, and the top soon became shabby in the raised position; the cover was difficult to fix in the lowered position and the top took up a large part of the luggage space when stowed. My preference inclined towards the Lincoln rather than the Cadillacs and I preferred the four-door Lincoln Continental sedan to the more expensive two-door Mk IV Continental. In the case of the latter model, I have never quite accepted the RR-inspired radiator shell and I dislike the vestigial hump in the boot-lid which no longer houses the spare wheel. I gather it is retained as a status symbol for US owners, but in my opinion it detracts from the otherwise acceptable lines of the car.

The Cadillac did give place to a Lincoln – but to a Mk IV, not a four-door Continental saloon! It came about in this way: ideas of buying a suitable used Continental in the US, during one of my visits and importing it came to nought by reason of the Common Market regulations – extremely important but not widely known relating to cars manufactured after 1 January 1972. I fear there are owners of such cars inadvertently using them here, unaware that the absence of an 'E' plate could invalidate their insurance cover in the case of an accident, while the resale value of their cars could be little more than the scrap price.

Accepting that the road to the purchase of a new or recent model in the States was closed, I turned my attention to the possibility of finding one here in the UK. When several months had passed without the smell of a four-door Continental I was tempted to look at a 1974 Mk IV Lincoln which Steve Ouvaroff – he owns the American Car Centre in Kingston-upon-Thames – was selling for a customer. It had several important features. First and foremost it was 'E'-plated, having been imported by Ford for their stand at the Motor Show at Earls Court in October 1973. Furthermore, it had done under 2,000 miles, was in immaculate condition, and was very reasonably priced. A short drive convinced me that the opportunity was one not to be missed, and so, the Mark IV superseded the Cadillac.

The first thousand miles were driven whilst

the 50 mph speed limit imposed temporarily in the interests of conserving petrol was in force. I used this car for commuting from home to the office. It is difficult to counter allegations of anti-social behaviour, using such a large car to convey a single occupant 20 miles each way instead of using such public transport as is available. So be it; until the law decrees otherwise I shall continue to use such cars as I can afford, preferring to enrich oil sheikhs, rather than tobacco and liquor barons. I have heard others who have been criticized for using large thirsty cars, but have not yet been at the receiving end of abusive remarks concerning the assumed high petrol consumption of the Lincoln which looks very large indeed. (Actually, the Double-Six Daimler is just about as thirsty, but is regarded as 'just a Jag' by the uninformed public and passes more or less unnoticed.)

Con and I planned to spend a week in the South of France in September 1974 and decided to take the new Lincoln. The small luggage boot posed no problem for us – until we invited two friends to join us for the journey home! Only by exercising great ingenuity in loading the boot and having one large suitcase on the rear seat between the passengers were we able to manage. Except for the difficulty of ingress and egress for rear seat passengers – a characteristic of two-door saloons, but made more difficult in this case by the totally unsuitable seat belt anchorages fitted to comply with British law – the Lincoln proved itself an excellent means of transport. Our route included motorways, main and secondary roads, mountain passes Grimsel and Nufenen; and pottering round Italian lakes and along the Côte d'Azur. At all times we travelled in supreme, air-conditioned, armchair comfort and more than once my passengers were enjoying a post-prandial snooze whilst cruising along at 100 mph. Petrol consumption for the 1,000-mile outward journey was 12.7 mpg, varying from 13.4 mpg on flattish main roads to 11.4 mpg over the mountains. Two additional passengers and luggage doubtless accounted for the drop to 11 mpg on the homeward run. The Lincoln consumed 180.8 gallons of petrol (Super in France, 4-star here) during the round trip of 2,120 miles, i.e. 11.7 mpg.

I saw only one other Lincoln Mark IV during the fortnight, but was intrigued by the coincidence when I found the only empty parking space at the Metropole in Beaulieu next to a 4-door Lincoln Continental saloon. I was able to compare the two cars side by side and to discuss their relative merits and demerits with the Belgian owner. Strangely enough, I preferred his model (four doors and larger boot) and he preferred mine, chiefly for its looks. If it hadn't been for the potential resultant Customs complications and expense, we might have made a level swap, for both cars were 1974 models, the same colour and had covered almost exactly the same mileage.

My car attracted a good deal of interest wherever it was parked. Several locals in Switzerland and France recognized it as being identical to the one used by the detective, Cannon, in the television series. Many people, including fellow countrymen, peered at the car to find out what make it was, staring at the radiator, wheels and rear-end without success. The name 'Lincoln' does not appear externally, only 'Mark IV' and 'Continental'. I would not be surprised if some holiday-members returning to the UK brought back tales of having seen a new experimental or prototype Rolls-Royce being tested on the Continent!

Whilst this book was going through the processes of the publishing business I seized an unlooked-for opportunity, despite earlier misgivings, to acquire a Cadillac Eldorado. My eye caught an advertisement in the 'Autocar' in October 1974 describing an Eldo offered for sale: as new, under 1,000 miles, nine months old, and at a figure not much over half list-price. As it was to be seen only 10 miles from my home I succumbed to the temptation to see and try. One look and a short drive round the houses, and I was hooked. Once again General Motors

71 *Change-over day: the incoming Cadillac Eldorado (left), beside the outgoing Mark IV Lincoln*

superseded Ford in the Sedgwick garage.

The petrol economy speed limits have been in force during the twelve months I have had this car and I have not yet taken it across the Channel. The 8,000 miles which I have driven have, therefore, been covered in somewhat restricted conditions and the majority of it commuting to and from the West End of London.

Do I like the car? Yes. Its six inches longer wheelbase and shorter overall length compared with the Mark IV Lincoln give it an improved appearance. Everything is, of course, automatic and has worked faultlessly – except the never-used electric sunroof which jammed open when operated late one night to enable Australian friends in the back seat to see the floodlit dome of St Paul's! The automatic air-conditioning and temperature control is superb. The Cruise Control is consistently accurate and the many other aids to effortless driving and comfortable travel work well. The quietness of the engine ranks with the best.

It was not long before I perceived the advantage of front wheel drive. One experiences a sensation of being pulled round bends instead of being pushed straight on as with the models having conventional drive. The resulting flat floor is a bonus making for comfort and mobility within the car.

Disadvantages? Yes – there are some, mostly arising because of the two-door coachwork. There is insufficient headroom for comfort in the rear seats for passengers of normal stature; the doors are large and heavy to close, and visibility for rear passengers is somewhat limited. For such a large car the luggage space is ridiculously small and it is difficult to accommodate quite modest suitcases because of the intrusion of the huge spare wheel.

Nevertheless, this two-year old Cadillac has several features which I was surprised not to find on the new Camargue, such as; pedal parking-brake, self-releasing when the selector level is moved to 'D' or 'R'; back of front seat released electrically when door is opened; fibre optic tell-tales for rear lights, brake lights and turn indicators; remotely controlled mirrors on *both* sides; lighting (variable intensity) on passenger's vanity mirror; antenna rising automatically when radio is switched on.

Having now experienced the two- and four-door versions of both Cadillac and Lincoln, I adhere to my selection of the Lincoln Continental four-door sedan as the Best Buy – for me anyway.

72 *Wishful thinking – Le Mans line-up 1953. From left to right: Briggs Cunningham's 1953 Continental Bentley, Bill Spear's Continental, Walter Sleator's Continental, and Briggs' 1952 model. (Only Sleator's car has Bentley wings on a dummy radiator cap.)*

Borrowed plumes

King for a day, or two, or more

R-Type Continental Bentleys

In the post-war years it has been my good fortune to be lent motor cars by other people; sometimes the manufacturers, sometimes trusting owners. I seize every opportunity to drive good cars, preferably large and fast, and am blessed with a total lack of the apprehension which deters many experienced motorists from enjoying borrowed plumes. Many's the time I have got into a strange car and driven off in London's West End rush-hour traffic on a wet and dark Friday night. This is not a boast, merely my good luck. Nor does it imply a lack of concern; quite the opposite, in fact, for I drive as if it were my own car and no one can ask for more than that.

One of the most enjoyable borrowings took place twenty years ago, when I had the use of one of Briggs Cunningham's R-Type Continental Bentleys for a holiday on the Continent.

Few motoring enthusiasts, except the small circle of journalists whose professional activities included the testing of cars, had yet driven the Continental Bentley. I was elated when, early in 1953, in the course of correspondence on the subject of Le Mans arrangements, Briggs Cunningham suggested I 'deliver' his new left-hand drive Continental to him at Le Mans and, after the race, borrow his 'old' one for a touring holiday. 'Old' in this case meant eleven months and 11,000 miles.

I collected the brand-new Continental at the Conduit Street showrooms of Bentley Motors and was pleased to find that my recollections of the fine qualities of this car had not been gilded by the passage of time. Two changes had been made which affected the external appearance of the car. The first was the fitting of more substantial steel bumpers designed to cope with transatlantic driving habits, in place of the original ones of light alloy. The second one was the outcome of public opinion and concerned the radiator cap. The prototype and the earlier

production models had had no filler cap, dummy or real but it was not long before a flat (dummy) filler cap surmounted by a small 'B' became a standard fitment. Both Briggs Cunningham's cars had the early type of radiator shell with no filler cap. Briggs had specified that the steering column gear-change lever customary on left-hand drive cars was to be replaced by a central gate change. This gear-change mechanism proved itself to be as positive and pleasant in use as its more usual right-hand counterpart. Briggs shared my view that the absence of rear-wheel spats improved the car's appearance. (Partly for this reason, and partly because of expensive-to-remedy corrosion at the anchorage points, I discarded 'Olga's' spats some years ago.)

The journey to Le Mans was uneventful but exhilarating. No one will claim that the Continental Bentley can accommodate comfortably more than four adults, but we managed to squeeze five grown men into the car and an incredible amount of luggage into the boot. This heavy load naturally detracted a little from the phenomenal performance of the car, but on several occasions the speedometer needle remained well over the 100 mph mark. Leaving Le Touquet at 4.22 pm, we reached Le Mans at 9 o'clock, where we checked in at the headquarters of the Cunningham team of which we were to form part. I was pleased to hand over my precious charge to its owner and very interested to find that the car was now one of three Continental Bentleys on the strength. During the vast amount of pre-race work which was going on I managed to collect Briggs and Bill Spear with their Continentals, and Walter Sleator, the Paris representative of Bentleys, with another of these cars, and to marshal them in front of the pits as if ready to start in the race. How dearly I wished that this was the shape of things to come.

After a very full week-end dominated by the great race, we left Mulsanne Corner in Briggs' 'old' Continental, on Monday at 11 am, having made a final lap of the course, with Guéthary – just south of Biarritz – as our destination. Con and I were accompanied by Bob Gregory (with whom I had done the week-end trip to Monte-Carlo and back in his 1904 Darracq three years previously) and his wife, Marjorie. Advantage had been taken of the considerable amount of room in the luggage boot by selecting the most suitable cases and adhering to a pre-arranged stowage plan. Our route went by Tours, Poitiers and Bordeaux; this road – N10 – was new to me, but I had been told that it was fast and straight. And so it proved, especially after Bordeaux, when I covered 70 miles in an hour – quite a respectable performance 20 years ago. It demonstrated the effortless high speed cruising capability of the car, and perhaps the most important aspect of it all was that the passengers' comfort (and peace of mind) remained undisturbed at speeds over 100 mph.

We reached our hotel, the Eskualduna, at Guéthary some 8½ hours after leaving Le Mans, 384½ miles away. The 18-gallon tank was filled to the brim as we left Le Mans and I could hardly believe the apparently optimistic figures resulting from mental calculations made during the day on the basis of instrument readings. I decided to satisfy myself beyond all possible doubt on the consumption figures by emptying the tank as nearly as possible.

The distaff side of my crew clearly expressed its views as to the undesirability of running out of petrol far from a pump and I was eventually prevailed upon to stop in Bayonne. We had covered 374 miles without running out of petrol and put in 83.45 litres (18.36 gallons) to replace the quantity used (I know that this is more than the capacity of the tank, but the filling tube holds a considerable quantity), and thus my computations were confirmed; the Continental was covering more than 20 miles to the gallon; on this day the figure was actually 20.37.

In the course of the evening, we drove into Biarritz and I said to my passengers: 'There will be lots of Rolls-Royces and Bentleys around, but I'll bet there won't be any Continentals.' At the next cross-roads we came face-to-face with another Continental, and didn't see another Rolls or Bentley all evening!

Our plan was to leave the Côte Basque the next morning and to drive the length of the Pyrénées, thence to Barcelona. Accordingly we set off and went through St Jean-de-Luz to St Jean-Pied-de-Port – a picturesque village clustered round an ancient fortified prominence which, when one looks down upon the house tops from above, looks as if a sackful of building blocks has been emptied into a heap. We made a detour to visit Pau. It was raining heavily, but this did not deter us from doing a couple of laps of the Grand Prix course before continuing our journey back into the mountains. The higher we went the worse the weather became. When we eventually reached the Hôtel Col d'Aubisque at the top of the pass, visibility was down to about 20 yards or so and remains of the winter snow added to the gloomy scene. Our depression was soon dispelled by the warmth of the welcome given to us by the patron and his wife, who were surprised to see us arrive in such weather in spite of a long-standing reservation.

Weather conditions had not improved by the next morning. The plot for that day was to follow the Route des Pyrénées and spend the night some 250 miles away at the Grand Hotel at the summit of the Col de Puymorens, but the clouds were so low as to obscure the scenery and to take the pleasure out of driving. We went into Lourdes and had a look round that remarkable religious city; thence to Barbazan where we finally made up our minds that the Pyrénées were not for us that year. We decided to turn southwards into Spain in search of sunshine, and sent a telegram of regret to the hotel on the Puymorens.

A study of the map revealed that the nearest frontier crossing was on a comparatively minor road near Luchon between Fos and Lés. We tanked up with Supercarburant at St Béat, the last village in France, and crossed the border on the road, if so it can be called, to Lérida. The formalities at the frontier caused no trouble. Although individual tyre numbers had to be declared in the Carnet de Passage, no one checked them, but an hour passed before we had cashed travellers' cheques and started off in the rain. I was told that of the two possible roads, one climbed the Puerta de la Bonaigua (6,798 ft) and the other went through a tunnel, but was very narrow. I chose the former and we were soon climbing steeply on a narrow, unsurfaced road which would have brought a flush even to the cheeks of rally organizers who describe execrable tracks as being 'of a non-chassis-breaking nature'. We were soon in the clouds, which mercifully obscured the precipitous drop from my passengers' eyes. I found it advantageous to lower the tyre pressures to secure maximum adhesion and steering on the narrow, muddy road, and blessed the good lock of the Continental on the hairpin bends. The mud was splashing everywhere and it was not finally cleaned out of the engine compartment until its return to England. We continued through occasional poverty-stricken villages and eventually reached Lérida half an hour before midnight, feeling hungry and tired. In spite of the lateness of the hour, the staff at the Hotel Nacional set about cooking a meal.

On driving the car out of the garage the following morning I found the side of the body caked with mud, in some places half-an-inch thick, which gave it the appearance of being finished in two colours. The sun was shining as we left Lérida for Barcelona, 100 miles to the east. This road, a section of the main route from Barcelona to Madrid, was a curious mixture of comparatively smooth finish and occasional stretches of badly broken surface. More surprising and dangerous was the existence of an occasional pot-hole of anything up to 6 inches deep in an otherwise good stretch of road. After a deviation to drive up to the Monastery at Monserrat, from which we had an unrivalled view across the plain to the foothills of the

73 *The Continental at Lerida, the mud giving the appearance of a two-tone finish*
74 *Crossing the bed of the Rio Tordera near Blanes on the Costa Brava*

Pyrénées, we reached Barcelona for lunch. The car was washed during lunch at the extremely low charge of 25 pesetas (23p), and I was surprised to find that one night's garage cost the same amount. We visited friends who themselves were keen motorists, although their activities were more than somewhat limited by the 250% import duty levied on foreign – and therefore all – cars. One of my friends was very keen on motor-racing and read all the English motoring journals. He was very interested in the Bentley – which would have cost a Spaniard about £17,500 – and I took him for a ride on the Peña Rhin circuit, during which we did 90 mph along the Avenida Generalissimo Franco.

The next morning Bob and I drove out to the Pegaso factory and presented our 'credentials'. We were ushered into the board room to meet several directors of ENASA and the chief designer, Señor Ricart. Imagine our surprise when we found Harold Radford, Pegaso concessionaire in the UK, in solemn conclave. The main activity of the factory was the production of impressive heavy commercial vehicles, but it was, of course, the Pegaso sports car section which interested us. We saw about 20 chassis and bodies in course of manufacture and were able to examine the partly dismantled car which Jover had crashed at Le Mans. Those Pegasos were undoubtedly fine cars, but necessarily appealed to a very limited and specialized market.

It was early afternoon when we filled up with 'Plomo', the best, but not so good, petrol available in Spain, and left Barcelona driving northwards along the coast road towards the Costa Brava. This we approached with mixed feelings. I had flown over the coast and had no doubt that the scenic beauty would live up to descriptions we had heard, but the reports of road surfaces given to us by motoring friends made me wonder just what we were in for. One of them had described the surface in some places as being made of loose rocks as big as footballs.

The road from Barcelona to Blanes, where the Costa Brava really started, was moderately good, but thereafter one left the main road to Gerona and took a secondary road following the coast. Very soon we came to a broken bridge across a wide dried-up river where the wheel marks of traffic led down to the river bed itself, with patches of treacly mud in places – to regain the road on the far bank. The road between here and Tossa was narrow and there was no wall on the 'drop' side, but the surface was reasonably good.

There was very little traffic on the roads in Spain and I could not help feeling a bit of a pioneer at times, especially in the sparsely populated areas, but my ego received a severe jolt upon entering a tiny place like Tossa only to find the streets blocked by cars bearing GB plates. (They had, of course, arrived from the north and not by our circuitous route.)

From Tossa we drove along the coast road, stopping frequently to admire the coastline, and on the recommendation of our Barcelona friends dined at the hotel at the point near San Sebastián marked on the map as Ermita y Faro (Hermitage and Lighthouse). The hotel was actually the old hermitage and was situated on a high promontory from which one had views of breath-taking beauty along the coast in both directions. From Palafrugell we cut across country to Figueras to avoid the longer road through Gerona. The route we chose was shorter but the surface was so bad that we had to keep our speed down to little more than walking pace for several hours. This section was covered in the dark, and was so bad as to defy description. Across the frontier, the roads of France seemed like a billiard table. It was a weary group of motorists which entered the Grand Hôtel at Perpignan at midnight and sought their beds without delay.

The following morning we sped along the road to Marseille where we arrived for a late lunch. We were due at Eze-sur-Mer, between Nice and Monte-Carlo, that evening and left Marseille in the late afternoon to follow the winding coastal road all the way. I was very pleased to find that our road out of Marseille took us past the block of flats on stilts built by Corbusier as I had often seen photographs of this remarkable architecture. We pottered along the coast, lingered a while in St Tropez and celebrated a wedding anniversary of the Gregorys' dining at the Tour de l'Esquillon at Miramar, another restaurant situated on a promontory with wonderful views along the coast. Before continuing our journey, we had to disconnect and remove a fog lamp, the bracket of which had fractured as a result of the pounding received on the Spanish roads. We discovered subsequently that the bracket supporting the other fog lamp had similarly broken and we had two new ones made and fitted. The breaking of these lamp brackets – not of Bentley manufacture incidentally – was the only trouble we experienced throughout the holiday.

We spent three happy days at Eze and one day I took Bob to Nice to see a fine collection of old cars that I had discovered in a breaker's yard the previous year. Here were about twenty veteran cars, some of them genuine nineteenth-century vehicles. Most of them were runners and had an annual outing during the Cannes Carnival. There were Darracqs, De Dions, Peugeots, Panhards and an Audibert-et-Lavirotte. The latter car had two wheels on the steering column, one above the other. The top one was used for steering in the orthodox manner and the bottom one to change gears, a quarter-turn representing each ratio. Truly a collector's piece.

We commenced our journey home by climbing up to La Turbie, thereby making the most of the last glimpses of the Mediterranean, and then following part of the Monte-Carlo Rally Regularity-speed Test course over the Col de Braus to Sospel. We crossed the frontier into Italy by the tunnel at the top of the Col de Tende and sped along fast straight roads to Turin for lunch. Leaving Turin we turned westward and drove over the Mont Cenis pass to Lanslebourg where we headed for the Col de l'Iseran, the summit of which is 9,088 ft above sea level. A flurry of snow at the top of the pass turned into thunder and heavy rain as we descended on the northern side. This rain persisted all the way to Geneva and marred what would otherwise have been a very pleasant run.

On arrival in Geneva, we went straight to the Hôtel du Rhône only to find every room taken. After trying half a dozen hotels, some of which were full and some of which were too expensive, we eventually found accommodation at the Angleterre on the lake. Next morning we left for Paris, taking the usual road through Morez, Poligny, Dijon, Sens and Fontainebleu.

In Paris, we shunned the expensive show places and left the following afternoon for Le Touquet to take a 'plane at 8.15 pm for Lympne. We stopped for half an hour at a pâtisserie in Beauvais for tea and reached the airport three hours after leaving Paris. Having a little time to spare, we drove into Le Touquet itself to do some last-minute shopping and caused some eyebrows to be raised when the Marchal Fulgor horns came on of their own accord and stayed on just as we passed a 'Zone de Silence' notice. The time-honoured panacea of a sharp bang with the hand remedied this fault for the time being.

Customs formalities were almost completed at Lympne when suddenly I was told that I would not be allowed to drive Briggs' car away as it was owned by a non-resident and could not, therefore, be imported on touring documents unless accompanied by the owner personally. I was dumbfounded and expressed my annoyance at length and in no uncertain terms to everyone within earshot. I pointed out that I expected some difficulty when entering a country like Spain with an American-owned British car on French 'TT' plates while travelling on a British passport and speaking no Spanish, but to be prevented from bringing the car into my own country, where I was known and could provide any guarantees or undertakings required was enough to drive anybody 'nuts'. Chapter and verse of the appropriate regulations (Notice No. 115 A) were produced and, sure enough, anybody resident in this country is prohibited from driving a car imported on touring documents by a non-resident owner. These regulations were, of course, designed to prevent the illegal use in this country of cars which had not borne Purchase Tax, but one would have expected there to be provision for exceptional cases. The Continental was impounded until it could be collected by a Bentley Motors driver. It was particularly irksome for me as I planned to take the Bentley over to France again the following week-end to assist the Cunningham team at Reims and then to bring it back to the Works for routine maintenance. The inconvenience of having to unload everything from the car and to finish the journey home (90 miles) by taxi can be imagined.

The Continental had carried us 2,576 miles in safety and comfort and had averaged 20.09 mpg over that distance. The remarkably economical petrol consumption was, of course, the result of lightness, good streamlining and a high axle ratio and showed just what could be done. (Petrol cost the equivalent of 29p, 23p and 22½p per gallon in France, Spain and Switzerland respectively.)

I found that as far as petrol was concerned the conditions of the previous year had been reversed. The Continental pinked on the best petrol obtainable in France, Spain and Switzerland, but not on the premium grade fuels which had become available in this country; of course, petrol here was still cheaper than almost anywhere else, in spite of the penal tax element included in the price. Another thought: I could have wished bottom gear synchro-mesh, as the change-down from 2nd to 1st, used on steep, tight hairpins, was by no means easy to make silently.

The cost of hotels and meals on this trip in June 1953 form an interesting basis for comparison with today's prices:

		Sterling Equivalent
Hotels		
Guéthary (Hôtel Eskualduna)		
Demi-pension, with bath	1,800 francs per person including service, etc.	£1.83
Col d'Aubisque (Hôtel d'Aubisque)		
Room, no bath, no running hot water ..	500 francs (for two)	51p
Dinner	500 francs each	51p
Service	10 per cent	
Lérida (Hotel Nacional)		
Double room with bath, two single rooms, no bath	115 pesetas (for four)	£1.06
Supper	35 pesetas each	32p
Service	15 per cent	
Barcelona (Hotel Condado)		
Room with bath	145 pesetas (for two)	£1.33
Lunch	45 pesetas each	41p
Service	15 per cent	
Perpignan (Grand Hôtel)		
Room, no bath	900 francs (for two)	92p
Service	15 per cent	
Eze-sur-Mer (Le Bananeraie)		
Demi-pension with bath	1,900 francs per person including service, etc.	£1.93
Demi-pension, no bath	1,700 francs per person including service, etc.	£1.73
Geneva (Hôtel d'Angleterre)		
Room, no bath	42 Swiss francs (for two)	£3.44
Service	15 per cent	
Paris (Hôtel Brighton)		
Room with bath (no restaurant)	3,000 francs (for two) including service, etc.	£3.05
Restaurants		
Barbazan		
Chez Bergé	800 francs plus 15 per cent	81p
Paris		
Le Madrigal	800 francs plus 15 per cent	81p

Miramar de l'Esterel			
Le Tour de l'Esquillon	.. .. ..	950 francs plus 15 per cent	97p
Poligny			
Restaurant de Genève	.. .. ..	750 francs plus 12 per cent	76p

The rates of exchange at the time were as follows:

	To the £
French francs	983
Spanish pesetas	102
Swiss francs	12.2

Jaguar XK 120

In July 1954 I had the opportunity of 'delivering' a drophead XK120 to the South of France for a friend, so Con and I, with 10-year-old Carol on a foam rubber cushion between us, commenced our summer holiday in this manner. I decided to go from Le Touquet to Nice by the shortest, not the quickest, route and many quite experienced continental motorists were surprised to learn that this took one into Switzerland, then into Italy and back into France. The detailed itinerary was as follows:

Route	*Intermediate Places*	*Roads*	*Kms*		*Miles*	
Le Touquet	Montreuil, St Pol	N318, N39				
Arras	Cambrai, St Quentin,	N39, N44b				
	Laon	N44	97		60	
Reims	Chalons-sur-Marne,					
	Vitry-le-Francois, St	N44, N4				
	Dizier	N67	169	266	105	165
Chaumont		N19, N67	180	446	112	277
Langres	Gray, Besançon	N67, No. 85	35	481	22	299
Lausanne		No. 9	226	707	140	439
Montreux	Martigny, Col du Gd	No. 9, No.				
	St Bernard, Aosta,	114, No. 27				
	Ivrea	No. 26				
		Autostrada	25	732	16	455
Turin	Cuneo, Col de Tende,	No. 20				
	Sospel	N204	243	975	151	606
Nice			216	1191	134	740

It will be seen that the journey could conveniently be broken by overnight stops at Reims and Montreux, making three stages of 165, 290 and 285 miles, respectively, and it was in just those stages that we decided to do the trip.

We left Le Touquet at 7 o'clock in the evening – after a six-hour wait at Ferryfield due to bad weather – and pressed on, arriving at Reims 3 hours 35 minutes later. The next two stages were covered in more leisurely fashion. We left the Hôtel Welcome at Reims at 9.50 am after two laps of the Grand Prix circuit and lunched three hours later in Langres. We stopped 20 minutes for tea in Pontarlier (233 miles), spent a quarter-hour at the Swiss frontier and arrived at our destination, Montreux, exactly nine hours after leaving Reims. The Jaguar, which had provided the cosy comfort of a closed car on the wet drive from the coast to Reims on the previous evening, proved its versatility by giving us a wonderful day of open-car motoring.

We left Montreux at 9.20 am in glorious sunshine for the most interesting part of our trip, and arrived at the summit of the Great St Bernard Pass soon after 11 am after a tedious climb behind slow-moving traffic. (This was 10 years before the road tunnel was constructed and the 8,114 ft high road over the top had not long been free from snow.) An hour later we moved off through the Customs into Italy having visited the kennels of the famous St Bernard dogs at the Hospice. We lunched at Aosta having done only 77 miles since leaving Montreux, and set off again passing through Ivrea and entering the Autostrada at 3.45 pm. The eight miles of Autostrada soon passed beneath the wheels of the Jaguar, which sped joyfully along at 100-plus in contrast to the mountaineering so recently finished. We passed through Turin, stopped for tea and petrol, and crossed the frontier back into France through the dripping tunnel at the top of the Col de Tende at 6.45 pm with 235 miles behind us. The remaining 50 miles of winding roads over mountainous country, the latter stages well known to Monte-Carlo Rally competitors, was covered in $1\frac{3}{4}$ hours. The journey of 285 miles from Montreux to Nice took us just over 11 hours and we enjoyed every minute of it.

This route to the Riviera may still be followed and may be shortened, if so desired, by using the Grand St Bernard Tunnel and/or the autostrada from Aosta to Turin.

300SL Mercedes-Benz

I am still not quite sure how it came about that Mercedes-Benz (Great Britain) Ltd came to entrust me with the Works demonstrator, but I was agog with anticipation from the moment my name was entered in the diary of the 'Silver Lady' until I stepped off a bus in Camberwell New Road one Friday afternoon in March 1955, and approached the new Service Department with fingers crossed lest some VIP's requirements had deprived me of 'PLB 23' for the ensuing 72 hours. The car was awaiting my arrival and, after satisfying the management that I had acceptable insurance cover, I listened to some well-chosen words of advice and instruction from 'Mac' and drove back to the West End conscious that the car was the cynosure of all eyes. I soon became accustomed to the car being stared at and was not surprised when one interested driver in an adjacent line of traffic in Hyde Park motored gently into the car in front before his attention was drawn away from the Merc.; my fair passenger said: 'Aren't men funny. He was looking at the car – not me!'

On reaching my office I was pleased to find my Chairman's Continental Bentley parked nearby and seized the opportunity to photograph the two cars side by side. Two fine cars, each designed with a different purpose in mind, which achieved perfection in their respective fields; the magnificent outcome of engineering skills so recently applied towards mutual destruction. What an excellent pair of cars for the man with £11,321 to spend.

At six o'clock the next morning Gerry Crozier, erstwhile owner of a 38/250 SSK model of the same breed, and I left my home to see the start of the AA Veteran Run to Hastings. The roads were lightly covered with sleet and melting snow. At Kidbrooke the 300SL contrasted strangely with the venerable cars carrying Guardsmen to the coast, and Bill Cook's 1908 Mercedes was singled out to render photographic evidence of the results of nearly a half-century of progress.

Thereafter, every opportunity was taken to keep the passenger seat of PLB 23 occupied by a series of discriminating motorists keen to have first-hand experience of the car. There were about a dozen of these chaps who owned, between them such cars as 57SC Bugatti, 2.9 supercharged Alfa-Romeo, C-type Jaguar, and DB2 Aston Martin; their standards of judgment were therefore, very high. They were prepared to be impressed by the Merc, albeit some were doubtful if it would live up to its reputation and a few were prejudiced by its country of origin. Having ridden in the car, they confessed themselves, without exception, astonished at the performance and praised its many qualities, finding little to criticize. One or two went off with that glazed look in their eyes which augured an unusual interview with their bank managers. Bill Cook placed an order for one within a few days and still has the car to this day.

Few will deny the beauty of the line of the 300SL. Its unorthodox appearance was characteristic of everything about the car – done that way for a purpose. Those supple and inquisitive enough to look underneath were met with the sight of an all-enveloping undertray which completed the streamlining of the whole car. The method of entry into the car was by the well-known 'gull's wing' doors. These enabled one to step over the high sill without bending double or banging one's head and, contrary to popular belief, the fair sex could get in and out gracefully – though the practising period was not without interest! My own two yards of skin and bone (me, not my wife) shot in and out of the driving seat dozens of times without taking advantage of the folding steering-wheel. Once in the seat it was apparent that the instruments were where they should be – it was a bit of a shaker to see that the speedometer registered up to 180 mph, not kph – and the controls were very well placed.

So much for the static – now for the dynamic. The first thing I noticed was that the indirect gears were noisy. It was a husky noise which was music to the ears of one brought up on vintage sports-cars, but might well have proved unacceptable to some drivers. Then – the acceleration. It was meteoric and consistent from tick-over to 6,000 rpm in all gears. The speedometer needle flashed round the dial and it was quite usual to reach 'the ton' in third before changing into top. Without the slightest exaggeration 100 mph soon became common-place. Cruising speed along traffic-free roads was limited only by visibility and the frequency of hazards. Quite long stretches were covered between 110 and 115 and the two-mile-a-minute mark was instantly attainable by further slight depression of the throttle pedal. Such was the steadiness of the car, the instant response to the finger-light steering and outstanding retardation afforded by the brakes, that highspeed motoring of this order engendered, in driver and passenger alike, a feeling of safety and control which would be difficult to surpass. In top gear the Merc. was as quiet as anyone could wish, but the 240 hairy horses in the engine compartment let out a throaty roar when the revs reached the 4,000 mark.

In the course of our wanderings in the southern-counties we called on Peter Hampton to find him fixing reflectors to the cars in his collection. After the inevitable demonstration run in the 300SL we pushed his 1903 Mercedes out of the motor-house – 'garage' does not seem an apt description – for another photograph of ancient and modern products from the same factory.

The next morning I opened an eye at 7.15

and realized that it was a case of now or never if I was to do any really fast motoring, so I hurried unshaven to the Merc. which stood outside covered with an icy film. I pulled out the petrol-injection equivalent of the choke and the engine started at once. I waited a few minutes while the de-icing fan cleared the windscreen and then motored slowly round the houses to warm up the engine before heading for Guildford and the Hog's Back. It was a sunny morning and the road was dry. Conditions permitted a rapid run towards Farnham with the needle between 100 and 125 mph most of the way. As the road became less open I turned round and commenced the return journey, this time accelerating rapidly until I perceived the needle at 135 mph before I decided that I was using up the available road awful fast and lifted my foot. At this speed the Merc. was rock steady and controlled with consummate ease. Incidentally, this car had the lowest of the then available axle ratios (3.64 to 1) and would poddle along quite happily and quietly in top down to 22 mph.

On reaching home I washed the car and then spent precious time shaving and breakfasting before going out again, this time with Dennis May, dug out of Sunday morning domesticity, on my right. This was the first of several more runs that day, each with a different passenger, and it became standard practice to do 100 mph in third and more on top on each occasion. What a car!

The week-end drew to an unwelcome close and 8.30 on Monday morning saw PLB 23 headed towards Town occupied by two bowler-hatted types apparently oblivious to the novelty of doing 'the ton' a couple of times on the way to the office. I drove into the Mercedes-Benz works as 580 miles came up on the trip-recorder and handed over the car, safe and sound, to the owners. The car had then covered a total mileage of over 13,000, was quite rattle-free and had that well buttoned-up feeling of a new thoroughbred car. I had made not a single adjustment and the engine had never missed a beat.

In retrospect, the Mercedes provided me with an unforgettable motoring experience. I found no vices in the car, but I should make it quite clear at this stage that my treatment of the car was somewhat different from that meted out by some motoring journalists and others who, self-confessedly, go out of their way to make a motor car misbehave. I drove the car as if it was my own: as fast as road conditions and commonsense permitted. I did not attempt to take bends and corners at a higher speed than experience had taught me to be safe; to me it seems a pointless pastime to drive a car faster and faster round a corner until it breaks away and then to say: 'It's all right until it breaks away and then you've had it' – ignoring the fact that the break-away occurred at a speed far higher than any sane driver would use unless racing. Likewise, I did not overdo it on wet roads and soon found exactly how hard I could step on it when accelerating without wheelspin making the tail wag. No doubt some purpose is served by the gallant chaps who, in the course of a road test, deliberately put a car out of control to see how it responds to corrective treatment, for this way lies the ultimate basis for comparing the road-holding qualities of different cars in similar circumstances – but such goings on are not for me.

A week-end with the Mercedes served to underline two things. Firstly, the complete failure up to that time of our road system to keep pace with the progress made by the automobile industry. Secondly, no matter how skilled and careful is the driver of a fast car or how well-fitted for high-speed motoring the car, the personal safety of the driver and passengers is dependent to a very great extent on the common-sense and skill of other road users. Ordinary concepts of motoring must be discarded when driving cars with the potential performance of the 300SL, and even more so in the case of much faster cars which have come on to the market since its introduction 20 years ago. Gaps and opportunities for overtaking, which just do not exist for the ordinary driver, occur all the time. It is more than ever necessary to exercise discretion in using the potential of the car so that others are not frightened or embarrassed, and it must be remembered that others do not always appreciate the speed of fast-travelling cars.

Truly, the 300SL 'Gull-wing' is now recognized the world over as a 'Classic' – and deservedly so.

Rolls-Royce Silver Shadows & 'T' Series Bentley

The 'Silver Shadow', – and its rarer version the 'T' Series Bentley, are now familiar sights on our roads; not surprising really, for they have been around since 1965 and up to the end of 1974 more than 16,500 had been manufactured. It was, however, a great privilege when, in August 1966, I was able to borrow the Works Demonstrator Bentley for a week-end.

When lending me this car ('1900 TU') Jack Scott, Sales Director of Rolls-Royce, wrote '. . . this is one of the very first semi-prototypes and the production cars have certain modifications and improvements, but with the shortage at the moment it is impossible to let you have one of the very latest. I hope you will bear this in mind . . .' The car was indeed the first of the new Bentleys and had done over 21,000 miles.

During the week-end I covered nearly 500 miles of most enjoyable motoring and this afforded me a taste of honey – as Tommy Wisdom described a similar drive in 'Autosport' – and generated an appetite for more.

Each time a new model has emerged from the Crewe factory it has been my good fortune to have one on loan for a week-end. On each occasion the car has stirred in me admiration, and I have felt that it would be difficult to improve on it, yet each successive model has, in the nature of things, been an improvement on its predecessor. But not since I first drove 'Olga' in 1952 had I thought that the new Bentley was so far in advance of the model it superseded as the 'T' Series.

For my part, the new Bentley gave me the fastest, safest, smoothest, most comfortable, effortless and untiring driving I had ever experienced. What more could one ask of a car? The individual characteristics which go to make up a car's performance can be found in some measure in every car. Different makes and models are notable for particular qualities and these features play a part in the choice of a car. If 140 mph cruising instead of 100+ is sought, then a Ferrari might be chosen; for enormous luggage capacity the American cars and station wagons cannot be beaten; habitual shoppers in congested areas would opt for a Mini and the seeker after superb cornering might go for a Lotus. These examples demonstrate that excellence in one direction is invariably achieved only at the expense of one or more of the others. It just isn't possible to incorporate the ultimate in all the qualities in a single car, but, in my judgment, the new Bentley incorporated 'the mostest of the bestest'. A compromise, if you like, but in the best sense of the word, and one which yielded nothing to the very high standard in all aspects which a person paying over £6,000 was entitled to expect.

At the risk of raising a laugh, I must report that most of the time the loudest noise in the car was the ticking of the clock – but this is absolutely true. There was some noise from the suspension occasionally, mostly at very slow speeds, and the engine was quite audible at – I was going to say speeds over 80, but I had better say – 70 mph. The fresh air inlets were very good and enabled the car to be driven with windows closed even in quite hot weather, so that the wind noise level was exceptionally low.

From the appearance point of view, whether or not the car appealed to one was entirely a matter of personal taste. I know that many Rolls-Royce and Bentley owners of long-standing expressed themselves disappointed with the lines of the new car. I think many of them were surprised that the designers, having paid heed to the criticism that the S-Types were old-fashioned in appearance, produced a car which looks like a car of today – and not a car of tomorrow. ('It looks like a Peugeot 403 or a Merc., etc.')

I accepted the design of the body for what it was: a car of the 1960s. I liked it and I think that the S-Types really did look dated beside the new car. The more I saw of the car, the more I considered it to be better-looking than any of its contemporaries. The model had not yet been road-tested by the weekly motoring papers and I had no opportunity of comparing notes with anyone else who had driven the car any distance. My impression was that it was a great car by any standards.

Never had I returned a borrowed car so reluctantly to Lillie Hall, even though the faithful 'Olga' was standing by for the completion of my journey to the office. (Oh, yes! The petrol consumption for the whole week-end was 14.6 mpg, which was slightly less than the average expected by the manufacturers.)

I have driven numerous 'Silver Shadows' since and recall a drive across France in December 1971. The car was a standard 'Silver Shadow' with under 1,600 miles on the clock. I left my office in the West End of London at 12.30 pm and pulled up at the Ferry Terminal in Dover exactly two hours later. It was half-past four when the Hovercraft beached at Boulogne and it was cold, foggy and nearly dark. It took two hours to reach the toll-gate at the Arras entrance to the autoroute (79 miles) and freezing fog was a nuisance the rest of the evening. I stopped to eat at Le Bourget Airport and then drove on, round Paris on the Boulevard Périphérique, and down the A6 to spend the night at the Novotel at Évry.

When I resumed my journey at 8 o'clock the next morning it was still dark and the freezing fog persisted all the way to Valence. I had covered 300 miles by noon at an average speed of 75 mph. I am not quite sure why I found it safe to drive at speeds between 50 and 80 mph in these foggy conditions on the French autoroutes, when I would have been driving at little more than half the speed on our own motorways. It was not that I was brave, or foolhardy; nor unheeding of the dangers of multiple crashes. I think it was largely because of the much lighter traffic encountered, which meant that such vehicles as were on the road travelled steadily along in different lanes. Heavies kept to the nearside lane; private cars to the middle and outer lanes. There was, therefore, no danger of running into the rear of a stationary truck and the likelihood of the sparsely-spaced cars running into one another was virtually non-existent. Even if one were to come upon a slow-moving or stationary car there would have been an empty lane to steer into to avoid a shunt. On reflection, maybe it wasn't so foggy, after all, but it certainly was freezing – the aerial trailed a fringe of ice! Anyway, the driving demanded unremitting concentration of a high order and the heated comfort of the Shadow certainly helped to reduce the fatigue.

I lunched at Montélimar and was pleased to see the last of the fog. I missed the turn-off for Nice at Salon and decided to stay on A6 to Marseille and then to take A52 and N 560 to N7 east of Aix-en-Provence. (I reached the end of A6 at Marseille at 2.40 pm with the day's mileage at 460 – 6 hours 40 minutes, including a 5 minute stop for petrol.) It was a mistake to go this way. In order to reach A52 from A6 it was necessary to drive through the streets of Marseille for 4 miles, taking 10 minutes, which seemed like hours. The autoroute eastwards was very short – 11 miles – and the N560 (and D1) was hilly and tortuous. I rejoined A7 near Trouves. At 5 pm I pulled into the Shell Station on the Promenade des Anglais at Nice – the journey of 576 had taken just 9 hours (including stops totalling 37 minutes) = 64 mph.

Checks against kilometre posts showed the speedometer to be $2\frac{1}{2}\%$ fast at 100 mph and the distance recorder to exaggerate by $1\frac{1}{2}\%$. Overall

75 *The 1965 '600' Mercedes alongside the 1910 '45/50' at Cobham Park 1966*

petrol consumption from Boulogne to Nice (807 miles) was 13.7 mpg.

I could not have wished for a better car for this trip, 500 miles of which had been in miserable conditions, and the experience served to confirm my high regard for the car. That I am not alone in this is evidenced by the ever-lengthening delivery time and the high prices commanded in the used car market. (An interesting drive in the 'Corniche' version is described later in this book.)

Mercedes '600'

Within a week or two of driving the 'T' Series Bentley for the first time, I was lent a '600' Mercedes for the week-end and drove this remarkable motor car for 300 miles. It was not the stretched version, just the standard saloon about 19′ long! This car was so responsive to the controls that its immense size very quickly ceased to be a factor. The suspension was superb – especially the way in which the car could be swept through a series of fast left and right-hand bends without the front end varying perceptibly from the level. I found the changing of gears very smooth. The hydraulic operation of seats, windows and boot lid I thought quite perfect. The most astonishing feature to my mind was the very small turning circle – the same as a Morris 1100 I had at the time. The front seats were very comfortable, but I thought the rear seat surprisingly below the standard of the car, too hard, bench-like and without any lateral supports.

I reckoned the '600' would appeal to many discriminating drivers in this country if only the body were not so (difficult to find the right word) aggressive (?), Germanic (?), heavy-looking? Doubtless designed with Heads of State in mind and bought by some, the '600' has found much favour with 'pop stars' – I wonder why?

Mercedes 280 SE

Would I like to take delivery of a new car at

the factory and drive it to Athens? Would I?? I cancelled the Stuttgart-Athens leg of an air ticket taking me to the Far East on a business trip and took Con with me for the ride from Germany to Greece. We took a taxi from Stuttgart Airport to the Daimler-Benz factory at Sindelfingen 20 kms away arriving there in time for lunch on Friday, 9 March 1973. We were impressed, but not really surprised, to find how well D-B were geared to deal with customers collecting their new cars. Luggage whisked away by porters as if arriving at a large hotel; comfortable lounge and restaurant; efficient paper-work and expert instruction on the use and operation of the car.

The particular Mercedes I was to take over had been completed some weeks previously and had to be brought from a nearby storage warehouse. This took some time and it was 4.32 pm before we drove out of the factory gates with a full tank and a recommendation not to exceed 120 kph for the first 1,000 kms. The owner had specified one of the most sensible 'extras' I have ever heard of, described in the export price list as 'Break-in 300 km (including first service) 325 DM.' A Works driver had driven the new Merc. for a couple of hundred miles and any faults found had been rectified and necessary adjustments made.

From the start I realized that this Mercedes was a first-class automobile. (Undistinguished-looking, I thought, but functionally designed with the accent on practicality and safety.) Cruising on the autobahn at not more than 75 mph, we arrived at the Schweizerhof in Lucerne having done 225 miles in $4\frac{1}{4}$ hours.

I planned to reach Rome, 520 miles away, the following evening and left the hotel at 8.05 am to catch a train at about 9.30 am from Göschenen through the St Gotthard Tunnel. Lunch at the Melegnano Tollgate at the start of the Autostrada del Sole south of Milan took an hour. The drive down the A1 at the running-in speed of 75 mph – which I strictly observed – was a contrast to my previous blind down this road in the Ferrari, but pleasant enough. We left the autostrada on the outskirts of Rome at 6.30 pm, and it was not until two hours later that I pulled up outside the Hassler Hotel! All sense of direction leaves me as I enter the Italian capital and, by the time I was within striking distance of our destination, the system of one-way streets and the Saturday evening congestion nearly drove me round the bend – not always the right one, at that.

We were due to report in Brindisi at 3 pm the next day to catch the boat to Patras, so we made another early start, again leaving the hotel at 8.05 am. With more than 1,000 kms on the clock I was now able to increase our cruising speed and reckoned that if I put up my limit by 20 kph every 100 kms. I would be able to drive at maximum speed on the last stretch of autostrada before Bari. And so it turned out. I covered 10 kms at a sustained 200 kph before we stopped for lunch at the AGIP Motel at 12.30 pm.

We boarded the 'Mediterranean Sea' and sailed at 5 pm. No small car-ferry this ship, but a converted ocean-going liner – quite an odd sensation driving down ramps from one deck to another. We very much enjoyed the voyage and disembarked in Patras in warm sunshine the next morning. I completed (as I thought) the necessary formalities to regularize the importation of the Mercedes into Greece and drove the 135 miles to Athens, and 15 miles beyond to the Astir Palace Hotel at Vouliagmeni.

The petrol consumption increased with the speed. From Basle to Milan (235 miles) it was 21 mpg; from Milan to Rome ($353\frac{1}{2}$ miles) it was 20 mpg; and from Rome to Korinth (443 miles) 18 mpg. (The distance recorder was accurate against kilometre posts.)

Our short stay at Vouliagmeni was interrupted when I discovered that I had mistakenly 'entered' the car with the Customs as a temporary tourist. This necessitated a 300-mile round trip to Patras with a Greek-speaking companion and a tiresome afternoon traipsing from office to office collecting rubber stamps and signatures until everything was at last in order. Before we went our separate ways by air – Con to Benghazi to visit daughter Carol, son-in-law Roger, and their two children currently resident in Libya, and I to Bangkok – I put the car in store to await the arrival of the owner. I really enjoyed driving that car; everything about it was right and it performed impeccably. Not a thing had gone wrong; not a squeak or rattle had developed in the 1,200-mile trip. This is a tribute to the inspection at Sindelfingen and, I like to think, to that initial 300 km break-in by the manufacturer.

Jowett Javelins in Monte-Carlo Rallies

Although not exactly lent to me, I feel justified in regarding my participation in the Monte-Carlo Rallies of 1950 and 1952 in other people's cars as falling within the description of 'borrowed plumes'.

I considered myself honoured to be asked by the Jowett company to be the third man in one of the three Works Javelins entered in the 1950 Rally and eagerly seized the opportunity to compete in this great event.

The Monte-Carlo Rally had been revived the previous year after a 10-year gap bracketing World War II, and was passing through a transitional phase when amateur owner-drivers could still take part with a good chance of doing well, manufacturers had not yet really got into the act with professional drivers, expensive pre-rally reconnaisance and immense support teams. Some manufacturers, realizing the publicity value of success in International Rallies, were assisting private owners with the preparations of their cars and others were participating with works-prepared cars, but with one or two possible exceptions their drivers took part on an 'expenses only' basis.

I travelled by train to Bradford in early January to meet those responsible for entering and preparing the cars and the other team drivers. 'My' car was in charge of Horace Grimley, a member of the factory staff, the other co-driver being Reg Phillips, a well-known trials driver. One of the other Javelins was manned by seasoned competitor John Eason Gibson, and Reggie Minchin who was responsible for supervising the operations of the Metropolitan Police Motor Driving School at Hendon. The third Jowett in the team was that of Tommy Wise and Mike Wilson.

In the event, that year's Rally turned out to be one of the hardest since the series started in 1911. Out of 283 starters, 101 failed to reach Monte-Carlo at all. Of those that arrived in the Principality, 62 were outside the time limit and only 5 cars completed the course without losing any marks for lateness. The reason for this thinning out of the ranks was, of course, the weather.

We started from Glasgow at tea time on 22 January in company with 64 others, facing 2,000 miles of night and day motoring to the Côte d'Azur to be covered at 31 mph plus – including all stops. Patches of ice on high ground in Scotland and the North of England presented no difficulties and it was a cheerful boat load of competitors which left Folkestone the following morning for Boulogne. In Northern France, Luxembourg and Holland the roads were dry – fortunately so as the temperature had been below freezing all the way from Glasgow. We felt it couldn't last and at Controls we heard rumours of snow in Central France. Sure enough by the time we reached Nevers snow was falling, slowly and relentlessly, as if it was in no hurry and would go on for ever.

By the time we passed through Lyon the snow was lying 6″ deep and still falling. Such were the delays incurred by competitors that only six of the Glasgow starters checked in here on time.

I can't remember how late we were, but the maximum lateness allowance of 3 hours at the finish was being whittled away. Between Valence and Digne conditions remained the same, but seemed somewhat less daunting in daylight.

76 *The Jowett Javelin team, from left to right, John Eason Gibson, Reggie Minchin, Horace Grimley, Reg Phillips, the author, (?), Tommy Wise and Mike Wilson*

77 *Bob Nelson-Harris and the author in a Jowett Javelin arriving at the Liège control during the 1952 Monte-Carlo Rally*

The Jowett Javelin flew along, Horace Grimley handling it in masterly fashion. The speed at which he went up and down the slippery mountain roads was really something. Reg Phillips, no doubt accustomed in trials to his car pointing only vaguely in the direction of travel, drove with commendable speed. Frankly, I was pretty scared at times and I fear that my co-drivers must have been irked by the pace which I deemed to be my fastest in the icy conditions when entrusted with the wheel.

Despite the most valiant efforts – especially on the part of Horace – we fell further and further behind our scheduled time. We arrived in a rainy Monte-Carlo without mishap and were placed 96th. Tommy Wise and Mike Wilson finished 44th. The Eason Gibson car had gone off the road in an uncontrollable slide when cruising at about 50 mph where the average motorist without the competitive urge would be driving at 10 mph. Later the windscreen wipers ceased working in most trying conditions, all of which resulted in his Javelin reaching the Finish Control one minute after it had closed!

The Rally was won by the Frenchmen Becquart and Secret in a 1939 3½-litre 'Paris-Nice' Hotchkiss, followed by Gatsonides' Humber Snipe and three Simcas. (It says a lot for the quality of the Hotchkiss car, for this make had won the Rally six times in the 1930s.)

The Rally had proved to be a severe endurance test for crews and, as a contemporary motoring journalist put it: '. . . a searching eliminator of inefficient cars.' The Jowetts gave us a fast, safe and comfortable journey and we were impressed by their performance. It was a very tired and worn crew which left the Javelin in the parc fermé and made for the hotel.

When I telephoned Con before falling into bed for a long sleep to tell her of our safe arrival, she told me that a friend of ours had been 'successfully delivered of a son.' Next morning I sent the joyful mother a telegram which tells its own story; it read: 'Congratulations, I nearly had a baby, too.'

Two years later a private owner of a Jowett Javelin, Bob Nelson-Harris, invited me to join him as co-driver in the 1952 Monte. This time there would be only two drivers. Again we chose Glasgow as our starting point and this year, too, turned out to be one of the most gruelling 'Montes' on record. It will live in our minds as Sydney Allard's year, for he won the Rally in a car of his own construction – a Type P Allard Saloon – being the first Englishman to do so since Donald Healey won in 1931.

The weather and road conditions presented no problems this side of the Channel and all was going well on the other side until we approached Bourges where it was snowing hard. The road from Le Puy down through the Rhône Valley to Valence was very bad. The N7 was narrowed by deep snow, and cars were involved in crashes and ditchings; many were fitting chains; others pushing in the hope that wheels would eventually secure a grip on icy gradients. Only 17 cars were on time at Valence. Sydney Allard, with co-drivers Guy Warburton and Tom Lush, was among them, but not so Mrs Allard and her two sisters, driving in a similar car. They had skidded off the road in the Rhône Valley and hit a kilometre stone. Sydney's Rally Number was fifteen higher than his wife's which meant that the ladies left each Time Control a quarter-of-an-hour ahead of Sydney. Going like the clappers on the black ice, Sydney recognized his spouse's car stationary on the snow-covered verge. He slowed down, wound down his window and yelled, 'You all right?' Back came the wifely reply, 'No.' Quick as a flash: 'Pity,' retorted Sydney, winding up the window and accelerating away without actually coming to a stop. Of such determination and dedication to the task in hand are Rally winners made!

The atrocious conditions persisted in the mountains to the East of the Rhône. One stretch of road was a shambles. Crews were taking hours to get out of ditches; others were stuck on hills and many were baulked by fellow competitors unable to get going. Ken Wharton's Ford went straight on at a corner, through a gap in a wall and dropped into a ravine, landing on top of a crashed Citroën, which was itself on top of another car.

And then it happened to us. Bob was driving at a commendable speed on the frozen snow when the car side-slipped into an invisible snow-filled ditch on a left-hand hairpin bend and bumped into a wall. It was beyond our human strength and other aids to get the Javelin back on to the road, so I trudged through the night in knee-deep snow to rouse a farmer, who unprotestingly (and suitably rewarded) brought a pair of oxen to the scene. The beasts were hooked up to the car and, on the command of their master, leaned forward and loped through the deep snow recovering the Jowett with no more effort than drawing a cork out of a bottle. Throughout the rescue operation competing cars were speeding past in the dark, our presence adding to the hazards of the slippery road, and our own situation being more than somewhat dangerous. Inspection revealed that the front suspension and steering had been bent and further motoring at competitive speeds was out of the question. We drove slowly to the next town, being at pains not to impede more fortunate competitors and, after effecting repairs, continued our journey to arrive in Monte-Carlo too late to rank as a finisher.

It was disappointing not to be among the finishers, but no disgrace, for more than half the 328 starters met the same fate, and only 15 reached Monte-Carlo without penalty.

The highest placed 50 cars on the road section were required to compete a couple of days later in a Regularity Test at 50 mph round a 50-mile mountain circuit inland from Monte-Carlo. Either the route or the speed – I forget which – was changed and I spent the 'rest' day before the Test reworking all Sydney's pace notes. The British contingent was overjoyed when he drove the Allard into the Palace square to receive the winner's laurels from Prince Rainier.

An incident on the non-competitive run home stays in my memory. About 150 miles south of Paris we took pity on a lonely figure thumbing a lift on a deserted stretch of road in very heavy rain. We sat him between us on the bench-type front seat, the rear compartment being 'loaded to the gunwhales', and at once regretted it, for we were enveloped in an aroma of garlic which persisted and increased all the way to Paris. I detest the smell of garlic and my discomfiture in the coude à coude accommodation of the Javelin can scarcely be imagined.

My Monte-Carlo Rally experiences in the Jowett Javelins gave me a healthy respect for these great little cars. They were easy to drive, willing performers and the road-holding qualities had to be experienced to be believed. What a pity that production ceased two years later.

Franglais

In the early 1950's the English translations issued by the Automobile Club de l'Ouest relating to the organization of the Le Mans 24-Hour Race left much to be desired, as witness the following privilege car park windscreen sticker –

> Cette carte de garage n'est valable que si elle est entièrement collée sur le pare-brise.
>
> Elle ne peut etre vendue sous peine de retrait immédiat et de poursuites judiciaires.
>
> For to be valid in the garage, this cart-board ought to be entirely glued on the windscreen. It cannot be selled under punishment of immediate shrinking and judicial pursuits.

Motoring for motoring's sake

For me motoring is an end in itself. In no way is this more clearly demonstrated than by the pleasure I derive from driving a good car a long distance, preferably alone, and with as few stops as possible.

As I have often said to incredulous friends, if someone were to offer me an expenses-paid choice of either a return air ticket to Rome with first-class accommodation there for a week, or a good car to drive there, twice round the Colosseum and straight back, I would not hesitate to choose the latter. I have been fortunate in being able to indulge myself in this regard in a variety of cars, but the first really long non-stop journey I did – 24 years ago – was in the capacity of a navigator/timekeeper – not as a driver at all – and, incidentally, it was my first experience of Veteran car motoring.

Veteran venture

The hero of this tale of adventure was a 1904 Darracq belonging to my friend, Bob Gregory. It was known as the 'Flying Fifteen' and had a 3-litre 4-cylinder engine, and carried a body consisting of two armchair bucket seats and a locker-cum-dickey behind.

The Idea

Most motorists at some time or other, when doing a long journey on main roads at a fairly high speed, have been surprised to find that they are overtaking heavy lorries which they have already passed earlier in the day. On such occasions it is quickly realized that one has stopped for a meal or for some other reason, whereas the lorry has just pressed on. It is very often the case that the commercial vehicle travelling at an average speed of 20–25 mph and rarely, if ever, exceeding 40 mph covers long distances in the same time as a car which has nullified its bursts of high speed by frequent stops en route.

It was this realization that led Bob Gregory to liken his Darracq to a commercial vehicle in this respect. He thought that the Darracq driven consistently with a minimum number of stops of the shortest possible duration would cover great distances in a comparatively short time. His theory was put to the test when he started from Land's End to the Veteran Car Club's Eastern Rally at Norwich early in 1949. On this occasion the Darracq covered 405 miles in 16 hours, averaging 25 mph, including stops, with a running average speed of 32.7 mph.

The Land's End run having been accomplished, it followed that John o' Groats should be the next extremity to receive attention. Bob declared this remote spot to be his starting-point for the VCC of Great Britain Northern Rally at Southport, and took the opportunity to make a non-stop run beforehand from Brighton to John o'Groats.

The Preparation

In preparation for the long run Bob decarbonized the engine and gave the Darracq a thorough going-over.

Safety considerations on a run of this nature suggested that something more than the ordinary oil and acetylene lighting should be provided. One electric headlamp, two side lights and a tail light were, therefore, fitted and a fully charged 12-volt 75 amp hour accumulator was slung alongside the prop-shaft. An additional 10-gallon petrol tank of contemporary design was fitted at the rear of the chassis, thus giving a total fuel-carrying capacity of 20 gallons. The relatively low position of this tank necessitated the use of pressure feed. An ordinary foot-pump was fitted on the floorboards – in a position only too convenient for the passenger's right foot.

In accordance with the traditional way of things, Bob completed the reassembly of the car only a few hours before the planned time of departure from Brighton, 70 miles away. After a rapid two mile test run, during which no trouble was experienced, the car was loaded and left for the South Coast.

Brighton to John o'Groats was a distance of 760 miles and to accomplish the journey in 24 hours entailed an average speed of 31.67 mph, including stops, no mean demand to make upon a 45-year-old motorcar. The selected route was the main road from Brighton to London and thence the Great North Road to Scotch Corner; westwards to Carlisle, then via Lanark, Stirling, Perth, Inverness and Bonar Bridge.

We decided not to aim at maintaining a steady average speed throughout, but to vary the planned average according to the terrain being crossed. Three separate hours, the first including Beattock Summit, the second Killiecrankie and Drumochter and the third Berriedale, were plotted at 25 mph each. The greater part of the run through England was planned at 33 mph. Most of Scotland was planned at 32 mph. Optimists that we were, the above hourly mileages were to include stops for petrol, food and other essentials. In other words, we would have to improve upon our self-imposed schedule in order to stop at all! Theoretically we would be forced to stop only once for refuelling but, as will be seen, it did not work out like that.

For the run from John o'Groats to Southport we planned to retrace our route as far as Penrith and then to proceed via Lancaster and Preston, a total distance of 522 miles, which we hoped to cover in little over 17 hours, including stops.

The Journey North

We arrived in Brighton about 10 pm, and were made welcome at the Brighton and Hove Motor Club. As the midnight hour struck we left the Palace Pier for points north.

A drizzle commenced and lasted nearly all the way to London. We made good time and arrived at Hyde Park Corner 1 min early at 1.34 am, where the driver's long-suffering wife waited to pass us two Thermos flasks of tea, two ditto of soup and two biscuit tins full of good things to eat. Ten minutes later we left with 9 mins to catch up. We did not stop again until four hours had passed, and the petrol tanks were switched over. We next stopped at 8 am to replenish the radiator (which had mysteriously started boiling) from a steam-roller crew at the roadside. We had covered 270 miles in the first 8 hours (one-third of our allotted span) and stops included in that time totalled 22 mins. We were, in fact, 7 mins ahead of schedule in spite of the stops.

We could not know that the radiator was to be a constant source of trouble and delay for many miles. It was made up from horizontal tubes, and the apertures for the passage of water were very small. Some scale had come loose, which was sufficient to prevent adequate circulation, and boiling resulted.

We pressed on, and in half an hour found a level-crossing at Leeming Bar closed in our path, so we pulled into a conveniently situated petrol station, topped up both tanks, and took on oil and water.

We took the opportunity of eating a sandwich or two and drinking a cup of tea. In fact, we established a drill which was followed throughout. When we stopped for petrol, the driver attended to the replenishment of the car, what time I dispensed soup or tea from flasks and produced food from our store. When we moved off both of us were still munching sandwiches. While driving we found chocolate a very satisfactory food and consumed many weeks' ration in as many hours.

The radiator soon boiled again and we stopped at a garage, whipped off the bottom hose and ran water from the mains in at the bottom of the radiator allowing it to flood out of the filler. This seemed to clear the stoppage, at least temporarily, and on we went. This porcedure was repeated a number of times in the course of the next 70 miles, and on each occasion took about 15 mins. One mile south of the Border the nuts of the prop-shaft were tightened and the radiator drill was carried out. We had aimed to reach the Border (367 miles) in 11 hours, but had actually taken 12 hours 36 mins.

After another 20 miles the radiator drill was repeated, as it proved, for the last time.

We then covered over 100 miles without any boiling and stopped only twice (once to change over petrol tanks and once to replace a plug lead) before reaching Perth (504 miles) at 17 hours 13 mins. We spent 25 mins here taking on petrol and generally preparing for the night section. We left Perth two hours late, but still full of optimism now that the radiator seemed to be behaving.

Less than 20 miles after Perth the pot-joint cover – improvised to keep out dirt – became excessively noisy and it took over half an hour to remove it. At Aviemore (588 miles) 20 hours 42 mins had passed and we were 2 hours 17 mins late. It was now dark and it was clear that we could not cover the remaining 150 miles within the desired 24 hours. We had been 'in the saddle' for a long time and succumbed to the temptation of hot soup and tea, the only occasion on this run on which we stopped specially for sustenance.

Over the Top

After half an hour we went on for another 50 miles when tiredness necessitated a 5-min stop for 40 winks just outside Maryburgh. Then on to Dingwall where we (that is, I) made the only navigational error on the trip; I missed the right-hand fork for Tain, and we reached Strathpeffer before realizing we were on the wrong road. We returned to Dingwall (in silence, but without having words!) and left by the correct road.

Midnight found us at Evanton, 648 miles from our starting point – and we stopped to celebrate the failure of our plan; the hooter, a hand klaxon, was given a wind, this being the only time it was used during the run. We were 112 miles short of our destination, but our stops had accounted for 4 hours 37 mins, of which two hours were directly attributable to the radiator trouble.

We were both admittedly tired by this time and the weather had deteriorated to rain and wind. It was on this stretch over the Struie that the only incident of the trip occurred. We were descending a steep hill and negotiating a real hairpin at slow speed with brakes hard on and the wheels on full lock. The Darracq decided that it was just a bit too much and gracefully turned right about and stopped in the middle of the road facing the wrong way.

Fatigue, filthy weather and wet roads considerably reduced our speed. Our object now was just to reach John o'Groats. This we did as dawn was breaking at seven minutes to six. (The 17 miles from Wick seemed like 70!) We had taken 29 hours 53 mins to cover the 760 miles, an overall average of slightly over 25 mph. Actual running time was 24 hours 21 mins, which is a running average of 31.2 mph, and during the first 12 consecutive hours' running time we had averaged over 35 mph, covering 424 miles.

We knocked up the proprietor of the John o'Groats House Hotel who had just retired, having waited up for us all night. From the moment we arrived to the minute we left Alastair MacKenzie and family went out of their way to be helpful and took a great interest in our doings. Our dripping clothes were dried and we fell into bed and were asleep at once.

We were up at noon, having had five hours sleep, and after lunch set to work on the car. Bob removed the prop-shaft and Alistair MacKenzie took me into Wick, where a keen garage mechanic set about making new pins and bushes at 4.15 pm. At 10.30 pm we set off to return to John o'Groats, complete with the new bits and the mechanic, who realized that he might never see another 45-year-old car and was intent not to miss this opportunity. During our absence Bob had removed the radiator and turned it upside down, flushed it thoroughly with a hose and refitted it.

It was 1 am before the prop-shaft was back and, as we planned a 6 am start for Southport, we went to bed without a trial run.

The Journey South

Our arrival and stay at John o'Groats had coincided with the worst spell of weather they had experienced for many a day, but this day dawned bright and sunny.

The Darracq started first pull up, and having loaded our replenished Thermos flasks and food containers we pointed the radiator southwards. We started at 6.45 am, and it says a lot for the interest and enthusiasm of the proprietor and guests of the John o'Groats House Hotel that they all turned out in their night attire to bid us 'Bon Voyage'.

We were pleased to be motoring along the east coast of Scotland in brilliant sunshine after the miserable trip in the opposite direction. After 82 miles, covered in 2 hrs 34 mins, we stopped to examine and oil the repaired universal joints, and drove on again for more than 100 miles before stopping for petrol and food, the latter for the first time at the civilized hour of 1 pm!

We then covered the longest non-stop distance of the whole trip, 191 miles in 5 hrs 50 mins, and this stop was necessitated because we could not get at the drum of oil without getting out of the car. Oddly enough, this stop, too, coincided with the normal mealtime of 7 pm, and we partook of refreshment with some relish. The border was crossed before dusk, the 407 miles being covered in 13 hrs 33 mins, including stops totalling exactly one hour – an overall average of 30 mph and a running average of 32.43 mph.

In Carlisle we refuelled and had a snack, setting off in darkness after 20 mins on the last lap of 105 miles to Southport – a piffling distance to us at the time. This we accomplished without stop, and the Darracq made light work of the well-known Shap Pass, needing second gear for 100 yds only, the rest being done in top gear. The weather deteriorated rapidly in Lancashire and we entered Southport in a howling gale and driving rain soon after midnight. Reading a street plan in very trying circumstances and groping for the Palace Hotel, we were hailed by two chaps who appeared from nowhere in dripping raincoats. They proved to be keen types of the local Press, who had waited up to get a story from the intrepid motorists from John o' Groats.

We stopped outside the Palace Hotel (closely followed by another newshound in a taxi) after 17 hrs 48 mins, 37 mins behind our optimistic schedule. Our four stops – many would shudder at so few in nearly 18 hours' modern luxury motoring – had taken up 1 hr 25 mins. Our overall average for the 522 miles was just under 30 mph, and we had maintained a running average speed of nearly 32. The run had been absolutely trouble-free by any standard, and the car had responded to every demand made upon it. It was after 1 am on Saturday by the time our belongings had been unloaded and the Darracq garaged, and as we had slept only nine hours since early Tuesday morning we were asleep as soon as our heads touched the pillows.

Next morning – not so early by recent standards – we were polishing up the Darracq's brassware in time for the midday parade. On the way to the Rally Point we had to divert to the local goods station to get a ticket from the weighbridge: 1 ton 1 cwt. In the afternoon the Darracq took part in the Speed Trials and covered a standing quarter-mile in 32.3 secs, winning its class. It was also a member of the winning Relay Race team.

Next day we left Southport for Slough, intending to keep a lunch date in Stoke on the way. The journey was uneventful and the distance of 225 miles was covered in a running time of 7 hrs 19 mins – 30 mph; rather slower this section, as I was permitted to drive three-quarters of the way.

So ended 1,600 miles of motoring in five days, and the bonnet had not been opened since leaving John o'Groats, now some 770 miles behind!

Retrospect

Bob and I derive much pleasure from recalling the reception given to the équipe throughout the journey, and the many incidents which come to mind will always be happy memories.

North of the Clyde most people had apparently never seen a veteran car at all. A flute player in Perth dropped his instrument from his mouth in the middle of a note, such was his astonishment. Another amusing incident was the arrival of the Darracq in the square of a Midlands town inadvertently at the head of a Battle of Britain procession, band and all, to the surprise of the waiting dignitaries.

With rare exceptions, the police and long-distance transport drivers were very co-operative and very interested in the Darracq. The look on the faces of the habitués leaving a Highland hostelry at closing time as the Darracq passed had to be seen to be believed. The Darracq was streaking through the village and must have been a truly ghostly sight with the driver protecting his face from the driving rain with a handkerchief worn highwayman fashion.

The Darracq had all the appeal of a Veteran combined with a performance not unworthy of a modern car of the time. We found that we could pass loaded motor coaches uphill, but that they could just 'do' us downhill. We passed a bus load of dockers returning home to Glasgow much to the delight of the occupants, but apparently the driver was a bit narked. The bus was definitely 'Vintage', and eventually came bucketing past at about 55 mph and really looked quite frightening. Few cars passed us, and we passed countless family cars, much to the astonishment of the drivers, most of whom hadn't been looking in their mirrors.

Several drivers of fastish cars raised their hats to us as they passed, and numberless drivers nearly ran out of road looking at the strange sight of a 45-year-old car getting along at no mean lick. Even Chris Jennings, the Editor of 'The Motor', who passed us in a 1950 Minx, found it difficult to believe his eyes and took a wrong turning in consequence!

Driving the Darracq called for no great skill, but the steering was very (repeat very) heavy. There must have been something wrong with the geometry as, although there was no difficulty on straight roads or curves, the turning of a corner or negotiating a hairpin called for herculean strength with which, fortunately, the owner is blessed.

Whilst not claiming to have done anything outstanding, it was a source of satisfaction to have completed a tour at which many would have boggled given a current model, and at a speed which would not have disgraced such a car. We had proved the 'press-on' theory and at no time exceeded 45 mph.

Mediterranean Weekend

John o'Groats having been visited in 'The Darracq', our thoughts turned across the water for a possible future foray, but the costliness of a Continental venture both in time and money deterred us from pursuing this idea. Imagine, therefore, the delight with which we received a suggestion from Auto-cheques early in 1950 that we should make a rapid trip to the South of France and back to publicize the cross-channel car-ferry operated by Silver City Airways and the hotel facilities provided by the former company.

The engine of the Darracq had not been touched since the John o'Groats run and it was decided to decarbonize it. A visit was made to Dunlops to fit a new set of tyres and tubes (815 × 105); what a blessing it is to veteran car enthusiasts that this concern continues to manufacture obsolete sizes. The improvised foot-pump hitherto used to pressure feed the fuel was replaced by a large capacity hand-pump, and Gallays made a replica of the original midships tank which had become work-hardened and was splitting.

Third Party insurance was effected for a modest premium and much work was put into

78 *The Darracq boarding the Bristol Freighter at Lympne*

79 *A routine refuelling stop for the Darracq*

the compilation of a road-book and a timetable based on an overall average of 45 kph. At the last minute it was decided by the sponsors that an A 70 Austin should accompany us and, although we saw little of this car for hours at a stretch due to the more normal feeding habits of its occupants it always turned up in a most friendly fashion.

We left the West End of London at 9.45 am on Friday, April 14 with the A 70, and a television cameraman in a Vanguard. A police motor-cyclist accompanied us to the outskirts of the Metropolis and we reached Lympne (66 miles) in 2 hours 22 minutes.

After a Press lunch the cars were loaded on to Bristol Freighters, the Darracq looking a little incongruous against this modern background. Twenty-five minutes later the Darracq was being filled with 'super-carburant' at Le Touquet by Shell, who went to a deal of trouble to provide refuelling facilities at prearranged points along the route, and at 4.30 pm we left for Nice.

We planned to stop only for the needs of the car and to feed while on the move or during refuelling stops. To contemplate thus crossing the 750 miles of France and passing by such gastronomic haunts as the Hôtel de la Poste at Saulieu and the Compagnons de Jehu near Mâcon will seem to many people to border on sacrilege if not insanity. Fortunately Bob Gregory and I find little difficulty in subordinating human demands to the job in hand and a gallon of hot soup in Thermos flasks, some sandwiches and a couple of pounds of chocolate suffice to keep us going for a day or two.

Abbeville (149.5 kms) was reached in 3 hours, but soon afterwards we had to stop to replace a punctured inner tube, a task which took 56 minutes. This was the only tyre trouble experienced. We reached Paris after 5½ hours on the road, including the stop, and called at the main French Austin Agency. This stop occupied 45 minutes and we proceeded down the Champs Elysées at 10.45 pm for Essonnes which was to be our first 'pit stop'. Fuel and oil tanks were

80 *The Darracq on the Promenade des Anglais, Nice*
81 *The author's turn to crank the Darracq*

replenished and we sped into the night. Our single white headlight caused approaching indigenous drivers to direct upon us a veritable Christmas tree of jaundiced gloom, but only one so far forgot himself as to drive across the road straight at us. Several stops were made during the night to change drivers and to grease the squeaking prop-shaft universal joint, and 12 hours after leaving Le Touquet found us at Avallon (458 kms).

Tanks were topped up at Villefranche-sur-Saône and Lyon was entered at 1 pm on Saturday. Another refuelling stop at Montélimar and at 4.30 pm, 24 hours after the start, we were 25 kms short of Aix-en-Provence. We passed through Fréjus at 7.30 pm, took the less hilly coastal road through St. Raphaël to Cannes and pulled up in the drive of the Continental Hôtel at Nice at 9.30 pm, exactly 29 hours after leaving Le Touquet, having maintained an average speed of 41.47 kph (25.8 mph) over the total distance of 1,202.7 kms (748 miles). Stops on the road had totalled 5 hours 20 minutes and the running time of 23 hours 40 minutes showed an average speed of 50.8 kph (31.6 mph). The greatest distance covered in any one hour was 60 kms ($37\frac{1}{2}$ miles).

Into Italy

The next day, having serviced the Darracq, we decided to skip lunch and drive along the coast into Italy to see the San Remo Grand Prix. Little did we know that the winner, a virtually unknown South American, was to become a future World Champion and his name a household word – Fangio! On our return into France, we were talked into starting the return trip from Monte-Carlo instead of Nice and accordingly left the car there overnight.

Early on Monday morning we returned to Monte-Carlo, collected the Darracq and, followed by greetings and good wishes from M. Anthony Noghes and his colleagues on the

Monte-Carlo Rally Organizing Committee, we were officially(!) started on the homeward run at 10.30 am.

On reaching Cannes we decided to go 'over the top' to Fréjus. The Darracq climbed gallantly although the radiator boiled for a short time. After 3 hours 20 minutes on the road the steering-column gear lever broke (came 'orf in me 'and, guv'nor!) and things looked somewhat difficult. However a 'Mole' wrench from the tool-kit was locked on to the remaining stub and, despite the loss of locating notches, we drove home changing gears with the wrench which remained in position throughout. We refuelled at Montélimar at 7 pm and again at Villefranche-sur-Saône after just 12 hours on the road (548 kms).

The night was cold. Driving rain set in at Saulieu and continued for the remaining 15 hours of the trip. It was most unpleasant and even caused us to erect the hood – an unprecedented proceeding.

At 8.30 am on Tuesday (22 hours after leaving Monte-Carlo) we reached Essonnes and refuelled, having covered the 960 kms at an average speed of 44 kph (27½ mph) including all stops. After a welcome cup of tea we proceeded into Paris and crossed the Place de la Concorde 23 hours 23 minutes after leaving Monte-Carlo.

Exercising Discretion

The Darracq was going like a bomb and we were surprised to hear the first signs of expensive noises in the engine about 80 miles from Le Touquet. Despite our disappointment we decided that it would be foolish to risk the possible breakage of irreplaceable parts for the sake of completing the last hop under its own power. Reluctantly, a tow-rope was attached and the journey that followed was the least pleasant part of the whole outing. The water (etc!) thrown up into our faces by the back wheels of the towing A 70, added to the 'stair-rod' rain, was very trying. (It was gratifying to find when the engine was dismantled on its arrival home

82 *The Darracq being started from Monte-Carlo for home by the Automobile Club de Monaco*

83 *Bob Gregory out and under the Darracq*

that the noise was caused by nothing more serious than a sheared water-pump drive.) The petrol consumption over the whole trip was 25/26 mpg.

It is difficult to do justice in words to the effect of the Darracq's passage upon French and Italian villagers and motorists of all nations. Everywhere we left behind a trail of shaken characters whose initial incredulity was frozen into astonishment at the sight of the receding 'GB' plate.

We had a wonderful time and one thing is certain: we carved up another notch in the annals of the 'mad dog the Englishman' and caused merriment among thousands of Frenchmen during five days of real motoring.

Doing it the Hard Way – the Easy Way

Two years were to elapse before I had another opportunity to dash across France again and this time my conveyance could hardly be more of a contrast to the stark reality of the Darracq.

An opportunity arose to 'deliver' a Mk VI Bentley to the South of France and I did not hesitate to seize the chance of achieving yet one more of my ambitions to drive solo and virtually non-stop from the English Channel to the Mediterranean.

The car was a 1951 Standard Steel Saloon with the 4½-litre engine and at 9,500 miles the original tyres showed no appreciable signs of wear.

I left the West End of London after a day at the office on Friday, 7 April 1952 with luggage equivalent to two adult passengers, stopped off at home for a meal, packed an overnight bag and drove to Southampton in heavy rain. I filled the petrol tank 'right up the spout' just outside the dock gates and waited to see the car safely loaded in the forward hold of the ss 'Normannia' making its second trip. The accommodation was well-appointed and very comfortable by the standards of the time, and its stabilizers were a welcome feature.

It was 8.30 am when I left the Customs Shed at Le Havre and pointed the bonnet to the South. The roads were wet enough to be slippery, but it was not raining, and these conditions existed for the first 100 miles.

Distances quoted in this report are based on the car's odometer, which recorded 707 miles on arrival at Cannes. The distances over the same route as given by the Guide Michelin, the RAC, and the AA are 706, 713 and 715½ miles respectively. It may be assumed, therefore, that the instrument reading is near enough for all practical purposes.

The accompanying table shows exactly how I progressed upon my way. I drove more or less as fast as road conditions permitted, but rarely exceeded 80 mph. I was interested to see whether or not an average speed of 50 mph could be maintained without overdoing it. It was one thing to cover 50 miles in an hour or even 100 miles in two hours, both of which I had done on several occasions in England, but quite a different thing covering ground at such a pace for hour after hour. It is surprising what a great effect a hold-up of short duration can have upon one's average speed.

A Speed Trap

I was stopped twice by police who examined the car – for contraband or Communists or something – and sent me on my way without question. When I was signalled to a stop for the third time I was beginning to find the procedure monotonous, but soon perceived that this was a stop of a different sort for the car following me was waved on to continue its journey. A policeman, one of three, then informed me that I had averaged 68 kph through the last village. I did not dispute it, deeming apology and promised observance of the 60 kph limit in future to be the politic course but I wondered how, if indeed at all, one could refute such an allegation. It seemed that I had been timed through a 'village' and my time and description had been radioed to a wireless car

parked at the roadside some distance farther on.

The first refuelling stop was at Avallon with 271 miles covered in 5 hours 20 minutes. It took 75.4 litres of fuel to replace that used since Southampton, indicating a consumption of 17.05 mpg. I drank a Coca-Cola, purchased two ham rolls and was on my way in ten minutes, resolved not to stop again until the flashing fuel indicator demanded attention. After the ham rolls, I reached into the dashboard pocket to make a start upon my supply of chocolate to discover only an empty paper bag – all the chocolate had been stolen on the boat.

The Need for Speed

Valence was reached 10 hours after leaving Le Havre, which meant that I had done 485½ miles in that time including the single 10-minute stop. It was dusk and I decided to combine replenishments of car and self. I entered the Hôtel de l'Europe and addressed the manager whom I had met previously in less happy circumstances when in – or rather out of – the Monte-Carlo Rally. I said that I realized that wining and dining in France was a pastime, an art, a means of passing an evening and altogether a leisurely occupation, but please could he whip up a quick omelette for me and call an hotel in Cannes to reserve a room while I went to fill up with petrol. He really did appreciate that hurry was the order of the day (the first time that I had ever succeeded in getting this point across in France) and when I returned from putting in 55 litres of fuel and 2 quarts of oil (taken out from England) the repast was ready and the reservation made. I went off again into the dark in exactly half-an-hour. The petrol consumption for the 204½ miles from Avallon to Valence worked out at 16.90 mpg.

The darkness and the tortuous nature of the road towards the end of the journey reduced the average speed. However, no further stop was made until I pulled up at the Carlton in Cannes 20 minutes after midnight. Seven hundred and seven miles had passed beneath the Bentley wheels in 10 minutes under 16 hours, with but two short stops totalling 40 minutes.

The Bentley was whisked away to be washed, and it is characteristic of this car that it was apparently in exactly the same state of mechanical efficiency as at the beginning of the trip; no rattles, squeaks, vibrations or other unpleasantnesses had developed on the way. I was tired – or rather sleepy – but not fatigued or worn out. The journey had been comfortable and I had not consciously changed my driving position to combat fatigue or cramp. Replenishment of the petrol tank next day showed that the consumption for the last section of the journey had been 17.54 mpg. The overall petrol consumption for the journey of over 700 miles reasonably rapid motoring had been 17.3 mpg.

Quicker by Road

Inevitably my mind went back to the days of 'beating the Blue Train'. The fastest train across France occupied 17 hours 39 minutes in its journey from Calais to Cannes, over 1¾ hours more than my time from Le Havre.

The journey served to confirm my opinion of the Bentley Mk VI. It was (and still is) an ideal method of getting from A to B in speed, safety and comfort and the greater the distance between A and B the more apparent and appreciated those qualities become.

Progress Tabulated

	Hrs	*Mins*	*Hrs*	*Mins*	*Miles*		*Miles in the Hour*	*Running Average Speed*
Le Havre (8.30 am) ..	0	0						
			—	30	21			42
			1	—	49	28	49	49
Rouen	1	10			55			
(Delay for obstruction = 5 mins)								
			1	30	67	18	46	45
			2	—	91	24	42	$45\frac{1}{2}$
	2	10			100			
			2	30	117	26	50	46.8
Versailles	2	45			130			
Just before Les Belles			3	—	139	22	48	46.6
Epines			3	30	165	26	48	47.1
Fontainebleau	3	40						
			4	—	194	29	55	48.5
(Champigny – police radio speed trap)			4	30	$224\frac{1}{2}$	$30\frac{1}{2}$	$59\frac{1}{2}$	49.9
			5	—	254	$29\frac{1}{2}$	60	50.8
Avallon	5	20			271			
(Stopped 10 mins for 75.4 litres of Super at 64.96 frs per litre = 4,900 frs, and ham rolls)								
Restarted	5	30	5	30	271	17	$46\frac{1}{2}$	49.3
Saulieu	6	—	6	—	$295\frac{1}{2}$	$24\frac{1}{2}$	$41\frac{1}{2}$	49.25
			6	30	322	$26\frac{1}{2}$	51	49.5
Chalons	7	—	7	—	346	24	$50\frac{1}{2}$	49.4
			7	30	373	27	51	49.7
Macon	7	40			381			
			8	—	399	26	53	49.9
Lyon			8	30	422	23	49	49.6
(Lot of traffic)								
Vienne	9	—	9	—	441	19	42	49.0
			9	30	466	25	44	49.0
Valence	10	—	10	—	$485\frac{1}{2}$	$19\frac{1}{2}$	$44\frac{1}{2}$	48.5
(Stopped $\frac{1}{2}$ hour (6.30 pm to 7.00 pm) for meal and 55 litres of ANTAR Super at 63.80 frs per litre = 3,511 frs. Put in $\frac{1}{2}$ gall Castrol XL.)								
Restarted	10	30	10	30	$485\frac{1}{2}$	—	$19\frac{1}{2}$	46.2
(Dark – driving with lights)								
			11	—	503	$17\frac{1}{2}$	$17\frac{1}{2}$	
			11	30	$525\frac{1}{2}$	$22\frac{1}{2}$	40	45.7
Orange	12	00	12	—	546	$20\frac{1}{2}$	43	45.5
Avignon	12	25	12	25	562			
			12	30	567	21	$40\frac{1}{2}$	45.4
			13	—	587	20	41	45.2

	Hrs	Mins	Hrs	Mins	Miles		Miles in the Hour	Running Average Speed
Aix-en-Provence	13	30	13	30	611	24	44	45.2
			14	—	632	21	45	45.1
			14	30	655	23	44	45.2
			15	—	678	23	46	45.2
Fréjus	15	10	15	10	684½			
			15	30	695	17	40	44.8
Cannes 12.20 am . .	15	50	15	50	707			44.7

EXCLUDING STOPS – 15 hrs 10 mins. 707 miles = 46.6 mph.
PETROL – 271 + 2 miles = 75.4 litres = 16.6 galls = 17.05 mpg
204½ miles = 55.0 litres = 12.1 galls = 16.90 mpg.
251½ miles = 63.7 litres = 14.0 galls = 17.54 mpg.
737 + 2 miles = 194.1 litres = 42.7 galls = 17.31 mpg.

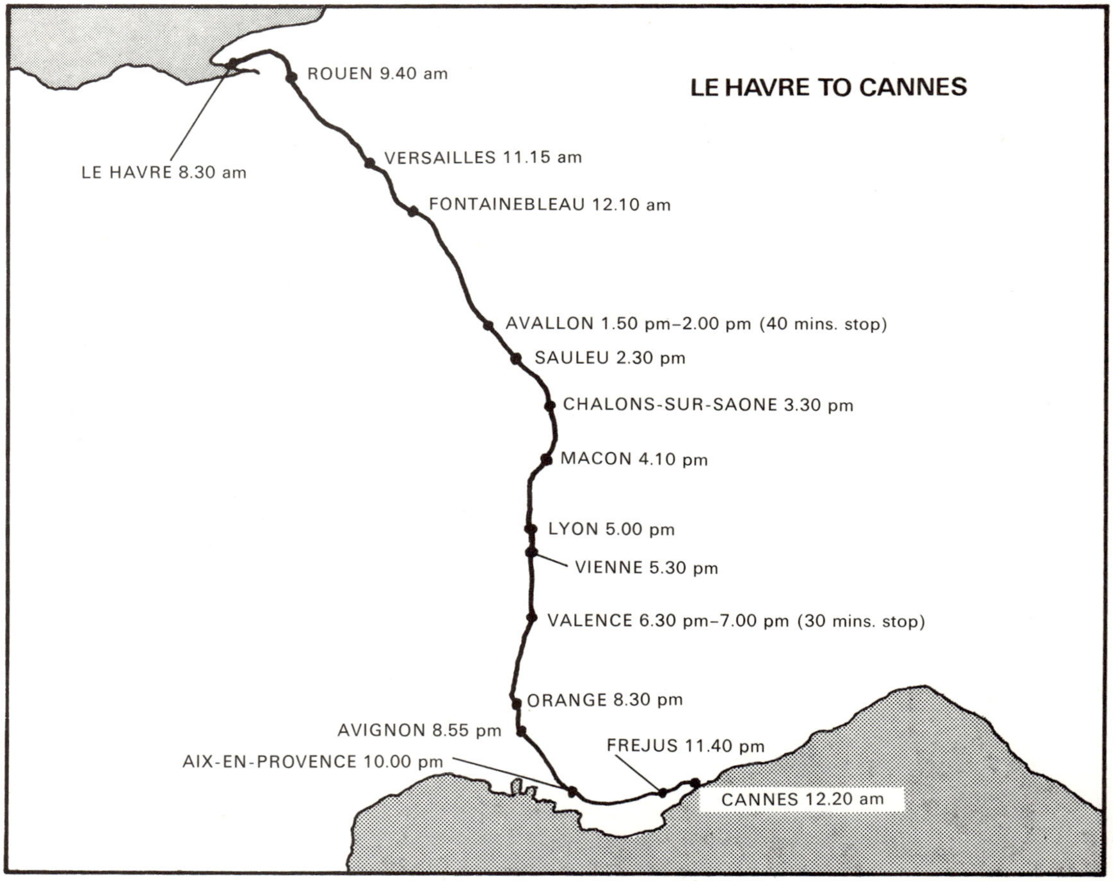

1 *The route from Le Havre to Cannes in a Mk VI Bentley*

Paris to London

Although not a long-distance run I feel it is worth mentioning a trip I did the following year in the same Mk VI from Paris to London.

I left Paris on a Saturday after an early breakfast passing the Arc de Triomphe at 7.30 am, crossed the Channel by the Le Touquet–Lympne Air Ferry and reached my home at Cobham, Surrey at 1.05 pm for lunch.

Total elapsed time was 5 hours 35 minutes occupied as follows:

Paris to Le Touquet (137.9 miles)	2 hours	43 minutes
At Le Touquet		22 ,,
In the air		20 ,,
At Lympne		25 ,,
Lympne to Cobham (77 miles)	1 hour	45 ,,
	5 hours	35 minutes

The distance from Lympne to Cobham was 10 miles more than the direct road to London and progress across country was necessarily impeded by Saturday morning shopping traffic in Godstone, Redhill, Reigate, Dorking and other towns en route. The total driving time was 4 hours 28 minutes, but I consider that only the overall door-to-door times are of any practical importance.

'Mini' Motoring

The only occasion when I have driven any length of journey on the Continent in a baby car was in October, 1962 when I brought a 'cooking' Mini Minor home from Monte-Carlo. This car was 'bog standard' and had covered less than 3,000 miles. This was before the days of the Autoroute du Sud and I saw it as something of a challenge to drive from Monte-Carlo to Paris in a day in a Mini.

I left Monte-Carlo at 6 am with a full tank and over 600 miles ahead of me. I resolved to stop only when it became necessary to replenish the tank, matching my needs for sustenance to those of the car, and (estimating the range at something over 200 miles) hoped that two pauses would suffice.

I passed Nice Airport at 6.30 am and at the end of the first hour had done 43 miles. I had the unique experience hereabouts of driving a car which could not reach the speed limit! It was on a curvy, uphill stretch of an excellent new road skirting the Estorel Mountains which had a limit of 100 kph and the Mini flat out was progressing materially below this speed. The next hour encompassed 49 miles; the following two another 90, the average being 45½ mph. I stopped 2 kms south of Montélimar at 10.45 am for petrol and breakfast. It took 23.9 litres (5.16 gallons) to fill the tank, showing the consumption to have been 42.44 mpg and confirming that only one more stop would be necessary before Paris. I resumed my journey after 23 minutes and did not stop again until La Rochepot (between Chalon-sur-Saône and Saulieu), 196 miles and 4 hours 10 minutes later. The tank took 19½ litres (4.29 gallons) and I took food and drink. Just before Auxerre 500 miles came up and 11 hours 47 minutes (including the two stops totalling exactly one hour) had passed since leaving Monaco.

By 7 pm it was dark and raining. Twelve hours at the wheel had covered a distance of 566 miles – an average speed of 47.2 mph. The remaining 48 miles to the Place Vendôme took 1 hour 10 minutes. The trip of 614 miles had taken 14 hours 10 minutes (including 1 hour of stops), the door-to-door average speed being 43.33 mph. The driving average was 46.62 mph and the overall petrol consumption 44.3 mpg.

Frankly, I was surprised to find that I was not exhausted and stiff. It says a lot for this little car that after a meal I was still sufficiently unfatigued to pay a visit to the Motor Show before retiring to bed.

The average speed seems slow in the context of the Autoroutes since opened between Paris and the Côte d'Azur, and the same journey could doubtless be covered in a similar car today in 3 or 4 hours less. In those days, the route via N7 to Fontainebleau, N5 to Sens, N6 to Lyons and N7 to Nice was 593 miles (955 kms) and one heard light-hearted claims to have 'done it in 10 hours flat, old boy.' The subject of average speeds will always be a bone of contention, but I feel sure that very, very few such claims would have stood up to close investigation. I do not contend that it was impossible to do the journey from Paris to Nice or vice-versa at a 'start-to-stop' average speed of 60 mph, but it must not be thought that a fast car and a good driver, both capable of sustained high-speed, non-stop motoring, were all that was necessary. Six hundred miles is a long stretch of road and I never did the trip without encountering one or more phenomena which caused unavoidable delays. Road repairs somewhere or other were almost certain to necessitate a lengthy deviation over minor roads; a mishap or police check may have brought traffic to a standstill; level-crossings could be confoundedly pro-railway (and why did one always come up behind a crawling camion on entering a 'No overtaking' zone?); these and other more unusual obstacles – markets, fairs, army manoeuvres, road-blocks manned by dissatisfied taxpayers, etc. – combined to make an unhampered run an outside chance.

In my view the completion of the journey in less than 12 hours, providing that safe driving was the keynote throughout, not only reflected great credit on car and driver, but meant that Dame Fortune had been sitting on the radiator cap.

A Day in the Life of 'Olga'

When crossing France, I usually made an overnight stop in Paris in each direction and the longest stretch in a day was the 600 miles or so between the capital and Nice; not a stupendous day's driving, but a different proposition in those pre-autoroute days.

It was not until September, 1970 that I drove all the way home from the Riviera in a single day, single-handed – and then it was unplanned. The car was my well-known R-Type Continental Bentley in which I had done 92,000 miles since having the car rebuilt 10 years previously and which was now in its twentieth year. After a few days in the sun at Cap Estel I was to drive home, leaving Con to follow by air a week later. I left Eze-sur-Mer – between Nice and Monte-Carlo – at 6 am on a Friday, aiming to spend the night in Paris and to complete the journey to my home in Surrey the following day.

In the event I made such good progress that I reached the Porte d'Italie, Paris, at 3.54 pm having made only two stops for petrol and sustenance totalling 50 minutes, and covered the 589.7 miles from Eze in a running time of 9 hours 4 minutes (65.04 mph). From Nice – 9 miles fewer – the driving time was 8 hours 49 minutes (65.86 mph). It was so early in the day that it seemed unnecessary to stop over in Paris and I had been calculating that I should be able to reach a Channel port in daylight. Would it, I pipe-dreamed, be possible to reach home that night?

With these thoughts in mind I turned on to the Périphérique and drove round Paris in about a quarter of an hour. I missed the exit for N1 and left the ring road at the Port Clignancourt. After a slow few miles on the suburban end of N14, I regained N1 for Beauvais.

As I sped northwards I was considering the possible courses open to me. I knew that N1 was closed for repairs for a considerable distance entailing a diversion between Montreuil and Boulogne, so I decided to go to the airport at Le Touquet to see if by any chance there was a space on a 'plane to Lydd. I stopped at the airport building at 6.43 pm having added an additional 143.9 miles to my drive since Paris without any further stop, thus covering 732.9 miles in a running time of 11 hours 53 minutes – an average speed of 61.67 mph. The average speed from Nice to Le Touquet (including stops) was 56.19 mph (723.9 miles in 12 hours 43 minutes).

The last plane for Lydd had left two hours previously; I learnt that the hovercraft was not operating from Boulogne due to bad weather in the Channel, but that a boat was due to leave Boulogne at 7.45 pm. A brief 10 minutes after pulling into Le Touquet Airport, I was on the move again to Boulogne, the RAC having telephoned ahead to secure a place on the boat and to notify my late arrival. I reached the boat at 7.25 pm with 752.3 miles on the 'clock'. My three stops had totalled exactly 1 hour, so I had been at the wheel for 12 hours 25 minutes. From Nice to Boulogne – 743.3 miles in 12 hours 10 minutes running time – produced a 61.08 mph average.

The ship was the 'Vortigern' and, although almost the last car on board, I secured a cabin, had a welcome meal and reported my whereabouts by radio-telephone to an astonished Con in Eze. I left Dover at 9.45 pm in the dark and rain for the horrible cross-country journey to Cobham in Surrey, arriving home five minutes before midnight with 847.3 miles now recorded.

I was delighted to have done something which had not previously entered my head as a possibility: driven from the South of France to my home in a day. It had taken 5 minutes under 18 hours. As they say in athletics, this was a 'personal best' for me, the longest distance I had driven in a day.

I do not claim any records, but what does impress me is that my magnificent Bentley was performing as when new, and how well those responsible for her conception knew the requirements for long-distance touring. Only two petrol refills were necessary to cross France – just over 300 miles on a tankful – and I was not fatigued after 14½ hours at the wheel. 'Olga' had required no attention other than filling with petrol during the journey and was running as sweetly at the end of the trip as when she had left home 10 days and 2,000 miles earlier.

The road included at that time some excellent stretches of autoroute (no speed limit); some good main roads (110 kph speed limit) and considerable distances on narrow roads where passing was prohibited or difficult – notably between Fréjus and Aix-en-Provence and between Mâcon and Pouilly-en-Auxois. I cruised between 90 mph and 105 mph on the autoroutes with occasional bursts of 110 – many miles at 100 mph (3,650 rpm) – and in 1 hour covered 91½ miles. About one-third of the journey in France was on wet roads and I experienced some delays at the scenes of seven major accidents and one caravan well ablaze on the roadside.

Incidentally, I was able to check the accuracy of my distance recorder over long distances by reference to the kilometre stones and determined that it was under-recording by 1 per cent. (Corrected figures are quoted in this report.)

Petrol consumption for the journey was 17.34 mpg. During the whole round trip of 2,196¾ miles, including messing about on the Riviera, some 123.88 gallons of petrol were used (4-star here – 'Super' in France) giving a figure of 17.73 mpg for the 3¾ in bore (4,887 cc) engine, compared with 19.4 mpg when road-tested by Autocar over twenty years ago with the 3⅝ in bore (4,566 cc) engine.

No wonder these R-Type Continentals have become collectors' pieces – but not, I hope I have demonstrated, museum pieces.

Across France American Style

A year later, in similar circumstances, I was again driving home from the South of France, but this time in a 'Continental' of a different kind – my 1966 Lincoln.

I left Eze-sur-Mer (9 miles beyond Nice) at 6 am and reached Cobham at 10.35 pm; i.e. 1 hour 20 minutes sooner than in 'Olga' the previous year and, if the Hovercraft had not been late leaving Boulogne, I could have been home by 10 pm. Yes, the journey in the Lincoln

84 *1966 Lincoln Continental at Cap Estel in August 1969*

was quicker than that in the Bentley Continental and even less tiring. Not surprising though, when one considers that nearly 80 miles of additional autoroute were open and that the Bentley was 13 years older than the Lincoln and had a manual gear-box and steering. I was not conscious of driving either one quicker than the other; certainly I would drive 'Olga' more quickly on twisty roads and on wet surfaces, but on the autoroutes which comprised most of the route I drove each car at the speed which seemed to be its natural cruising speed. The Lincoln Continental settled down beautifully at about 90 on the speedometer, which reads about 7 per cent slow. Apart from the short stretch of autoroute from Nice to Fréjus (32 miles), the road to Sénas, about 20 miles south of Avignon, was undulating, curvy and narrow, divided for long stretches by a solid white line with a resulting lack of opportunities to overtake the slow-moving vehicles which abound in this area. I reached the autoroute (A6) at Sénas at 8.40 am after covering the 143.8 miles in exactly the same time as in 'Olga' the previous year and settled down to fast cruising to Lyon nearly 160 miles away with the object of crossing that city before its inhabitants burst upon the streets for the noon dash home to lunch. One disadvantage of the Lincoln is its thirst for petrol, an average consumption of a gallon every 11 miles – which increases to 10 mpg on motorways – necessitating refuelling stops at intervals of 180/200 miles. The first such stop was at Montélimar (205.5 miles) for breakfast. (Checks of the distance-recorder against kilometre markers over long distances established that the instrument under-recorded by $6\frac{1}{2}$ per cent – corrected mileages are given throughout this report.) The tunnel in Lyon was reached at 10.55 am (300.3 miles) – 33 minutes sooner than in the Bentley – and another stop for petrol was made at Beaune at 12.03 pm (388.2 miles). This was on the stretch of autoroute opened early that year – a distance of 74 miles from Mâcon to Pouilly-en-Auxois – replacing a twisty, hilly 77-mile section of N6. This section took 1 hour 22 minutes in the Bentley and I estimate that it took half an hour less in the Lincoln on A6. We (I had my motoring enthusiast niece, Anthea, as a passenger as far as Paris) left 35 minutes later and in each of the next three consecutive half-hours covered 44.7 miles, 47.9 miles and 48.9 miles respectively, i.e. 96.8 miles in the last hour.

The Péage at the end of the toll-paying section of the autoroute at Fleury (Fontainebleau) was reached by 2.20 pm (3.25 pm in 'Olga) and soon afterwards I left the autoroute to drive to Orly Airport over some 8 miles of miserably congested suburban roads. After negotiating the seemingly endless feeder roads and spirals inside the airport – some of them at least twice – I disgorged Anthea and her luggage, filled up with petrol and set off again at 3.00 pm. On towards Paris and on to the Boulevard Périphérique, which I left at Porte de la Chapelle at 3.32 pm, with 589.7 miles behind me, having decided to take the autoroute (A1) as far as Arras. The 101.5 miles to the exit for Arras took 1 hour 13 minutes and the remaining 79.1 miles to Boulogne via St Pol and Montreuil another 1½ hours, bringing me into the Hoverport at exactly 6.15 pm. The total distance from Eze, including the detour into Orly, was 770.3 miles which had been covered in 12 hours 15 minutes. I pulled into the Hoverport exactly 12 hours after driving along the Promenade des Anglais in Nice, stops on the road having totalled 1 hour 15 minutes. The overall average speed (including stops) was 62.8 mph and the distance 770.3 miles had been completed in driving time of exactly 11 hours – i.e. at an average speed of 70 mph.

Comparing this with the run in 'Olga' – the distance was greater by 18 miles, mostly by reason of travelling from Paris by autoroute instead of RN1, and the point-to-point time taken was 1 hour 10 minutes less. (I see from my notes that I passed Montrueil at 5.48 pm, only 33 minutes earlier than in the Bentley, having lost time deviating into Orly, but did not then deviate into Le Touquet as I had done in the Bentley). I had caught the 7.45 pm boat for Dover with only 20 minutes to spare when driving the Bentley and I was hoping to leave on the 6.30 pm Hovercraft on this occasion. I did, but it left late and I spent 55 minutes waiting about with no opportunity to eat. No food was served on the Hovercraft, so part of the time saved compared with a boat crossing had to be spent in Dover taking sustenance. I left Dover, after topping up the tank, at 8.20 pm and savoured the delights (I don't think!) of motoring again in England for 2¼ hours in the dark to arrive home in Cobham, 94.2 miles away, at 10.35. So I had been at the wheel for 13¼ hours during which time I had covered 864.5 miles at an average speed (including this speed limit restricted country of ours) of 65½ mph. Apart from slipping accessory-drive belts squeaking on acceleration, the Lincoln was running as sweetly as ever and I really was not tired. Some American friends of mine commenting on my trip in 'Olga' have said that they could not understand what was remarkable about driving over 800 miles in a day – until they had experienced road and traffic conditions in Europe! Journeys of greater distances are not uncommon in the States, but they take place entirely on motorways with no need to stop except to replenish car and drivers. Admittedly, the American motorways are subject to speed limits, but the limit (? plus 5) tends to be the average, so it is simple arithmetic to determine in advance the likely duration of a journey. A 900-mile trip at 60 mph would take 15 hours; at 70 mph just under 13 hours.

1,000 Miles in a Day

Motivation

Who in his right mind would want to drive 1,000 miles in a day – and in England, too? Well, me for a start, for this was no ill-considered jaunt, but a planned effort to achieve a self-imposed task.

Why? Well – for fun really. The 1,000 miles in a day target had been sculling around in the back of my mind for some time. Having twice driven from the South of France to my home in Surrey in a single day, a distance of some 860 miles, I had on each occasion wished that I had farther to go to bring the day's mileage up to the magic (for me) figure of 1,000.

Inspiration

It was not until the opening of several stretches of motorway at the end of 1971 that it occurred to me it might be possible to drive that distance in a day in this country. The prospect of being able to do it without the expenditure of time and money involved in crossing the Channel was pleasing indeed.

Preparation

When? What route? How long would it take? Which car? Also, who should I invite to accompany me?

The answer to the first question was easy. It made sense to undertake the journey in midsummer to have the advantage of long hours of daylight and to choose a day in the middle of the week to avoid week-end traffic. As I could not expect the weather to be fine all over England in a single day I decided to go on a predetermined date irrespective of the weather and forecasts. The day fixed was Tuesday, 20 June 1972 when lighting-up time terminated at 4.13 am and began again at 9.51 pm.

After many permutations on the motorway system, aimed at covering as much of as many different motorways as possible with a minimum of doubling back, I settled on a route starting near London Airport so as to eliminate slow suburban driving from home to a motorway.

The route selected on was as follows:

M4 London Airport to Chiswick Flyover
A406 (North Circular Road) to Brent Cross and A41 to Fiveways Corner
M1 to end at Junction 43 (near Leeds)
M1 back to Junction 32 and M18 to edge of Doncaster
A1(M), A1 and A194(M) to end near Newcastle-upon-Tyne
A194(M), A1(M) and A1 back to Scotch Corner
A66 to Penrith
M6 to end at Junction 44 (near Carlisle)
M6 back to Junction 30 (near Preston)
M61 and M62 to end at Junction 23 (near Huddersfield)
M62 and M61 back to Junction 30 and northwards to Junction 31 to join
M6 to Junction 8 (near Birmingham)
M5 to Junction 15 (near Severn Bridge)
M4 to end at Junction 28 (near Newport, Mon)
M4 to London Airport.

Of this route only the following sections would not be on motorways:

	Miles	
Chiswick Flyover to M1	$10\frac{1}{2}$	Urban dual carriageway
A1 between Doncaster Scotch Corner	$68\frac{1}{4}$	Dual carriageway
A66 Scotch Corner to Penrith	49	Narrow, hilly single carriageway
	$127\frac{3}{4}$	

The remaining 870-odd miles would be on seven different motorways and two 'A' roads built to motorway standards, i.e. dual carriage ways with no intersections.

I assumed an average speed of 60 mph except between Chiswick Flyover and M1 (40 mph) and Scotch Corner to Penrith (49 miles in the hour). This indicated a driving time of 17 hours 10 minutes and, allowing for three stops of half-an-hour each, the time on the road looked like being about $18\frac{1}{2}$ hours. With a 4 am start this meant a finishing time of about 10.30 pm – virtually all in daylight.

Which car? I could have used my Cadillac, which had by then replaced the Lincoln – if ever a car was designed for motorway driving this was – and enjoyed air-conditioning, stereo and effortless motoring, but, as the 70 mph limit would have to be observed, it was obvious that the proposed journey was well within the capacity of my Vintage Bentley which I had cruised at 85 mph for long distances in France. The idea of doing the trip in a 40-year-old car had a special appeal for me and how nice it would be to be driving all of a midsummer day in an open car. Little did I know what a flaming (awful) June was in store for us. Having decided to use the 8-litre I proceeded to make sure that it was in every way fitted for the journey. The car needed little attention. A new exhaust system was fitted, rear flashers installed and a dynamo cut-out switch inserted to avoid overcharging the battery. The new silencer was so effective that I then appreciated the volume of engine noise caused by a worn crankshaft damper. A new one was fitted which transformed the car. A new set of Dunlop Fort 6.50/7.00 × 19 in tyres was fitted, petrol tank filled to the brim (just over 30 gallons) and the car was ready for the road.

So far, so good. Now, who had the qualifications to fill the passenger seat and – what was equally important – would accept an invitation to accompany me? My criteria required someone who could endure 18 hours as a passenger in an open car with me; who could gear the demands of nature – both input and output – to match the refuelling stops dictated by the size of the petrol tank and the petrol consumption; who could keep an intelligent log of the journey; who could apply himself to any mechanical adjustments or work which might prove necessary; and who could take over the driving if I should tire before completing the distance. It goes without saying that he would have to be an enthusiastic Vintage motorist and that the prospect of each other's company would have to be a mutually pleasing one. A telephone call to Graham Woodrow Hill in Esher, whom I knew met most of my desiderata, revealed that longish intervals between stops for food and drink would not be a cause for concern and, to my delight, that he would like to join me on the run.

Realization

And so the 8-litre quietly burbled out of the hotel car park in the early dawn light carrying two figures enveloped in fur-lined coats and waterproof clothing which was to be worn throughout the day. The sky was clear, the roads dry and almost devoid of traffic. The time was 4 am and breakfast nearly a tankful of petrol away.

What a pleasure to drive on an empty M4 and North Circular Road. Alongside a solitary Scammell at traffic lights the driver shouted, 'Best car in the world – had a 3-litre once.' By the time we reached M1 (33 minutes) the engine and transmission had warmed through – water temperature was steady at 68 deg C and the oil pressure settled down at 57 psi at 2,500 rpm – 70 mph in top gear.

The sun was rising to our right and we soon ran into ground mist which characterizes this section of motorway. It gave rise to no problems in view of the almost complete absence of other vehicles, but one had a sense of potential danger – especially seeing fields full of thick mist spilling over on to the road. However, it was not long before we had finished with the fog, switched off wipers and lights, and settled down to enjoy a beautiful day.

I decided to drive consistently at 70 mph and can honestly say that, although the needle tended to stray up a point or two, the speed never exceeded 75 mph at any time during the 1,000 miles. It was not necessary to keep an eye constantly on the speedometer as a marked increase in the whine from the straight-cut rear axle was audible as soon as the speed exceeded 70.

We reached our first turning point at the end

of M1 near Leeds at 7.04 am – 26 minutes ahead of schedule – having done 201.5 miles. We had already checked the trip recorder with the distance posts on the road and found it to be accurate over a 34-mile stretch. The sun was shining and after back-tracking on M1 and taking M18 we pulled up at the Selby Fork Motel for fuel and breakfast at 8.02 am, with 266.1 miles on the clock after just over four hours. It took 25.9 gallons to refill the tank to the brim, confirming the expected petrol consumption of about 10 mpg, and three quarts of oil in the sump. (It holds five gallons!) Thirty-one minutes later we were on the road again and encountering more traffic – especially 'heavies'. At 9.07 am three hundred miles came up making the average speed just under 60 mph including the breakfast stop. The end of A194(M) was reached at 9.59 am (357.6 miles) still more than half-an-hour ahead of schedule and we retraced our path to Scotch Corner. The hour I had allowed for the cross-country section from Scotch Corner proved to be more than enough and we joined the M6 at Penrith at 11.40 am with 446 miles behind us, encouraged to note that the rest of the journey would be on motorways. A smattering of rain reminded us that the forecasters had predicted wet weather on the west side of the country.

The end of M6, north of Carlisle and our furthest point from home, was reached at exactly noon – 468.8 miles in eight hours (58.6 mph including the stop at Selby). We turned southwards for the run along M6; then it started raining. The half-way distance (500 miles) was reached at 12.28 pm. The weather over Shap was appalling and we searched hopefully ahead for a break in the clouds. It was still pouring when we made our second stop at the Anderton Service Area after turning off M6 to go the length of the M61 and M62 motorways over the Pennines to Huddersfield and back. We had now covered 572.6 miles and took on 30.3 gallons of petrol – must have been close that time as I thought it was a 30-gallon tank – and a gallon of oil. Lighter by £11.35 (it seemed a lot at the time!) we went into the cafeteria to eat whilst it rained and rained. We must have lingered there, for 47 minutes elapsed before setting off into the soaking hinterland. Even in the rain we enjoyed driving on this motorway. It is a triumph of engineering and provides a constantly changing vista of moors, mills, towns and countryside, skillfully weaving up hill and down dale between large centres of population. As we approached the end of M62 the wiper blade – slow and inefficient even when working properly – gradually reduced its swept arc and finally stopped. We took the opportunity to enjoy a moment of shelter in the underpass at our turn-round point to dig out a spanner and tighten the wiper arm on its spindle. This cured its ills and was the only occasion on which we did anything to the car throughout the run. This welcome five-minute stop brought the total time of stops up to 83 minutes, but when we turned southwards again on M6 at 655½ miles we were still well ahead of schedule.

Just before 4 pm we had covered two-thirds of the 1,000 miles. Traffic and weather entailed slowing down to about 65 mph, and after two hours of rain we cheered up when it eased off and stopped as 700 miles came up on the 'clock' at 4.22 pm. Three-quarter distance (750 miles) was passed at 5.09 pm. I was able to drive consistently at 70 and averaged very nearly this figure.

The Severn Bridge towers hove into sight as we pulled into the Aust Service Area at 6.25 pm for our third replenishment stop (840.3 miles). Fifteen minutes later we left having taken on 26.4 gallons of fuel and another gallon of oil and drove over the Severn Bridge in a gale of drizzle. Traffic was confined to one lane, the bridge not having been passed as strong enough to carry more traffic, except at week-ends when presumably there are fewer heavies, and proceeded at about 25 mph. We had a wet run to the end of M4 beyond Newport and back again to the Bridge. It was nice to know that we were now really on the home stretch. The cross-wind on the bridge was unbelievably strong and took off my cherished cap. As I turned between the cones into the unused lane to stop and retrieve it, Graham said 'It'll cost you a fiver if you stop.' It didn't need a computer to tell me that it would be cheaper to buy a new cap and I turned smartly back into the traffic stream and continued with a very numb skull until I could stop to find my spare headgear.

I now focussed my mind on the telephone call I had undertaken to make between 7.30 and 8, to the BBC television studio in Birmingham to record a progress report in conversation with Cliff Michelmore for inclusion in the 'Wheelbase' programme to go out later in the evening. We decided to stop at the service area at Leigh Delamere and pulled into the car park at 7.48 pm able to report a trouble-free, uneventful run to that point of 908.1 miles. This interlude occupied 28 minutes bringing the total time of our stops to two hours nine minutes. We had no need of petrol, decided to postpone eating and set off on the last 90 miles or so along M4. The rain had stopped and the road was dry. As we approached London Airport we had to do a bit of calculating so as to complete the 1,000 miles as near to our starting-point as possible. In the event it necessitated continuing along M4 to Junction 3, doubling back to Junction 5, then turning on to A4 eastwards again. The trip recorder turned up all the noughts again on the Colnbrook By-pass at 8.34, and we came to a stop in the hotel car park three minutes later having covered 1,000½ miles since we left there 17 hours 37 minutes earlier in the day. I then drove home to Cobham and put the Bentley in the garage running as sweetly at the end of 1,016.2 miles as it was at the beginning. Great cars these 8-litres.

The start to finish average speed worked out at 56.9 mph – but for the assignation with 'Wheelbase' it would have been 58½ – and the driving time was 15 hours 25 minutes, i.e. an average speed for the 1,000 miles of 64.8 mph.

I filled the tank right up the spout again the next day and established that 99.6 gallons had been consumed in 1,016¼ miles giving an overall consumption of 10.2 mpg. Oh yes, the oil fill-ups totalled 3¾ gallons – more lost than burnt. Rather a lot, but oil is relatively cheap and I don't believe in pulling down for overhaul an engine which is running well. (I used Duckham's oil, but couldn't understand why it cost 42p per quart in a service station and only 26p in Woolworths!)

Evaluation

As for myself, I did not feel tired out. I could have continued driving quite happily and, in my judgment, I was driving as well as in the morning – Graham said 'Better' and I didn't quite know how to take this. I really do rather lose patience with organizations and individuals who pontificate about how long people should drive at a stretch, or in a day. It is quite impossible – and therefore a waste of time – to generalize on this subject. Every driver is different in his physiological and psychological make-up, and the importance of such variables as comfort, weather conditions, type of road, the designed performance of the car and the margin within which it is being driven, and the condition of car, cannot be exaggerated. (As for sitting in a simulator for four hours with an optical contraption strapped on one's head – a procedure used by a research organization – the very thought of it makes me tired!)

The seats in the Bentley are very comfortable and I can remember consciously changing my position on only one occasion. Doubtless the ease with which the Bentley ran along at 70 mph – so well within its compass – contributed to the lack of tiredness. This relaxed speed, plus the absence of the need for gear-changing and slow-speed steering, greatly reduced the fatigue factor. It is true that the run demonstrates that it is possible to observe the 70 mph speed limit and to cover long distances in a relatively short time, but this should not be interpreted as an endorsement of the validity of a 70 mph limit on motorways. If there had been no speed limit I would have driven 15–20 mph faster for most of the time. The higher speed would have been more demanding, but the journey would have taken less time. The safe speed limit in any particular circumstances can be determined only by reference to the skill and experience of the driver and the designed performance and condition of the car. Many cars overtook the Bentley during the day. Most of them were probably not exceeding 80–85 mph, but we saw no cases of bad driving in these circumstances. Most journeys on motorways are not long-distance ones and it seems to me that there should be no speed limit on motorways at all. I would, of course, support the meting out of severe treatment for careless, selfish and dangerous driving – and for unfit vehicles.

The most remarkable thing about the drive was that it was uneventful. We were not held up by road-works; we saw no accidents; we saw no interesting cars; we had no 'moments'; we made no wrong turns; the car performed impeccably; neither of us experienced any fatigue or ill-effects – both Graham and I were at work in our respective offices the next morning at the usual times.

The drive confirmed my view that our motorways will stand comparison with any on the Continent. From a driving point of view the three-lane motorways are excellent and have been made much safer since the heavies have been stopped from using the outer lane. On the two-lane motorways in any country one lorry slowly overhauling another can soon cause a queue of impatient motorists – a most undesirable state of affairs, so please let us not build any more of these. A welcome addition to our motorways would be rest or picnic areas, similar to those on the Continent, with simple toilet facilities.

Motorway design and landscaping have come a long way since the southern part of M1 was built. The best of them are, in my view, now an enhancement to the landscape rather than an eyesore. Surfaces vary and even new stretches are sometimes more uneven than the best main roads. The sign-posting is good on the whole and, providing he knows where he wants to go, the spaghetti junctions need hold no terrors for the inexperienced motorist – one flows along one's own particular road barely conscious of the enveloping cat's cradle of concrete.

Appreciation

Another memorable drive added to my personal experience. It would be ungracious of me not to acknowledge the part played by others in this venture, so my thanks to W.O. for conceiving and building these wonderful cars; to Fred Hofmann and Basil Mountfort for keeping my personal example in good trim; to Dunlop for making tyres in small numbers to keep Veteran and Vintage car owners on the road – no measurable wear on mine at the end of the run; and to my navigator/timekeeper/companion, Graham Woodrow Hill, for his patient, uncomplaining participation.

– and Commiseration!

The reactions of friends (and others!) on hearing of the run varied from congratulations from like-minded enthusiasts to the more common – 'You must be mad' and 'Rather you than me.' Others said – 'Sedgwick doing his Thing' – 'All that beautiful money wasted on petrol' – 'When does your case come up?' – and so on.

* * *

This drive received fairly wide publicity and no one has yet come forward to answer the question I posed at the time; has anyone else driven 1,000 miles in a day in England in any car?

Across France and Back in a Day

On returning home from the South of France in my (then) Lincoln Continental in September, 1971 having driven 864 miles in the day, my

85 *The Rolls-Royce Corniche at the Aire de Service de Nemours*

feeling of self-satisfaction was quickly deflated when I opened the current issue of Autocar and read the following statement in the Road Test of the Ferrari Daytona – 'Across Europe it would undoubtedly prove the fastest touring car that traffic conditions would allow, easily coping with a trip from the Channel to the South of France and back in a day'.

This struck me as an assertion worthy of demonstration and I resolved to see what could be done about it if an opportunity arose. Realization proved less easy than I had hoped, none of my Daytona-owning friends appearing to be in need of a co-driver to put hundreds of miles on the clock with the object of finishing up where they had started, so the idea went into the memory bank.

I had since driven my open 8-litre Bentley 1,000 miles in a day in England in a total time of 17 hours 37 minutes and I perceived that the same length of time at the wheel of a fast, modern, closed car – on roads free from speed limits – would encompass a considerably greater distance. It followed that I could drive all the way across France and back in a day myself given a suitable car. On further consideration I came to the conclusion that such a journey would be more meaningful if accomplished in a full-size saloon instead of an out-and-out sports-car. Thus it was that I asked a mildly surprised John Craig – Marketing Director of Rolls-Royce Motors – if I could borrow a Corniche for the trip. I was even more surprised when he said 'Yes', and I proceeded to make plans.

Preparation

I was faced with the usual questions – When? Who with? What route? The answer to the first question was easy. It made sense to undertake the drive when the daylight hours were longest, but before the holiday rush, and to choose a day in the middle of the week to avoid week-end congestion. I decided upon Tuesday, 22 May (1973) and tackled the next question – who should I invite to accompany me? The occupant of the passenger seat had to be prepared to take three days' leave; to match his bodily needs to the mandatory stops for petrol; to keep a detailed record of time and distance throughout the trip and be prepared to be driven uncomplainingly at high speed in my sole company for 18 hours or so. I was fortunate in recruiting a Canadian friend, Hugh Young, to this (mobile) office which, in the event, he fulfilled untiringly and meticulously. What is more, he enjoyed every minute of it.

The choice of route to be followed gave me food for thought. Obviously the maximum use was to be made of autoroutes and this presupposed using A1 to Paris, A6 to Lyon and A7 beyond. Hitherto I had joined the A1 at Arras having driven from Calais, Boulogne or Le Touquet, but this is a tedious drive of about 70 miles passing through many villages and several towns which takes anything between $1\frac{1}{4}$ and $1\frac{3}{4}$ hours according to conditions. I was pleased, therefore, to discover that a new stretch of autoroute had been completed from Dunkerque to Lille which entailed only a short distance through the outskirts of the latter city to reach the start of A1. I decided to use this new route feeling sure that the additional mileage would be more than justified from a time-saving point-of-view – and so it proved. I selected Marseille as the turn-round point, for this met the fundamental aim of crossing France from Channel to Mediterranean, and set about building up a target timetable.

From a study of maps, AA and RAC routes and my own records of previous journeys, I computed the mileage from Dunkerque to Marseille to be 657.6. The target timetable, i.e. a yardstick of possible progress – against which to assess the actual, which I devised was as follows:

Urban areas –	Miles	Hrs	Mins
Lille	2.5		4
Paris (Boulevard Périphérique)	8.5		12
Lyon	3.0		5
Vienne	5.6		8
	19.6	—	29
Autoroute – 638 miles at 90 mph	638.0	7	6
	657.6	7	35
Stops for petrol (and refreshment) 2 × 20 minutes			40
		8	15

Allowing for a 45-minute meal break in Marseille, and the same time for the return journey, the total time (including stops totalling 2 hours 5 minutes) added up to $17\frac{1}{4}$ hours, thus a 4.30 am start indicated a return to the starting-point by 9.45 pm – just about the duration of daylight at the time of year.

Realization

Another happy coincidence was the opening of 'La Motellerie' at Armbouts-Cappel on the outskirts of Dunkerque just off the 'Voie Express' (dual carriageway road) which becomes the autoroute A25 after 8 miles. So we crossed from Folkestone to Calais on the 5 pm ferry 'Hengist', drove to Dunkerque, filled the petrol tank to the brim, and turned in early at 'La Motellerie' after requesting a 4 am call. The astonished night-porter couldn't believe his ears when I said that we were going to Marseille for lunch.

We left the motel at 4.20 am and drove back into Dunkerque to the roundabout at Petite Synthe, 3 miles west of the ferry terminal, where the 'expressway' leaves the coastal road N40. I stopped there to take a photograph of the Corniche against the dawn sky before we set off at 4.31 am. The cloudless sky augured a fine day and the sun was soon shining brightly. As the engine warmed up I increased my cruising speed, mindful that the 45 miles to Lille should be covered in half an hour, and was surprised to find that 4,000 rpm corresponded with an indicated speed of 110 mph. Knowing that the true speed at 4,500 rpm was 118 mph I assumed that the rev counter was correct and that the speedometer exaggerated. I speeded up to find that 4,200 rpm equated to 120 mph on the speedometer and, at 4,500 rpm (which marked the start of a yellow segment covering the next 500 rpm before changing to red at 5,000 rpm), the needle was going 'off the clock' at 130 mph. Thus it was evident that an indicated 130 mph corresponded to a true ground speed of 118 mph – an error of approximately +10%. I knew, therefore, that so long as the instrument reading did not indicate more than 130 I would not be stressing the engine in any way. (Actually, my mandate from Rolls-Royce Motors was '. . . there should be no need to place any restrictions on the maximum speed for sustained cruising other than those dictated by road and traffic conditions.')

Just before reaching Lille we overtook our first car – it was a light grey 3½-litre Bentley saloon pursuing its gentlemanly progress, presumably having crossed on the night ferry. (We didn't see another UK-registered car for another 400 miles and only five all the way across France). Odometer readings, only 0.2 per cent out, were taken as accurate. The distance to the toll-gate at Arras was 75 miles and we passed through 51 minutes after leaving Dunkerque – only two minutes later than planned – thus endorsing the choice of route. The traffic was light and the trip recorder registered 139.7 miles at the end of 1½ hours.

We reached the end of the toll section at Survilliers (159.2 miles) at 6.13 am, having averaged 98 mph from Lille. The large number of cars approaching Paris at this early hour surprised us, and traffic was running in all lanes on the Boulevard Périphérique. It was, however, maintaining a speed of 55 mph so that the drive round to the Porte d'Italie took only a minute longer than I had allowed. We sped off down A6 mentally calculating where we should replenish the tank and take our first sustenance of the day. Rolls-Royce Motors had indicated that I could expect to do not less than 11 mpg. This meant a range of about 250 miles – hence my plan to make five stops for petrol. We stopped at the Aire de Service Principale de Nemours at 7.14 am and put in 94.6 litres (20.81 gallons) of Super to replace that used in covering the 233.5 miles to this point plus 5.7 miles the previous evening. This showed a consumption of 11.49 mpg at an average speed of 86 mph.

We partook of a 'continental' breakfast at a stand-up counter and the wheels were turning again after only 23 minutes. The next stage would take us to Lyon and we could not have had better conditions for the journey – dry road, sunshine, moderate traffic not too frequently obstructing the overtaking lane and only short stretches of single-working due to road works. I was cruising with the speedometer needle rarely dropping below 120 – a true speed of about 110 mph – and was conscious of the readiness of the car to exceed this gait without effort – but more of this later.

The first hour after breakfast saw another 96.4 miles behind us and then we were overtaken for the first time – by a 280CE Mercedes – as my speedometer showed 130, i.e. 118 mph. We repassed it 10 minutes later at the same speed and did not see it again. At 9.31 am, five hours after leaving Dunkerque, I had driven 418.7 miles (=83.74 mph) and 23 minutes later, i.e. after five hours driving time, 455.6 miles, which made the average driving speed 91.12 mph. We reached the toll-gate at Villefranche at 09.52½ (dead accurate, this Young fellow) and five minutes later at Les Chères (458.5 miles) I put in nearly 22 gallons. We decided not to eat – it was not yet 10 o'clock in the morning – and the stop took only 7 minutes. We reached the entrance to the Tunnel de Fourvière at Lyon at 10.12 am (469.3 miles). This tunnel has eliminated the slow, twisty, downhill run through the 'agglomeration' to the river bank and takes all the strife out of crossing Lyon. Five minutes after entering the tunnel we had resumed high-speed cruising on A7.

It always surprised me how rarely one was held up in Vienne where the main road ran between the town and the River Rhône and narrowed to a single lane over a temporary flyover at the main intersection. We were on top of this flyover at 10.28 am (489.3 miles) and passed through the Péage at Reventin four minutes ahead of our target timetable, fuelling stops having occupied only 30 minutes against a budget of 40. The 137½ miles of autoroute to the Péage at Salon Nord, including 8.2 miles of single lane working, took exactly 1½ hours (=91.67 mph).

We arrived at the large roundabout encircling the triumphal arch which marks the end of A7 at Marseille at 12.29 pm and pulled up at the Cathedral on the Quai de la Joliette at 12.31 pm, exactly eight hours after leaving Dunkerque and a quarter of an hour ahead of our target time. The point-to-point average speed for the 666.3 miles had been 83.29 mph and, deducting the two stops aggregating 30 minutes, the driving time of 7½ hours (5 minutes less than planned) represented a driving average speed of 88.84 mph.

Instead of stopping in Marseille for lunch as programmed we decided to wait until we reached a 'Jacques Borel' restaurant which we had noted 26 miles out on the autoroute. So, after a stay of four minutes in the South of France to photograph the Corniche against the background of Cathedral and docks, I turned the car and headed back to our starting-point. The mistral was blowing strongly, but the weather was still fine and sunny.

We stopped for lunch and petrol as planned. Two litres of oil went into the engine as a safety measure for none had been added for nearly 900 miles. The press-button oil-level indicator was not designed to give a correct reading at the speeds I had been doing, when most of the oil is doing its job elsewhere than in the sump, and the engine hadn't had a chance to cool sufficiently to obtain a valid reading on the dipstick. We were lucky to be on the move again after 49 minutes. This meant that our stops now added up to within a minute of my original target timetable. As Hugh put it, we rejoined the autoroute as our ghost went past.

Just after 3 pm with over 800 miles behind me I sensed what I described as a lowering in my threshold of awareness. This is not really sleepiness, but I become conscious of blinking and of taking fractionally longer to refocus my vision when transferring the eyes from road to instruments. After five minutes 'zizz' in an appropriately named 'Aire de Repos' I was completely refreshed and resumed this most enjoyable drive. (Inured by this time to making calculations from recorded data my indefatigable Clerk of the Course wrote in the log; 40 winks in 5 minutes = 8 winks per minute!)

The traffic was lighter in this direction and the Corniche purred happily along in the manner of the fast, well-mannered touring car that it is, as is evidenced by the fact that the distance of 196.4 miles between the toll-gate at Villefranche and the Courtenay/Sens Junction was covered at an average speed of 99 mph. I see from the log that I averaged 100.17 mph over the last 117.7 miles of this stretch.

At 5.23 pm we had clocked up 1,000 miles which had entailed 11 hours 18 minutes driving at an average speed of 88.5 mph. Just after 6 o'clock we were overtaken by our second car – a Citroën SM going like the clappers – and the weather deteriorated rapidly. Clouds gathered, lightning danced round the horizon and by the time we passed the exit for Courtenay and Sens it was raining very hard indeed. There was a brief respite at Fontainebleau and then a torrential downpour commenced which was to continue unabated for more than an hour and a half. The traffic was heavy approaching Paris and was reduced to a crawl and stationary jams by shunts and breakdowns. The Périphérique was congested and it took 23 minutes to drive from the A6 to the A1. At Le Bourget the thunderstorm continued, it was as dark as night though only 7.35 pm, and the torrential rain

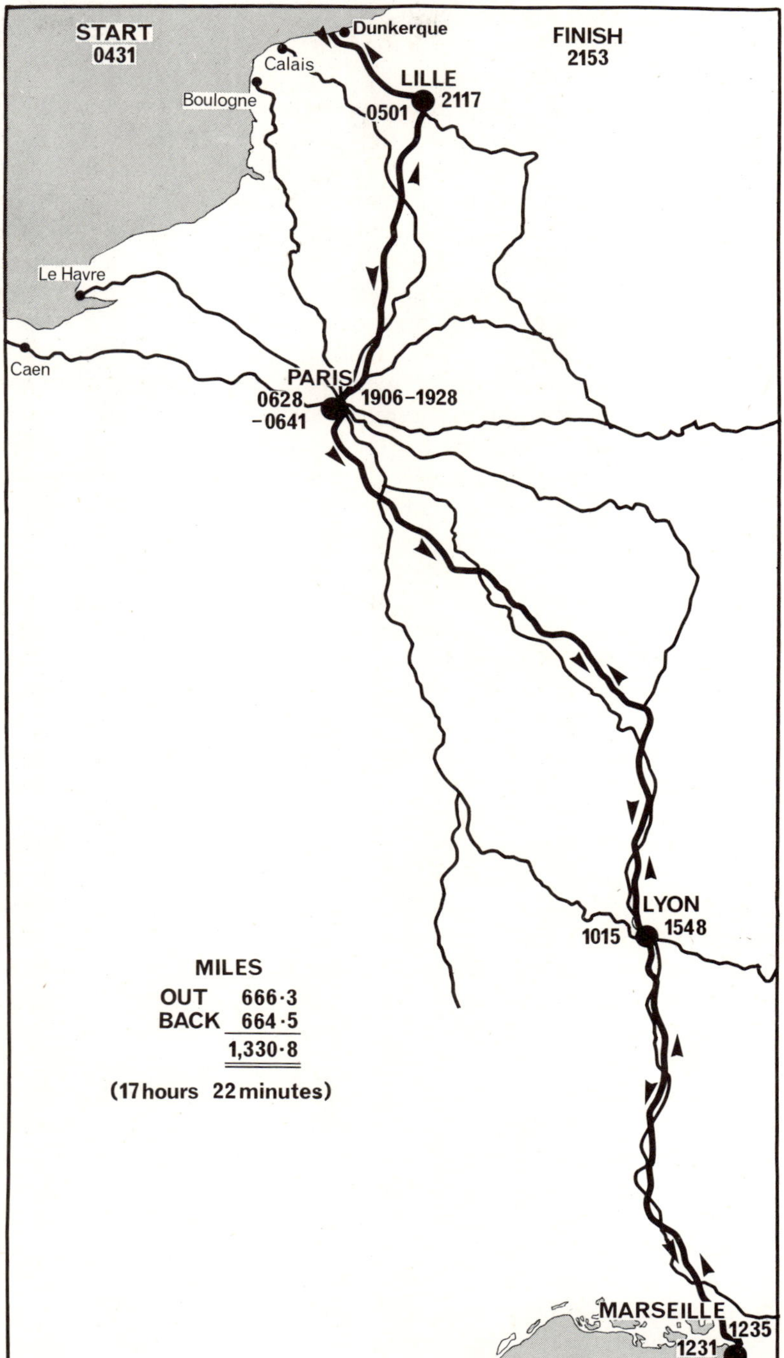

2 *The route from Dunkerque to Marseilles and back July 1973*

was bouncing high off the road. We took advantage of a covered petrol station to refuel for the last time.

The weather cleared before Lille and we found the rather tricky route round the town using the partly-constructed Boulevard Périphérique whereon happened the only 'untidy moment' of the whole trip when I found myself faced by an unlit barrier marking the end of the completed surface and an unsignposted deviation to the other carriageway. I stopped without touching anything and the biggest surprise was the cloud of self-raised dust which overtook the car after it had come to rest on the unmade surface! It is not difficult to imagine the thoughts that went through our minds at this happening so near to our goal. As we joined the A25 auto-route west of Lille for the final run-in Hugh told me that according to our target timetable we were due in Dunkerque, 40.4 miles away, in a quarter of an hour! The road was dry and traffic-free and we made it in 23 minutes, thus producing a sprint finish to our 1,330 mile run at 105.5 mph. We stopped at the Petite Synthe roundabout at 9.53 pm, eight minutes later than our target arrival, shook hands and drove back to the motel for supper and to honour our reservations.

The return trip had taken longer than the outward run, which had been made in as favourable conditions as one could ever hope to get. The following is a summary of the journey:

Dunkerque–Marseille (666.3 miles)
Total Time
8 hours = 83.29 mph
Driving Time
7 hours 30 minutes = 88.84 mph

Marseilles–Dunkerque (664.5 miles)
Total Time
9 hours 18 minutes = 71.45 mph
Driving Time
8 hours 14 minutes = 80.74 mph

Round Trip from Dunkerque to Marseille and back to Dunkerque (1,330.8 miles)
Total Time
17 hours 22 minutes = 76.57 mph
Driving Time
15 hours 44 minutes = 84.54 mph

I reckon that, on the basis of the above-reported progress, and remembering that 25½ miles were driven on single lanes where speeds were often restricted by heavy trucks to 40 mph or less, I must have driven more than 1,000 miles at speeds in excess of 100 mph. The overall petrol consumption was 11.35 mpg. It was rather better on the run south (11.95 mpg) than on the way back (10.83 mpg) – presumably because progress was more free-flowing necessitating fewer bursts of acceleration. (Incidentally, the SP Radial 205 HR 15 Dunlop tyres were inflated to 34 psi rear and 30 psi front compared with the recommended all-round pressure of 28 psi for normal running).

The following breakdown of the times taken to drive the various stages on the outward journey will serve as a basis for those interested enough to compare their own progress on the way to the Côte d'Azur without going to the unlikely destination of Marseille:

Miles		Hrs	Mins
178.0	Dunkerque to Paris (Porte de la Chapelle)	1	57
9.3	On the Boulevard Périphérique		13
282.0	Paris (Porte d'Italie) to Lyon (Tunnel de Fourvière)	3	1
20.0	Lyon (Tunnel de Fourvière to Vienne (top of flyover)		16
153.9	Vienne (top of flyover) to where the auto-route to Aix-en-Provence and Nice forks off 8 miles south of Salon	1	42
643.2		7	9

Evaluation

That neither of us was really tired at the end of this long run says a lot for the Corniche. We wore the seat belts all the time and, although we expected to be uncomfortable because of the relatively low top anchorage point (dictated by the construction of the two-door body) necessitating the strap coming up from behind the shoulder, we were not, in fact, inconvenienced. It is true to say, however, that the belts were more comfortable when not wearing a jacket.

Once placed in the right position the seats were so good as to call for no further adjustment and neither of us found it necessary to change our postures; nor were our joints stiff on getting out of the car. Two other factors played a tremendous part in making such a long journey unfatiguing: the air-conditioning and, because this enabled one to drive with all the windows closed, the insulation from outside noise.

The Speed Control device is not designed to function at speeds over 90 mph, so it was not much use on this drive. I did use it once, however, when we were confined to a single lane by road works, to check the speedometer reading at 100 kph against a timed kilometre – this distance took 38 seconds which is a speed of 94.74 kph indicating that the instrument was over-reading by about $5\frac{1}{2}$ per cent at this speed. (It should be said that it is almost impossible to time accurately from a moving vehicle – especially at high speed – even using a split-second chronograph. At around 100 mph an error of only one-fifth of a second in reading the time between one kilometre marker and the next makes a difference of more than $1\frac{1}{2}$ mph).

The Corniche performed impeccably. The fact that this particular example was built prior to the introduction of the major changes to the front suspension made little difference in this type of motoring. Only one fault manifested itself – in addition to the annoyingly optimistic speedometer – and that was the interior mirror being loose on its stalk. The right size Allen key would have fixed it in a moment but it was aggravating having to reposition it at frequent intervals. When I handed the car back with 33,882 miles on the clock it was as smooth and quiet as when delivered to me.

Altogether I consider that the Corniche proved itself to be a very, very good fast touring car. Not quite fast enough, mind you, and I make this open plea to those at Crewe to offer a higher axle ratio as an option for those who habitually drive on the Continent. I feel that the car has reserves of power and that the resulting slight falling-off in acceleration, if any, would be a small price to pay for an available top speed nearer to 140 mph and a cruising capability in the region of 125–130. (If not an option on the Rolls-Royce version, I suggest that it should be standard equipment on the Bentley!) Such a modification would meet the oft-heard criticism that the top-end performance of the Corniche does not match up to the standards set by certain other manufacturers of very good, but less costly cars.

To those who cringe at the price of the Corniche – and I am one – and who, having read this are inclined to say . . . 'So it should,' my reply would be 'Well, it did, didn't it?' Of course, no-one in his right mind would wish to drive across France and back in a day, but it shows that a four-figure mileage on the Continent in daylight is well within the capability of this car. A few more miles of autoroute, and destinations way down in Italy (normally thought of as being at least two days away) could well be reached between an early breakfast and dinner – especially if two people were to share the driving.

Justification

I offer none. I undertook the drive solely for the pleasure I would derive from it ('one man's meat . . .'). I was not disappointed. It cost a good deal of money and didn't last very long, but I can't think of anything which would have been more rewarding to me in terms of sheer enjoyment and I don't anticipate ever again using nearly £60 worth of petrol (119 gallons) and paying out over £12 in tolls in a day.

Thank you RR for a lovely day and thanks to H.J.T.Y. for bearing with me.

Rumination
It is interesting (to me, anyway) to note that the 1,330 miles took 15 minutes fewer than the 1,000 miles in the Vintage Bentley in England. Just to think of it – the average speed across France and back, including all stops, was nearly 10 per cent above the maximum speed allowed in this country.

My average speed for the round trip (76.57 mph) was slightly higher than that of the winning Speed Six Bentley of Woolf Barnato at Le Mans in 1930 (75.88 mph). I realize that the Bentley's average was maintained for 24 hours, but there were two drivers! There has been some progress in automobile and road engineering in the intervening years.

Was this the longest U-turn in history?

Marseille Revisited

Early in 1973 I acquired a new Double-Six Daimler (fancy Jag. – you know!) and it will come as no surprise that in the course of a holiday trip to the Cote d'Azur I took the opportunity of making a comparative 'outward only' drive in this car. It had covered 6,000 miles and certain teething troubles had been overcome.

Accordingly, after a 4 am wake-up call at the Dunkerque Motellerie on the first Friday in September, I found myself once again at the Petite Synthe roundabout making a 4.30 am start for Marseille. I was not out to beat the RR time, but to drive in a similar manner, i.e. as fast as weather, road and traffic conditions permitted and at a sustained speed at which the car settled down happily. I expected to be able to cruise somewhat faster than previously, but fully realized that (say) 10 mph on the cruising speed would not increase the average speed by the same increment.

First the good news:
In the event, the total point-to-point time from Dunkerque to Marseille, including stops, was 6 minutes less than that taken by the Corniche. Stops for petrol and sustenance totalled 35 minutes – 5 minutes more than the Rolls-Royce as the result of the need for an additional refuelling stop – making the driving time 11 minutes less than the Corniche.

The elapsed times and average speeds were as follows:

	Daimler Double-Six	*Rolls-Royce Corniche*
Total Time	7 hrs 54 mins	8 hrs 00 mins
Stops	35 mins	30 mins
Driving Time	7 hrs 19 mins	7 hrs 30 mins
Mileage (corrected)	665.5	666.3
Average Speed – Overall (including stops)	84.3 mph	83.3 mph
Driving	90.95 mph	88.8 mph
Petrol Consumption	10.45 mpg	11.95 mpg

The bare figures do not tell the whole story. I started at the same time of day (4.30 am), this time alone, but whereas it was just getting light in May when I did the journey in the Corniche, on this occasion it was dark and there were patches of fog which brought my speed down to 20/30 mph more than once before reaching Lille. The first glimmer of dawn appeared as I passed through the Arras Toll, running 10 minutes behind RR's schedule! I turned on to the Boulevard Périphérique at Paris at 6.34 am, the darkness and the fog contributing materially to the 7 minutes lateness compared with the Corniche. I circumnavigated the City to the start of A6 in 11 minutes – 5 minutes less than previously – and thus turned south again only 2 minutes down.

The likely petrol consumption was an unknown factor and prudence called for replenishment at a 'Petrol only' service area before reaching, 7 minutes later, the planned breakfast stop at Nemours. Leaving the latter at 7.39 am

86 *The Daimler Double-Six at the Cathedral at Marseille*

with 233.1 miles completed, the Daimler was now running 3 minutes behind the Corniche's timetable. The weather was perfect and, although the traffic was noticeably heavier than in May, one could not have wished for better conditions. It was at this point that I really began to move and covered the next 164.8 miles in 1½ hours – an average speed of 109.9 mph. I would have liked to have completed 2 hours non-stop, but the beast was getting thirsty again and I had to stop to refuel after only 1 hour 43 minutes, albeit having driven 186.8 miles in that time (108.8 mph). I took on 101.1 litres (22¼ galls) of Super which is rather more than the manufacturers give as the combined capacity of the two tanks – so I must have cut it fine. Expressed as a gallon every 5 minutes at 50p per gallon it sounds horrific, but conventionally interpreted as 8.8 mpg, I consider it satisfactory at this speed. (The overall consumption for the journey to Nice was 10½ mpg and just over 11 mpg for the 2,100 mile round trip.) The mileage completed during the 2 hours after breakfast, including the 6 minute stop for petrol, was 205.

I entered the Tunnel de Fourvière at Lyon 5 hours 31 minutes after leaving Dunkerque, the Corniche's 'ghost' now trailing by 10 minutes. By the time I crossed the 'fly-over' at Vienne I had lost 2½ minutes, but from here on gradually improved on the Rolls, being 15½ minutes to the good at the Sénas Toll. Mental calculations now confirmed that I could not reach Marseille without another stop for petrol and this clipped 7 minutes off my time advantage. I lost another 2½ minutes in traffic before pulling up at the Cathedral on the dockside at Marseille at 12.24 pm, thus having completed the journey in 6 minutes less than the Corniche and, after deducting stops aggregating 35 minutes, had been on the move 11 minutes less; i.e. a driving average speed for the 665½ miles of 90.95 mph.

The sustained high-speed cruising capability of the car is further evidenced by the time of 4 hours 44 minutes (excluding stops) taken for the 455.5 miles from the Porte d'Italie to the point on A7 where the A8 forks off for Aix and Nice, which, of course, includes negotiating Lyon and Vienne, i.e. an average speed of 96.24 mph.

As for the car, it behaved impeccably. A check on the odometer over a distance of 100 kilometres showed it to be over-recording by 1.9% and stop-watch tests by a passenger on a previous run in France indicated that the speedometer was exaggerating by 4%. The needle remained between 120 and 130 most of the time with occasional stretches at an indicated 130 and 140, usually when a BMW, Citroën SM, Mercedes or Porsche was in the vicinity – note, the order is alphabetical. The silky smoothness characteristic of this car was somewhat marred above 100 mph by slight vibration. It felt like out-of-balance wheels, but I had had them balanced statically and dynamically before leaving home. Incidentally, tyre pressures were 6 psi above normal.

I found the Daimler no less comfortable than the Corniche, but the air-conditioning was not man enough for the job and, although absorbed in the general noise level experienced in any car at high speed, it was much too noisy when operating fully. It must be remembered that I drove only one way in the Daimler and, although I cannot therefore say how I would have felt if I had driven straight back to Dunkerque, I would have undertaken the double journey in the Double-Six without hesitation had the circumstances arisen. The efficiency of the Rolls-Royce air-conditioning system made driving in the hot weather more pleasant than in the Daimler. I was pleased to learn that the 1974 Jaguars and Daimlers were to have automatic temperature control. An excellent feature this and one which has been available on quality American cars for years, but which RR have delayed introducing . . . 'until the system has been developed and proved to their customary high standards of performance, reliability and silence'. It is to be hoped that this 'leap-frogging' of Crewe by Coventry has been accompanied by increased refrigeration capability, for it would be no improvement to be automatically too warm instead of manually not cool enough!

– And now the bad news:

My enchantment with the Daimler plunged below zero when, a week later, returning home almost as quickly, the engine stalled (an irritation which I had been living with since just before leaving England) in the toll-gate on the autoroute near Fontainebleau and the starter refused to work! I was pushed clear of the slot and there I stood between ten streams of returning holiday traffic not knowing exactly what the trouble was or what to do about it. (I think I received a few metaphorical 'Harvey Smiths' from drivers who had reluctantly yielded the overtaking lane to the speeding Daimler during the previous hour or so!) I suspected a stuck Bendix, (now I know it hasn't got one!), but the bonnetful of machinery and the low ground clearance did not make for easy examination of such things and eventually I succumbed to the ignominy of a suspended rearward tow (to which owners of immobile automatic-transmission cars are committed) to the Jaguar agents, Île de France Automobiles in Fontainebleau 16 miles away. It was 7 o'clock on a Saturday evening, but managerial and technical staff were available to assist me and in no time at all the trouble was diagnosed as a flat battery due to the alternator having ceased to work. The appropriate warning light indicated this fault, but I find it difficult to believe that it was illuminated whilst I was driving the car as my eyes were flashing to the instrument panel every minute or so though not, apparently, to the voltmeter which would have warned me of the dying battery. We proceeded to Paris for the week-end to await further investigation on the Monday morning. By noon on that day I learnt that the trouble was a good deal less serious than I feared, the alternator drive-belt having worn itself to the thickness of a boot-lace and finally ceased to function. There were not many 12-cylinder Jaguars in France and I give full marks to this garage for finding a replacement belt and completing the fitting – a tedious job involving the removal of the other drive belts – to enable us to resume our homeward journey the same day.

And the Conclusion:
Had I completed this account before commencing my return journey – i.e. before experiencing the alternator belt trouble – then it would have concluded with virtually unqualified praise for the car. I still hold this view (when the car is in motion under its own power), but a delay of two days and the consequent expense of taxis, hotels, meals, etc., must detract at least temporarily from any car's appeal in the eyes of the most patient owner – even when the breakdown is caused by something comparatively trivial.

However, it is surprising how quickly breakdowns and inconveniences of this sort fade in significance in one's memory when one likes a particular car and, if one accepts that such a failure could have occurred on any make of car, then I feel that the already-drafted paragraph is still valid.

The drive served to confirm my opinion that the 12-cylinder Daimler/Jaguar is the best value for money in the world and that both the Rolls-Royce and Daimler cars do great credit to the British Motor Industry.

What Next??

Well, it would be nice to commemorate the 70th Anniversary of the famous race by driving from Pekin to Paris in 1977 – but it remains to be seen whether or not petrol, politics, time and money will make it possible seriously to consider the materialization of such a pipe-dream.

* * *

Re-read at the end of 1974, these pages have a nostalgic ring, for speed limits imposed in France (and most other countries) in the interest of petrol conservation seem unlikely to be lifted in a hurry – if at all.

How fortunate I am to have been able to do these fast runs before the Third World took the fun out of motoring – except, of course, for Veteran and (many) Vintage car owners who have not been much worried by speed limits anyway.

Like I Said . . .

We insular-minded Britons write letters in English to hoteliers in foreign countries taking it for granted that they will reply in our language – and not their own.

Manfully, even the most humble innkeeper will do his damnedest best to comply – often with results which cannot fail to raise a smile.

With great respect to the writer I treasure the following letter from the proprietor of an Auberge near Reims to my request for two twin-bedded rooms:

> 'I can reserve for you: two rooms with one bed for two persons, but no two rooms with two beds for one person.'

Motoring the world over

Twenty-five years ago I was appointed to two jobs and I still hold both of them, though with greater experience, responsibilities and rewards in both cases. A Chartered Accountant by training, I became an executive in a ship-owning company; and, a Vintage Bentley enthusiast by inclination, I assumed the cloak of the President of the Bentley Drivers Club on the death of Woolf Barnato. To these two offices I owe a great deal. The former provided the wherewithal to indulge my hobby of motoring and the opportunity to travel to many parts of the world. The latter contributed greatly to the pleasure Con and I have derived from the many friendships formed with like-minded enthusiasts, and nowhere has this kinship been more evident than on our visits to foreign parts. However romantic the names of foreign cities may sound, one's enjoyment can be minimal if you are a stranger in town. To be friendless in a foreign country usually induces a loneliness which cultivates dislike for the place and, unless one meets the 'natives' on their own ground – and, preferably, in their own homes – it is not possible to gain a meaningful impression of life as it is lived there. Fortunately for us, enthusiasm for interesting cars transcends all national and social boundaries, and in countries all over the world we have been welcomed into family circles where an instant rapport has been engendered by the common interest in motor cars and motoring for its own sake. Holidays have been planned to include such meetings and most business trips have permitted an evening's or week-end's diversion into this wonderful world of motoring enthusiasts.

I find that I have driven cars in forty different countries or territories – excluding such technical qualifiers as Gibraltar and Monaco.

On one of my visits to New York – in November 1958 – I borrowed the latest Jaguar saloon from Briggs Cunningham and drove to Washington with that extrovert motoring enthusiast James Tilling, whom I had met by chance on 6th Avenue. I had not been to the capital city before and wanted to spend a day unashamedly rubber-necking. Everything went according to plan and we enjoyed the excursion – except for two incidents! The first one was when I ran out of petrol in the rush-hour traffic on one of Washington's bridges. (In my defence I reckon J.T. shares the blame for this contretemps, having misdirected me, when looking for a filling station, into a lane of traffic from which I could not extricate myself to regain the right road without covering several circuitous miles.) There I was – stationary and causing a solid and impatient traffic hold-up. Almostly instantly a police patrol man riding a motorcycle and sidecar was on the spot and took charge. Without demur he told the driver of the car behind to push me off the bridge bumper to bumper. This he did, fortunately with no damage to the Jag. Was my face red?

The second incident occurred when we were bowling along an almost deserted twin-track highway in New Jersey on the way back to New York. I said to James, 'What do these radar speed traps look like?' He said he didn't know. Scarcely were the words off his lips when I knew the answer – I was caught in one and was told to follow the Highway Patrolman to the Court House where I paid a summary fine of $25.

It was in 1963 that I realized we had motored in most of Europe and, if we wished to explore further afield, it would be necessary to fly to the area and start motoring when we got there. Our first target was the Middle East and, much as I would have liked to have driven there and back, the time needed was just not available. So we planned the first of our do-it-yourself 'fly and drive' holidays. We flew to Istanbul and were fortunate in having a car and English-speaking driver placed at our disposal. Having visited the sights in the city we drove along the Bosphorus towards the border with Russia and for part of the way were in company with one of 'our' tankers on its way into the Black Sea to load. On a subsequent business trip to 'Constantinople' I enquired about old cars and a colleague remembered having seen one in the Military Museum. Needless to say, I was soon there making a bee-line for this car. It turned out to be a Mercedes in which a Turk, Shevket Pasha, had been shot in 1913. The bullet-holed glass was still in the windows. It was not a runner, one cylinder block being missing, and the non-original 'LACRE' radiator fooled me until the similarity to my own car was pointed out to me.

From Istanbul we flew to Beirut in the Lebanon and rented an Opel to see the surrounding country, the fabulous ruins at Baalbeck and the Dead Sea. We then drove via Damascus the 270 miles to Jerusalem and certainly felt very adventurous crossing the Syrian desert in searing heat. We had a good look at Jerash on the way and then visited all the Biblical sites in Jerusalem and Bethlehem, but had to forego a hoped-for trip to Petra for lack of time. The drive back to Beirut was uneventful and after a night's rest we went by air to Cairo and checked in at the Hilton.

In Egypt we were greatly indebted to the Egyptian head of our Agents for driving us around in his Mark IX Jaguar. Not only did we see the Pyramids and the Sphinx, but spent a night at Suez and then drove the whole length of the Suez Canal to Port Said before returning to Cairo. It was extremely interesting driving alongside the canal passing a convoy of ships in transit. The terrain was such that on some occasions an approaching vessel looked as if it was on the road. Con had her moments when we visited the National Stud and she was mounted on a pure-bred Arab for a few swift laps round the paddock.

Reluctantly leaving Egypt we flew to Athens, where once again our motoring was of the chauffeured variety. Plenty to see in this part of Greece and we made the most of it before leaving for home.

I would like to drive to the Middle East – the signpost outside Damascus pointing across hundreds of miles of desert to 'Baghdad' at-

87 *The Mercedes in which Shevket Pasha was shot on 11 June 1913. The car is now in the Military Museum in Istanbul*

88 *The Mark IX Jaguar by the pyramids of Egypt*
89 *Approaching vessels on the Suez Canal gave the illusion of being on the road*

90 *Lenin's 1922 Silver Ghost Rolls-Royce in the V.I. Lenin Central Museum, Moscow*

91 *Two Mercedes owned by HIM The Emperor of Japan lined up for the author's delectation in the Palace Grounds in Tokyo*
92 *Guy Slaughter's Straight 8 1930 Packard Phaeton in Hawaii*

tracted me – but such has been the changing political situation in that part of the world that it has been scarcely possible to plan a trip with any certainty of being able to execute it.

Immediately after our daughter Carol's wedding in October 1964, Con and I embarked upon a trip round the world by air. It occupied 33 days and, although that may sound a bit rushed, we found time to see what we wanted to and time to relax, due to meticulous planning beforehand.

Our first stop was Moscow, but the only motoring we were able to do here was in taxis provided by Intourist. There were very few private cars, but they were all clean, it being an offence to drive a dirty vehicle. The main avenues in the city were wider than any I have seen and on some roads the central reservations marked out in white lines on the road surface were so wide as to eliminate the need for left turns, cars being able to make U-turns in the centre of the avenue and then turn right.

In the course of a visit to the V.I. Lenin Central Museum, I did seek out the 1922 Rolls-Royce Silver Ghost used by Lenin. On my return home I wrote asking for some information about the car and received a reply from the Deputy Director as follows:

> 'In answer to your enquiry, we send you details of the Rolls-Royce used by V.I. Lenin. Engine No: 207H, chassis no: 17KC,* Coachwork: torpedo, no. of cylinders: 6, diameter of cylinders: 114 mm.
>
> 'By order of the Council of Peoples' Commissars of the Russian Soviet Federated Socialist Republic, a number of such vehicles were obtained. The motor car at Gorky was the same series, but it was transferred to the Putilovsky Works for use on snow-covered roads and in places where roads did not exist.'

*This must have been 17KG.

The Director of the Polytechnic Museum admitted to there being some cars at a garage outside Moscow, but said that they were in a terrible state and so was the building, and for this reason it would not be possible to see them. I gathered that they were all Soviet vehicles except one, which may have been either a Steyr or Stoewer. He did, however, take me into the basement of the Museum and there (amidst displaced busts and statues of Stalin) were three vehicles, one a 1902 NAG, a 1924 AMO and a 1927 NAMI. The AMO was a lorry and seems to have been the first Soviet vehicle built. The NAMI was also a Russian vehicle, but rather a dull-looking saloon.

Whilst Con was seeing art treasures, I was strolling towards the British Embassy when I saw a convoy of big, black (ZIM?) limousines approaching and sweep swiftly through a gate in the Kremlin wall. Little did I realize at the time that I was probably witnessing history of the USSR in the making, for on that day Kruschev was removed from office.

Next stop was New Delhi, and we were very excited at the prospect of seeing something, however little, of the teeming sub-continent of India. It seems to be a quirk of air time-tables that all flights in and out of Delhi happen in the small hours of the morning – and so it was with us. The inconvenient hour did not stop Johnny Marshall, Rolls-Royce Aero Engine Service representative in India, and his wife, Bobbie, from turning out to meet us and whisk us to the Ashoka Hotel. After a day's sightseeing we left the city in Johnny's Ford station-wagon to see the Taj Mahal at Agra, and to stay overnight with his friend the Maharajah of Bharatpur. My mind was turning to all those magnificent Rolls-Royces, Hispano-Suizas, etc. bought by the dozen in more affluent days and now said to be standing unused and unloved on vast estates. I knew that the Maharajah had a Rolls or two, but did not know what they were. On arrival at Moti Mahal, the Maharajah's palace, I lost no time in enquiring about cars, but found only a couple of interest. One was a 1926 20 hp Windover Cabriolet with a polished aluminium saloon body which the Maharajah's mother had bought new and the other was a well-used Phantom II Hooper Limousine, which followed us to a duck shoot full of servants and bearers. His Highness was charming and we treasure this glimpse of the magnificence that once was India.

(Lest it be thought that ironmongery always takes precedence over beauty and even wonders of the world, I hasten to say that the Taj Mahal lived up to all the pictures and descriptions.)

After a stop-over at Bangkok we went straight to Tokyo. Our motoring in Japan was limited to taxi rides in the notoriously congested capital city – more than usually throttled by the additional traffic caused by the Olympic Games.

We did, however, have an astonishing piece of good fortune. I had told our Japanese guide – a charming young lady named Keiko – that I would like to see the Emperor's cars! She opened her eyes in incredulity and said that the Palace grounds were open only on one day each year and then not the Palace itself. Clearly I had asked for the Moon. Imagine my surprise, therefore, next morning when the smiling Keiko arrived at the hotel to say she had arranged through the Emperor's chauffeur for me to visit the Imperial garages! There I first saw the moderns – a Phantom V Rolls-Royce and an S3 Bentley in current use. Then the chauffeur produced a pre-war Mercedes in immaculate condition with the engine running beautifully. He indicated that there was another similar car and showed me a third, adding that a fourth was away being 'fixed'. They were the Type Nurburg, first produced in 1930 and in limited numbers thereafter until 1938 against special orders. The three cars seen in the Palace left the factory in March 1932 and January 1934.

After a short stay in Hong Kong, during which we were driven around the colony in a Mercedes placed at our disposal by business associates, we made the long overnight flight to Sydney to spend the week-end in Australia. Forewarned of our arrival, John ('Jumbo') Goddard invited all members of the Bentley Drivers Club living in New South Wales and – on the off-chance – Victoria to a party at his home. The response to his invitation was astonishing and resulted in an 80 per cent turn-out of those living in NSW. This was not all – members came from other parts of the Continent – some by Bentley; some in other cars and some by air. The distances travelled by Members to meet me as President of the Bentley Drivers Club were quite something and the effort, time and cost involved speak themselves for the high regard for the Marque.

Among those travelling long distances by road were Doug Jarvis from Adelaide (1,000 miles); Malcolm MacDonald from Brisbane (600 miles); Ian McColl and Albert Gladwin from Melbourne (600 miles); Jim Ryrie from Michelago (250 miles) and Ted Lobb from Grenfel (250 miles). Campbell Jaquet drove from Rowena – a mere 430 miles – in his fine Vanden Plas Saloon 8-litre. This car – one of the only two of this model in Australia – provided me with first class transport during a well filled 48-hour stay in Sydney. Bill Hands completed a rebuild of his open VdP 3 litre just in time to set off for Sydney – 600 miles away – without any time for a trial run. He had minor troubles on the way, but turned up at John's place in good shape.

The 'Oscar' for enthusiasm went to Arthur Vance – no millionaire and no youngster – who flew from Perth to Sydney for the week-end especially to be present at the meeting – a distance of 2,128 miles each way. Arthur Vance's pilgrimage (no lesser word suffices to describe his journey) was accepted by all as the seal on this spontaneous evocation of respect and regard for W.O. and his Bentleys.

All too soon we were winging our way to New Zealand. Con and I had accepted a very kind invitation to stay with the late 'Max' and Eilidh Maxwell-Stewart in Wellington. They met us at the airport in their R-Type Continental which I had been instrumental in purchasing for Max in England earlier in the year, and which he had collected personally and used for a holiday here before shipping home.

Again a gathering of Bentley enthusiasts was arranged – this time at the newly-opened Motor Museum of Len Southward. The Museum was most interesting and contained a wealth of motoring miscellany in addition to a collection of Veteran and Vintage cars, including Len's 3-litre awaiting restoration.

The next two days were spent in touring northwards to Auckland (530 miles) in the Continental and I revelled in the opportunity to drive this car in conditions which approached a motorist's paradise. Few cars and fast well-surfaced roads through scenery reminiscent of Wales, Scotland and occasionally Switzerland.

Whilst we were checking in at Auckland airport and digesting the news that our departure would be delayed by 3 hours, the distinctive burble of Vintage Bentleys announced the arrival of A.B. Seccombe and his daughter in his beautifully turned-out open Speed Six, followed by his son driving his 4½. These were soon joined by N.C. Adams' 3-litre and R.S. Mills' 4½-litre Park Ward Saloon. Also present were several other Vintage car enthusiasts. The waiting hours were spent happily – albeit in an uncomfortable and 'dry' airport lounge – talking Bentleys. The party gradually dispersed, but a few stayed until the bitter end to see us off to Fiji around midnight.

After a very short night in bed at Nandi I hired a Holden and we set off for the 70-mile drive along the beautiful, unspoiled coastal road to Koru Levu. The couple of days complete rest here was enough for me, but Con would have stayed a good deal longer and often talks of Fiji as the place she would most like to go back to. At the end of a two-hour drive to the airport in the dark, during which we saw scarcely a soul or habitation, we left Nandi for Hawaii.

On arrival at Honolulu – you've guessed it – we were met by Guy Slaughter, the owner of a 4½-litre Bentley, and his wife Betty, who placed the traditional leis round our necks in welcome. In the car park was the only Vintage Bentley for at least 2,000 miles in any direction and a Vintage

Packard Club Sedan to transport us and our luggage to the Hotel.

As far as was known there were only about half a dozen enthusiasts in the Islands and you can imagine how the three I met welcomed a personal contact with one closely connected with the cult in the UK. The inhabitants appeared to have little appreciation of Vintage cars and their lack of knowledge was quite surprising – it took quite a thick skin to drive around in an old car at the receiving end of laughs, jibes about 'Model T's' and countless daft questions and suggestions.

The afternoon was spent in motoring round the island of Oahu in the open Bentley, which Guy had finished putting together with new big ends only the previous day. It ran like a bird and we enjoyed our sightseeing trip immensely. That evening we dined with one of the few Vintage car owners in Hawaii – Judson Ihrig – whose garage housed a PII Rolls-Royce, a 1926 37.2 hp Hispano-Suiza, a 1913 EMF and a small Vintage Rolls. Another enthusiast in Hawaii – then without any Vintage machinery – was Warren Kernaghan who had owned until recently the 12-cylinder Packard used in the film 'South Pacific'.

Our second day in Hawaii included a 100-mile drive round the main island in a most elegant Straight 8 1930 Packard Phaeton from Guy's stable.

From Honolulu to San Francisco where we found awaiting us at the hotel, a letter from a Club Member, Jay Heumann, inviting us to spend the following day with him and his wife. This turned out to be a guided tour of San Francisco in his R-Type Continental with lunch and dinner included. This hospitality we accepted appreciatively and spent a most pleasant day sightseeing. Not far behind the Golden Gate Bridge and the giant redwood trees ranked Jay's $4\frac{1}{4}$-litre (MX series) Bentley. This car had been completely rebuilt by Jay and it did him great credit. Incidentally, Jay really has mastered the change down into bottom gear on his Continental – he had to, living in a City where nearly all the streets are steeper than any encountered in this country. Con and I agreed that San Francisco would be our choice if we had to live in the States.

An invitation to visit the almost legendary Harrah Automobile Collection caused me to dent our itinerary between San Francisco and Los Angeles and thus we arrived at Reno at 11 o'clock one morning with a bare five hours to do less than justice to this unique car museum. We were met by Bud Catlett, the Purchasing Supervisor of the Collection, who devoted his day to showing us the cars and answering innumerable questions. It would be quite impossible to give an adequate description of Mr (Bill) Harrah's collection in anything less than a volume, but I will give just a few facts and figures as a bare framework in which one's imagination may wander.

There were then 940 cars, about 300 of which were on display, the majority having been restored in the plant which was the backbone of the collection. This plant covered 5 acres and, in addition to two large showrooms, included a large workshop area and separate buildings for coachwork, upholstery, plating and sandblasting. In these shops were employed 70 craftsmen and there did not seem to be a single job arising in rebuilding cars which they could not tackle – I saw radiators, wheels and lamps being repaired and, where necessary made from scratch, for veteran, vintage and classic cars undergoing restoration.

Bill Harrah had brought out on the occasion of my visit, a Supercharged $4\frac{1}{2}$-litre Bentley awaiting its turn for face-lifting and an 8-litre bought from an owner in the Eastern United States. I also saw another 8-litre recently bought from Briggs Cunningham and a 100 mph 3-litre. We were joined at lunch in the staff cafeteria by Bill who, once his natural reserve had been overcome, enjoyed a stimulating discussion on motor-cars in general and Bentleys in particular.

After the breath-taking tour of the showrooms and workshops we visited and lingered in the library. Yes – this, too, defied description. Thousands of volumes covering every aspect of motoring and a research staff – all maintained to one end – the authentic and true-to-original restoration of cars in the collection.

And so to our last port of call, Los Angeles, where Briggs Cunningham met us at the airport and drove us to his new home at Newport Beach where we were to spend the next two and a half days. I had asked Briggs if he would arrange a meeting of Club members in the area and if those attending might then see his collection of cars. He did more than this. Briggs wrote personally to all the members resident in California and neighbouring States inviting them to a lunch at his home and to see the cars afterwards. So great was the response that the venue of the lunch was moved to the garage itself.

The Saturday of the Club party arrived and much effort had gone into cleaning up the cars and especially sprucing up the Bentleys. In the morning I enjoyed driving around in, successively, the ex-Pierre Marechal Speed Six; the ex-Peter Bell 8-litre; the Eddie Hall TT 4¼ and my old Phantom III Rolls-Royce. We parked the three Bentleys and three others (4½-litre Supercharged; 4¼-litre Overdrive and 'R' Type Continental) outside the 'warehouse' containing the remaining 40 or 50 cars in the collection and awaited the arrival of the guests.

First to arrive was Norman Brooks from San Diego without his 8-litre, which was still undergoing coachwork restoration at the hands of an unhurried craftsman. He was closely followed by Arthur Rippey who flew in from Denver, a thousand miles away, thus providing further evidence, if any were needed, of the enthusiasm of we car-minded people. Members began arriving thick and fast. Amherst Villiers (designer of *the* Blower) took time off from rebuilding a Supercharged 4½-litre – now owned by Phil Hill – to join the party.

Briggs and Laura had set up a U-shaped lunch table for 40 in the garage and we sat down to the groaning board in the presence of as fine a selection of cars as one could wish for. This very happy occasion concluded with a vote of thanks to Briggs and Laura for arranging the meeting and for their generous hospitality. The guests reluctantly departed in ones and twos as the air was shattered by the Bentleys being driven back under cover.

In January 1967 Con and I decided to see something of Africa and my carefully planned itinerary enabled us to visit countries in East and South Africa in a three-week round trip.

After a most worthwhile visit to Murchison Park in Uganda and an unpleasant experience at the hands (and rifle-butt) of a guard outside the palace of the deposed Kabaka, we flew to Nairobi. There were only four Club members living in Kenya at the time and I had written to each of them suggesting getting together one evening, perhaps in Nairobi. The response was prompt and enthusiastic. In fact, each one had suggested different ways of making the most of our short visit to Kenya and extended invitations to us to stay a day or two with them, which, unfortunately, my closely planned itinerary would not permit. Eventually, we all lunched at Nakuru, 100 miles from Nairobi, on Sunday, 22 January, a private room at the Stag's Head echoing to Bentley talk for a couple of hours or so; but first let me go back to our arrival in Nairobi. At the airport we were met by Ken Rhys-Maitland – Dental Officer in the RAF then stationed in Kenya – and his wife, Joan.

There were no Bentleys in Nairobi, but Ken took me to see a 1913 London-Edinburgh Silver Ghost being restored by its owner Willy Balabanoff.

The drive to Nakuru was pleasant enough and the first car I saw in the main street was a very clean and standard open 4½. This belonged to John Jeeves and was the only Bentley present. Stewart Hamilton had burned a lot of midnight

93 *John Jeeves (centre) with his $4\frac{1}{2}$-litre Bentley in Nakuru, Kenya*

oil in an effort to get his Standard $6\frac{1}{2}$ on parade, but was beaten by drain tubes which had been incorrectly threaded. These two, together with Ken Rhys-Maitland who had accompanied me from Nairobi, represented a 75 per cent turnout of the whole membership of the country, plus an erstwhile member, Roddy Williams, who had a $3/4\frac{1}{2}$ at home – in bits hanging on the wall, as far as I can gather. Those present were exhorting him to 'build up' or 'part up'. Another non-member present with his Mk VI was Stephen Hempstead, who also owned a 1915 Alpine Silver Ghost. Thereafter, some of us, including John Jeeves in his $4\frac{1}{2}$, went to the nearby lake famous for being the home of flamingoes said to number up to two million at times. There were so many that the edge of the lake was fringed in pink as far as the eye could see, and the level lake shore invited driving antics.

In Mombasa I rented a 'bread-and-butter' car and drove several miles into the bush to see what Kenya was really like. I found that only a mile or two off the main road the land was free from all the trappings of so-called civilization, the people going about their daily life in the villages as they must have done for centuries. Now I know why it is necessary for makers of cars intended for East African markets to drive them through dust-bowls to ensure that they are leak-proof! I noticed that the most popular makes of cars were those which had done well in successive Safari Rallies.

Only one Member was living in Dar es Salaam, our next port of call – Francis Spencer – a temporary immigrant from the UK and a dyed-in-the-wool Vintage Bentley enthusiast.

He took me off in a taxi to the house of a friend, 6 miles out of town, to show me his Bentley. We arrived at this house amid palm trees and as I followed him round to the back I was surprised to see under a lean-to a bodyless 3-litre chassis in an advanced stage of rebuild.

The car was then complete mechanically, as was demonstrated to me when I went for a ride

94 *Francis Spencer's 3-litre Bentley in Dar es Salaam*

95 *Briggs Cunningham's 275GTB4 Ferrari and his wife Laura's mother-of-pearl Lamborghini Miura at Costa Mesa*

on the bonnetless machine, standing on the chassis frame and gear-box with the driver seated in a bare, bucket seat. The body work was to be started soon and an entirely new body fabricated.

Francis had recently discovered in Dar es Salaam a Vintage $4\frac{1}{2}$ Bentley with a Mk VI radiator owned by a Mr William Boddy. The log book showed Chassis No XF 3517 and Engine No XF 3515 which belong to the 1929 Paris Show car. It had a VdP body, was running on one set of ignition and had a Fordson dynamo. The replacement parts used from time to time looked distinctly agricultural. The front brakes had been converted to hydraulics using lorry parts. The Tanzanian Registration No was IR 1231 and it had been imported before the War.

We then went to Livingstone and found the Victoria Falls to be one of the most impressive sights we have ever seen and afterwards headed south to Johannesburg, where our visit would coincide with the Annual Dinner of the local members of the BDC.

Whilst Con's hair was having attention in readiness for the dinner, I was taken to Jeffs Watson's lovely home in his drophead Mk VI Bentley. I saw his very nice, standard VdP $4\frac{1}{2}$, which was driven during the rest of the week-end by Jeffs' eldest son, Roy, who, incidentally, had recently rebuilt a Tiger Moth from scrap and raced it with satisfactory results. Jeff had a collection of Veteran and Edwardian cars, and being restored in the garage were a Type 35 Bugatti (with a Type 38 engine) and a curved-dash Oldsmobile.

In the evening we were collected at the hotel by Gordon Strauss in his well-preserved, high-mileage, early Mk VI and taken to the venue for dinner. This was, in fact, the most off-beat imaginable – a prison and the waiters were inmates. Sounds awful, doesn't it? Well, it wasn't. The establishment was a rehabilitation centre for first offenders – an open prison at which they were taught trades and vocations with a view to keeping them out of trouble when they were released. It catered for both black and white and was seemingly doing a good job. For our part, the table, the service and the food were beyond criticism and the room could have been the banqueting room of any provincial English hotel.

Before we sat down to dinner I was able to meet and talk to all the members present – no less than 18. Some of these had driven several hundred miles to be there, Waldie Greyvensteyn from Bloemfontein probably scoring top marks in this respect. The party, including families, numbered 46 in all. The usual toasts were proposed and the meaningful words spoken on the subject of the Club, our Patron and Bentleys generally, reflected exactly the same sincerity of admiration and feeling as on similar occasions in the UK.

Gordon Fisher presented to me a handsome, inscribed copper tray as a memento of the occasion. I replied suitably, I hope, and the party dissolved for conversation. As always, I was impressed with the enthusiasm and the detailed technical knowledge of these chaps who did miracles in maintaining their Bentleys far from the comparatively easy sources of spares and technical know-how available to UK members. Anyone overhearing the post-prandial conversation in Johannesburg would have thought himself at a Club meeting in the 'local' at home.

At Cape Town we were met by Luccio Labia from whom I had acquired my Mercedes. He showed us round and then lent me his Alfa-Romeo for the duration of our stay. Two members of the Bentley Drivers Club, Tony White and Rudi Reitz, on hearing of our 48-hour stay in Cape Town, contacted all Members within reasonable distance and arranged a meeting. Thanks to the generous hospitality of Tony and his wife, this took the form of a supper party at their home. Driven there from our hotel by Rudi Reitz we were greeted, as we entered the drive of the White house, by the sight of the two open $4\frac{1}{2}$s of the Rohr brothers, Bert and

Ralph, standing side by side, with Cecil Harris's S-Type discreetly parked in the shade. In all 12 members attended, Rudy Reitz having driven nearly 300 miles from George. Dr Clarke came from Worcester, 70 miles away, to which town he had recently moved from Livingstone in Zambia. (The Secretary of the Club had notified Tony White of this change of address specially for the purpose of the gathering and, when Tony telephoned John Clarke from out of the blue and said, 'Are you a member of the Bentley Drivers Club?' the surprised medico replied, 'Yes, but how the hell did you know?')

We soon repaired to the garage where Tony White's Standard 6½ awaited commencement of the complete rebuild scheduled for it. Alongside it Barry Morton was rebuilding his 4½ from the ground up and was in the middle of mounting a replica VdP body imported from England in kit form.

Our Cape Town visit terminated on a very happy note when Cecil and Ann Harris insisted on picking us up at the Mount Nelson Hotel at 6.15 am (!) and driving us to the Airport in their S1 Bentley.

This was the start of our journey home, but we had yet one more country to visit – Rhodesia.

Not many members were then living in Rhodesia, but a tentative enquiry about the possibility of a get-together to E.J.L. ('Charles') Griffith brought a speedy response with a promise to meet us at the airport and to arrange a dinner in Salisbury. I had known Charles in the immediate post-war years before he left the UK and well remembered his prowess in competition in a Blower Bentley in those days.

He met us on arrival in a more pedestrian, but well-maintained 3½-litre saloon and drove us to the City centre, where I picked up a Hertz car to leave at once for the Vumba Mountains 180 miles away. Charles' last remark as we left Salisbury was: 'If you are in trouble in Umtali, chief 'Itala-swinger' Jack Sanderson – a reference to VSCC Silverstone meetings years ago – is with Meikle's Garage there.' I wasn't in trouble in Umtali, but I did call on Jack – happily married with a growing family – and he did not need much persuading to drive 20 miles over a mountain road (187 bends) to dine with us at Leopard Rock that night.

I found motoring in Rhodesia a joy – perhaps the best of any country I had visited. The road from Salisbury to Umtali (160 miles) was surfaced all the way, gently curving and undulating and interesting – and traffic-free! I needed only 160 minutes to cover the 160 miles in a 'cooking' Cortina in which I rarely exceeded 65 mph, and never 70.

It was thus no hardship to leave the Vumba three days later to drive to Salisbury in time to catch an 11 am hair appointment for Con in preparation for the evening party. The afternoon was spent at Charles' house where his chain-driven Frazer Nash and other automotive projects occupied some time.

Four Club members – Charles, T.E. Barlow Pye and his son, J.B. Pye, who had flown in from Ndola in neighbouring Zambia, and C.A.L. Meredith were present at the dinner party in the Ambassador Hotel. Several other Bentley owners were there. Also Joan Rowland, a niece of W.O.

Again, we spent a most pleasant evening and the kindness and hospitality extended to us was further evidence that the interest of Members in Bentleys transcends not only social, financial and geographical boundaries, but also thrives with complete indifference to political barriers.

Altogether, during our trip, we met no less than 40 Club members. Each one of them – and the wives of the married ones – contributed something to our enjoyment which cannot be assessed in material terms.

In June 1968 in the course of a business trip to Australia and back in the short space of 13 days I managed to contact Club members in several places. Over the Pole to Tokyo via Alaska – no BDC members there – then via Hongkong and Manila to Sydney. John Goddard was here, instead of there, but a telephone call to Jack Jeffery brought forth an invitation to dine at his house and a visit to his garage – presently devoid of Bentleys, but boasting a fine Mercedes-Benz.

In the course of a 24-hour visit to Melbourne, 460 miles away, Gregor Rusden managed to gather together a party of Members and Bentley enthusiasts at his home where I spent a very pleasant evening. I am always amazed at the perseverance and tenacity of these Australian Bentley lovers who rebuild and maintain their cars under difficulties scarcely imaginable to those who are within two-day postal delivery of most spare parts and a local call away from expert knowledge and advice.

Next stop was Honolulu, to refuel and pass through US Customs. An air mail warning of my passage to Guy Slaughter brought him hot-foot from his place of work at Pearl Harbour to the airport in his $4\frac{1}{2}$. We spent a pleasant hour in the Coffee Shop – it was breakfast time – talking of matters Bentley and Vintagery generally. Five hours and 2,400 miles later I landed at Los Angeles to be met by Briggs and Laura Cunningham who whisked me away to Bruce Fagan's apartment. Here we were joined by Bill Anderson and John Milchick and later adjourned to a Beverly Hills restaurant for dinner and talked about – you've guessed – Bentleys and ancillary subjects until nigh on midnight, when Briggs drove me south to his home at Newport Beach.

Early next morning I was in Briggs' Automobile Museum at nearby Costa Mesa relishing once again his wonderful collection of cars. I then drove his 275 GTB4 Ferrari and Laura's Lamborghini Miura, before being driven to LA to catch the 1 pm flight to New York. On arrival I picked up a Hertz Ford Galaxie and drove out to spend a night in Bernardsville, New Jersey, with daughter Carol and her family.

I flew to Bermuda the next morning and, after lunch with friends at the Mid-Ocean Club and three business meetings in Hamilton, I took a taxi out to Stanley Sears's home for tea. (Guess what we talked about!)

Charles Noble, owner of no less than four supercharged $4\frac{1}{2}$-litre Bentleys, was awaiting my arrival at J.F. Kennedy Airport having driven out from the City especially to spend an hour with me between flights and – yes – we talked Bentleys until about 1 am. Such is the dedication of Bentley enthusiasts.

A visit to Mexico for the Olympic Games in 1968 provided an opportunity to taste the joys and hazards of driving in Central America. On the way there we stopped off in New York to visit Carol and Roger, and our grandchildren, in New Jersey and again in Washington where I enjoyed driving Con around the capital city, this being her first visit there, in a Mustang belonging to Mr Hertz.

We were met at Mexico City Airport by Porfirio ('Sunny') Diaz, who owned the only Vintage Bentley in the country. It was an 8-litre, particularly interesting in that it was the only one fitted with American coachwork when new, a roadster body by Murphy. It was not in good shape. The engine was dismantled pending rebuilding and motive power was provided by an International diesel truck engine – sounded rather like a Vintage Bentley, I must admit, but not like an 8-litre. I drove it with some trepidation as the ancient tyres had that rather tired 'dried-up mud' appearance. Another unusual feature of this Bentley was the wooden-spoked wheels. When Sunny acquired the car it had no wheels at all; it was only by good fortune that he found four wheels off a Mercedes in a breaker's yard which fitted the splined hubs. (This 8-litre and all the bits have since been acquired by Don Weber of Texas and is currently undergoing a once-and-for-all restoration at the premises of Hofmann & Mountfort at Henley-on-Thames where the car and pieces were delivered in huge crates from Mexico.)

Whilst in Mexico City we visited some of the nearby ruins in our rented Ford Galaxie, the

96 *Stanley Sears gives the author a ride during a visit to Bermuda*

97 *The author with Sunny Diaz and his 8-litre Bentley in Mexico City, now owned by Don Weber of Texas and undergoing complete restoration*

98 *Arthur G. Rippey and the Mk VI Bentley in his museum at Denver, Colorado*

pyramids at San Juan Teotihuacan impressing us perhaps most of all. The relics we saw in the City itself and in the Museum of Anthropology whetted our appetite for the planned excursions to Uxmal and Chichen-Itza from our next stopping-place, Merida in Yucatan. Motoring in this part of Mexico was very enjoyable and exploring the Mayan ruins filled us with awe and admiration for their creators – tinged with disgust at the barbarity of some of their ways.

We continued our journey by air to Kingston, Jamaica and rented a car to drive across the island to Ocho Rios where we were to stay a few days. There was some unrest and labour trouble in Kingston and not long after leaving the town an attempt was made by a Jamaican driving an old banger to run me off the road; I can only think he took exception to being overtaken by a more modern car and retaliated in anger.

In May 1969 we were fortunate enough to be on the belated maiden voyage of 'Queen Elizabeth II' from Southampton to New York. A contingent of old Rolls-Royces and their owners were on board at the start of a tour in the United States, so motoring talk was predominant throughout the trip. After visiting New Orleans and Williamsburg – where I rented cars locally – we joined up again with the RR party in Washington and rode with them to attend a reception at the British Embassy. Afterwards, everyone was entertained to dinner by members of the Rolls-Royce Owners Club (of America) in the Smithsonian Institute. Films were shown of the previous year's Rolls-Royce and Bentley Pageant at Goodwood and I was called upon to make impromptu remarks each time a Bentley appeared on the screen – a task I performed indifferently, I'm afraid, not having seen the film before, but it was made intelligible and enjoyable by John Dymock-Maunsell's commentary, for he had organized the event and knew nearly every car.

In June 1971, bidden to attend the opening of a mammoth dry-dock in Lisbon, we flew to

Faro, borrowed a Toyota from Sr Hertz and spent an interesting week in the Algarve before allowing business to raise its ugly head. This was my first experience of Japanese motoring and the car provided perfectly adequate transport. We took the attractive inland road to Lisbon and whilst staying there revisited Cascais, Guincho and Sintra, which we had first seen in the Mk VI in 1959, and, of course, drove over the magnificent new bridge spanning the Tagus.

In February 1972 Con and I decided to get away from the English winter for a week's sunshine in Tunisia. Whilst staying at Hammamet we hired a car and drove southwards 100 miles or so to see Kairouan and Sousse. We then spent a few days with our old friends the Scheels at Carthage, during which Ditlev took us for a long drive in his Opel Diplomat to the fantastic, but perhaps not so well-known, ruined city at Dougga.

Oil business took me to Colorado and California in May 1972 and I decided to take a few days holiday to see the Indianapolis '500' Race on the way home. First call was on Arthur G. Rippey in Denver, Colorado, who had flown nearly 1,000 miles to Los Angeles to meet me when Briggs Cunningham gave the lunch party in his 'garage' in 1964, and I was glad of the opportunity to repay the courtesy. On his retirement from business at the end of 1966, Mr Rippey sold his original collection of Veteran and Vintage cars, but then found it possible to indulge his hobby once more by running a purchase-and-sale business alongside his museum. The collection was not a large one and included a majority (I think) of post-Vintage and post-World War II cars. My first choice would be the 1933 Chrysler Custom Imperial with Le Baron phaeton coachwork.

After an overnight stop in LA, a non-stop flight in a DC-10 took me to West Palm Beach in Florida where I stayed overnight with Bill Spear. There were no longer any Bentleys in his stable, but I seized the opportunity to drive his 3-litre BMW (named the 'Bavaria' in the States by the manufacturers to dispel the prevalent impression that it was a British car!), Wankel-engined Mazda and his latest acquisition – a Dino Ferrari.

I made a side trip to the Bahamas to inspect some land I was misguided enough to purchase some years ago, and then flew from Nassau to Toronto where I had been invited to a private preview of a collection of about 50 Veteran, Vintage and Classic cars to be unveiled to the world at large three weeks later. This collection had been put together quietly during the previous year by selected purchases made for the sponsors, Rothmans of Pall Mall Canada Ltd, through 'The Craven Foundation'. The shopping list was compiled by an advisory Committee of enthusiasts in the field of Veteran and Classic cars in Canada and a prominent part was played by Ralph Turner whose personal Speed Six was well-known in those parts. Many desirable cars had been acquired, including an 8-litre Bentley costing £15,000 which I was privileged to be the first to drive on the road there. I rode as a passenger in a 'J' Duesenberg and fifty-one thousand dollars-worth of Packard – an immaculate, dual-cowl phaeton '734' model of 1930; also a rare 1930 Ruxton and a Graham.

Later that week, having completed business matters in New York, I flew in to Indianapolis to see the '500' on the following day. I had been looking forward to seeing the famous race at Indianapolis. I felt my education in the motor-racing field was lacking until I had seen this race – once! I knew that it was unique and surrounded with a lot of bally-hoo, but the speeds were fantastic and my impression from films and photographs – which actually concentrated on spectacular crashes – was that the event was becoming too dangerous. The start was spectacular and I saw one heart-stopping crash in which the car returned to the paddock as a crumpled ball of metal dangling from the crane of a rescue track but, mercifully, the driver survived. As the race progressed and cars spread out it became less enthralling and for many laps it was frankly boring. The speed of the cars did not appear to be near the 200 mph mark and certainly the whole thing looked relatively safe to me. The protection for the spectators is so good that the track tends to provide 'slot-racing' with the result that when a driver runs out of road, he is, in fact, bounced straight back on to it in the path of following cars. As there is no verge between the outer edge of the track and the barrier, the following drivers have less chance of avoiding a car in trouble, and are, therefore, more at risk from the misdoings and mishaps of others than would be the case on most European circuits.

Right after the race I flew to Detroit and was the guest of Dick Mertz, President of the Rolls-Royce Owners Club of America who very kindly took me to the Ford Museum at Dearborn, and allowed me to drive his immaculate Phantom III. A direct VC 10 flight to London terminated that trip.

In March 1973 I seized the opportunity to visit the Chinese Peoples' Republic in connection with the British Industrial Technology Exhibition in Peking. After flying to Stuttgart, and driving from there to Athens (reported elsewhere), I decided to stop off for a week-end in Bangkok on the way to Hong Kong, the jumping-off point for Pekin. In anticipation of my stop-over I wrote to 'Bira' (Prince Birabongse Bhanubandh) asking if H.M. King Bhumibol of Thailand owned any old cars and, if so, could he arrange for me to see them?

Soon after checking in at the Intercontinental Hotel, I called him at his apartment in the Dhusi Thani Hotel to learn that he did not know whether his Royal cousin had any old cars or not. 'Bira' was busily engaged running his own airline and had lost interest in motor racing and motoring. Nevertheless, he readily agreed on a voyage of discovery and first took me to the garages at the King's residence, Chitrlada Palace, where three cars, one Veteran and two Vintage, were to be seen among the fleet of modern cars.

99 *The author out in Toronto with Ralph Turner on the first trip in Canada of the 8-litre Bentley recently added to the Craven Collection*
100 *Mike Mosley's car returning to the Paddock as a crumpled ball of metal during the Indianapolis '500' in 1972*

The Veteran, a beautifully kept – presumably restored – four-cylinder Renault four-seater tonneau with a fringed canopy was pushed out into the open so that I could take photographs. The two Vintage vehicles, not in pristine condition, but apparently complete and in workman-like shape, were a Hotchkiss and a Voisin.

The former had a Saoutchik body, and the latter coachwork by Ottin of Lyon.

My appetite thus whetted, and 'Bira' and his beautiful wife now infected by my enthusiasm avidly searching for identification plates in dusty and oily darkness, we were then piloted by a couple of Royal Mews employees to another palace the name and whereabouts of which I failed to note. On arrival we drove past many modern cars and several immaculate post-war Delahayes which, I believe, the King himself had acquired during the time he lived in Paris, and perceived promise of better things to come as two Rolls-Royces came into sight.

On blocks was a Silver Ghost (chassis No. 108AG) with an enclosed drive cabriolet body by Hooper. This car was supplied to H.E. Buri Navarash on 4 October 1921. I noticed that it was fitted with apparently original Dunlop Limousine 895 × 150 tyres. Its later sister was a Phantom III (chassis no. 3DL 158) with a limousine de ville body by H.J. Mulliner finished in the Royal deep cream. It was immaculate and was driven out of its garage as silently and smoothly as any PIII I have known. The records show that this car was shipped from Southampton on 21 August 1939 to HRH Prince Aditya Dhipya Arbha in Bangkok. The radiator shutters were fixed in the open position, presumably to cope with the tropical climate.

Next to the Rolls-Royce a pair of (to me) less interesting cars stood on blocks, a Mercedes with rear wheels hanging grotesquely on their swing-axles and a Daimler with a Charlesworth body. My failure to pursue further investigation of these cars was due to a glimpse of a group of large radiators visible in a series of open-fronted garages further down the road. Impatiently approaching this Aladdin's Cave, my eyes popped out of my head when I realized that the five giants from left to right were a Cadillac, a Pierce-Arrow, a Mercedes, a Hispano-Suiza and a Voisin! The Pierce-Arrow, a 1930 or 1931 Straight Eight with a phaeton body was unusual in having bracket lamps instead of the traditional ones faired into the front mudguards. The Mercedes was a six-cylinder supercharged car of 1929, almost certainly a Type 630B. The chassis had been sent by train from the factory in Stuttgart to Paris in July 1929 where the coachbuilders, Saoutchik, fitted a touring body.

The Hispano-Suiza was the well-known H6B 37.2 hp six-cylinder car of 1927. And last but by no means least, the V12 Voisin. Time was getting short and I did not look for identifying information on this car, but my attention was captured by an interesting feature: an extra radiator under the bonnet. Was this for water or oil, and was it a standard feature or a tropical extra?

I left the Royal mews with mixed feelings. Gratification that examples of these Grandes Marques still existed; sorrow that the prevailing climatic conditions must have wrought severe but not irreparable damage; regret that there was no prospect of the cars passing into the hands of enthusiasts able and prepared to restore them to new condition – the latter sentiment tempered by the knowledge that any self-seeking dealer contemplating a trip to Thailand with a view to making a kill would be more likely to be on the receiving end of Royal disapproval – for the King never sells anything.

The best hope was that something may be done to restore the cars and put them on exhibition in Bangkok – a course of action which I enjoined 'Bira' to commend to His Majesty.

I dodged about a bit in Japan and then flew from Hong Kong to Pekin in a chartered BOAC VC 10 on the first-ever direct airline flight between these two cities. Of motoring in 'Red' China, there was virtually none. Lots of trucks, seemingly millions of bicycles, some taxis, motor-coaches and Chinese-built cars used by Government officials and employees, but the only private cars to be seen were those of foreign diplomatic staff. The roads were wide and motorized traffic sparse. The biggest hazard

101 *'DL' Series Rolls-Royce Phantom III limousine de ville by H.J. Mulliner*

102 *Prince Birabongse Bhanubandh with the 1909/10 Renault*

were the ubiquitous cyclists – who were not required to carry lights at night – causing drivers of the few taxis and other vehicles to blow their horns incessantly.

There were 900 Brits. in Peking on this occasion and the Chinese certainly made us welcome. It was, for me, a never-to-be-forgotten experience to stand upon the Great Wall of China and I left the country feeling that, given political stability, it had a great future. It seemed to be developing slowly and surely, and if the will to continue is maintained there is a great opportunity to raise the standard of living, at the same time avoiding the pitfalls which have plagued Western civilization. I am conscious that any views I express about China, based as they are upon a week in two cities without any knowledge of the language, are virtually valueless, but I know what I saw – and that is an apparently healthy and contented people working hard. Nevertheless, I must confess to a feeling of freedom regained as I got off the train from Canton and walked across the border bridge to Lo Wu into the New Territories of Hong Kong. I continued the same day by air to Tokyo and across the Pacific to Los Angeles.

And so to California where I found that Acton Cochrane had once again risen to the occasion by arranging not one but two Bentley meetings on the same day – a concours in the afternoon and a dinner in the evening. Accordingly, Barry Hon called for me at the Beverly Hilton early on Saturday morning and I drove his S1 Continental out to the Santa Anita Park Racecourse (horses, not cars) on the outskirts of Los Angeles. Here I found myself in unfamiliar surroundings when asked to be in the Winner's Circle to welcome the winning horse and jockey of a race named 'The Rolls-Royce and Bentley

103 *'Aladdin's Cave' – from left to right are a Cadillac, a Pierce-Arrow, a Mercedes and a Hispano-Suiza*

104 *V-12 Voisin with supplementary under-bonnet radiator*

105 *A 'Red Flag' limousine in Peking, manufactured in Changchun No 1 Factory, which produces between fifty and a hundred cars a year for official use. The limousine has a 5.65 litre engine, a weight of $2\frac{3}{8}$ tons, and is understood to come with varying degrees of armour-plating and bullet-proof glass*

Owners Purse' in honour of the two clubs. I then presented the prizes to winners of the Rolls-Royce and Bentley Concours.

In the evening the basement hall of the elegant Bank of America Building outside the dining-room was graced by the presence of three Bentleys, a gesture I appreciated very much.

I was pleased to be able to reciprocate in some measure by showing my films of the Club visits to Le Mans and Aubusson, thereby bringing to life the photographs of Bentleys seen in the pages of the Club's magazine by the many who might never be able to come to the UK to see the cars themselves.

A fitting close to this day was when, at somewhere approaching midnight, the Speed Six driven by Dave Clark, and the Blower $4\frac{1}{2}$ driven by Phil Hill, had a drag race down Flower Street, in the heart of the financial district. As the Club's local scribe, Don Taylor, put it – 'The Bentley Burble and the Blower whine echoed and re-echoed from the walls of glass and steel that were only a quarter their age, or even less . . . The Perfect Epilogue.'

Brief stays in Toronto and New York, where I renewed motoring friendships, ended this, my third circumnavigation of the World.

And that is about the sum total of my globe-trotting experiences in the world of motoring. South America has been on my list as a 'must' for some time and I hope I shall be able to visit that part of the world whilst I am still 'young' and fit enough to enjoy it.

Meantime, I consider myself very fortunate to have travelled so widely and thus been afforded the privilege of meeting fellow enthusiasts on their home ground. For my part, the hospitality and friendship which has been extended to me in so many places overseas has been more than adequate reward for work I have put into the Club over the years. It is not too much to say that life has been enriched beyond measure by friendships formed all over the world.

My sincere thanks go to all concerned.

Index

(Place names are indexed under countries)